'*Taking Back Desire* represents a monumental step forward in the under-standing of the relationship between psychoanalysis and queer theory, espe-cially as evidenced on the screen. James Lawrence Slattery provides a breathtaking series of analyses that show how a psychoanalytic queer theore-tical approach can uncover radical insights where we wouldn't necessarily expect to find them. It's a book not to be missed for anyone interested in how to think about what we're watching today'.

Todd McGowan, University of Vermont, USA, author of *Capitalism and Desire: The Psychic Cost of Free Markets*

'In an era of rainbow capitalism, James Lawrence Slattery's *Taking Back Desire* reasserts the conceptual specificity and radical potential of *queer*. Crucially, Slattery addresses queerness not at the referential level – where an emphasis on representation might too easily be assimilated to the politics of identity and commodity – but in a variety of audio-visual strategies across diverse media. *Taking Back Desire* affirms that queerness cannot be precisely located or delimited to a specific practice, but seeks its resonance in align-ments between the socially abject and the aesthetically disjunctive that threa-ten to destabilise the logic of neoliberalism and its future-oriented temporalities. Combining erudite scholarship, meticulous analysis and admirably lucid prose, *Taking Back Desire* offers engaging and vital readings of contemporary culture – with the discussions of *Sharp Objects* and *120 BPM* offering particular standout moments – to insist upon the renewed and enduring necessity of bringing together screen media, psychoanalysis and queerness to address the contemporary political scene'.

Ben Tyrer, Lecturer in Film Theory, Middlesex University, UK, author of *Out of the Past: Lacan and Film Noir*

Taking Back Desire: A Psychoanalytic Approach to Queerness and Neoliberalism on Screen

Taking Back Desire studies film, television and video art texts through a Lacanian prism to restore a sense of queer as troubling identity and resistance to neoliberal forms of inclusion.

James Lawrence Slattery illuminates how the framing of desire, identity, enjoyment, resistance and knowledge contributes to the investment in neoliberal formations of being and success, despite the corrosive effects neoliberalism has had for much of society. The book does not read queerness on screen as a discernible group of characters or narrative formulas, but as a point that meaning fails in the visual and temporal field. Examining the interrelation of the real, the imaginary and the symbolic in contemporary politics and contemporary media, Slattery investigates how a diverse selection of moving image texts forge queerness as a relationship to the lack, while crucially resisting the creation of a new or definitive 'canon'.

Taking Back Desire will be essential reading for academics and scholars of Freudian and Lacanian psychoanalysis; queer theory; late capitalism; film, television and media studies; sexuality studies; critical race theory; cultural studies and feminist theory.

James Lawrence Slattery completed their PhD in English and American Studies from the University of Manchester in 2023, funded by the Arts and Humanities Research Council. They also hold a master's degree in Film Aesthetics with distinction from the University of Oxford, formally organised the Manchester Queer Research Network, and have published essays and reviews in academic journals, edited collections and cultural publications. Their work investigates the moving image and visual culture to rethink identity and subjectivity in late-stage capitalism.

The Lines of the Symbolic in Psychoanalysis Series

Series Editor:
Ian Parker, *Manchester Psychoanalytic Matrix*

Psychoanalytic clinical and theoretical work is always embedded in specific linguistic and cultural contexts and carries their traces, traces which this series attends to in its focus on multiple contradictory and antagonistic 'lines of the Symbolic'. This series takes its cue from Lacan's psychoanalytic work on three registers of human experience, the Symbolic, the Imaginary and the Real, and employs this distinctive understanding of cultural, communication and embodiment to link with other traditions of cultural, clinical and theoretical practice beyond the Lacanian symbolic universe. The Lines of the Symbolic in Psychoanalysis Series provides a reflexive reworking of theoretical and practical issues, translating psychoanalytic writing from different contexts, grounding that work in the specific histories and politics that provide the conditions of possibility for its descriptions and interventions to function. The series makes connections between different cultural and disciplinary sites in which psychoanalysis operates, questioning the idea that there could be one single correct reading and application of Lacan. Its authors trace their own path, their own line through the Symbolic, situating psychoanalysis in relation to debates which intersect with Lacanian work, explicating it, extending it and challenging it.

The Origin of the Subject in Psychoanalysis
Rethinking the Foundations of Lacanian Theory and Clinic
Alfredo Eidelsztein

Decolonization and Psychoanalysis
The Underside of Signification
Ahmad Fuad Rahmat

Queer Theory, Lacanian Psychoanalysis, Sexual Politics
From Norm to Desire
Luiz Valle Junior

Taking Back Desire: A Psychoanalytic Approach to Queerness and Neoliberalism on Screen
James Lawrence Slattery

For more information about the series, please visit: https://www.routledge.com/ The-Lines-of-the-Symbolic-in-Psychoanalysis-Series/book-series/KARNLOS

Taking Back Desire:
A Psychoanalytic Approach to
Queerness and Neoliberalism on
Screen

James Lawrence Slattery

Routledge
Taylor & Francis Group

LONDON AND NEW YORK

Designed cover image: Jenkin van Zyl, *Looners* (2019).

First published 2025
by Routledge
4 Park Square, Milton Park, Abingdon, Oxon OX14 4RN

and by Routledge
605 Third Avenue, New York, NY 10158

Routledge is an imprint of the Taylor & Francis Group, an informa business

British Library Cataloguing in Publication Data
A catalogue record for this book is available from the British Library

ISBN: 978-1-032-86371-9 (hbk)
ISBN: 978-1-032-86370-2 (pbk)
ISBN: 978-1-003-52724-4 (ebk)

DOI: 10.4324/9781003527244

Typeset in Times New Roman
by Taylor & Francis Books

Contents

Foreword

Neoliberalism plays a number of cruel tricks on our sense of self and what we want, including, crucially, structuring the very forms of desire that it appeals to as the ostensibly universal basis of personhood. It is necessary here to grasp the way that neoliberalism operates: As an individualisation of experience that locks desire into each separate subject, so foreclosing possibilities of collective action; as a political process of a restructuring of the state apparatus that removes the forms of support that sustain us as a community; and as a securitisation of everyday life that exposes us to the kinds of violence which enforce obedience and, at the same time, generates fear of otherness, indeed of other people, as well as otherness ideologically located in particular social categories, of the symbolic.

But, more than this – and this is where the book provides an invaluable cutting edge to open up neoliberalism in cultural production and in the process of reading and rereading – neoliberalism invites a peculiar misleading understanding of 'resistance' that draws us more tightly into its grip. The trap, which psychoanalysis discerns and warns us against, is to buy into the idea that there is, bubbling below the surface, an already coherent form of self and its desire that simply needs to be harnessed and mobilised as an alternative. That ideological process then also traps us into lines of the imaginary that entertains us with fantasies of sameness and difference.

Desire is not an orientation to something, to particular objects to which it is chained and which then define it, but, as James Slattery tells us, it is an orientation to lack. Reorientating our relation to desire, not as a substantive thing but as movement bound up with others, desire as desire of the other, enables us to queer what neoliberalism sells to us as 'identity', whether that is our own identity, the identity we are told will be good for us or the kinds of identity that, we are told, are a threat to the core of our being. Those threats are configured as if they are 'real', traumatic.

This book is part of a process of queering underlying neoliberal assumptions, taking it back but, through a Lacanian reading of how desire works, reformulating it along the way, seizing not only our desire from the grip of neoliberalism but also the conceptual apparatus through which we might follow our desire as we engage with the screen productions that invite us into culturally and historically specific modes of subjectivity.

Clinical and theoretical psychoanalytic work circulates through multiple intersecting antagonistic, symbolic universes. This series opens connections between different cultural sites in which Lacanian work has developed in distinctive ways, in forms of work that question the idea that there could be a single correct reading and application. The Lines of the Symbolic in Psycho-analysis series provides a reflexive reworking of psychoanalysis that transmits Lacanian writing from around the world, steering a course between the temptations of a metalanguage and imaginary reduction, between the claim to provide a god's eye view of psychoanalysis and the idea that psychoanalysis must everywhere be the same. And the elaboration of psychoanalysis in the symbolic here grounds its theory and practice in the history and politics of the work in a variety of interventions that touch the real.

Ian Parker
Manchester Psychoanalytic Matrix

Acknowledgements

My greatest thanks to David Alderson and Jackie Stacey who have been immensely supportive and provided invaluable feedback on this work, to Hal Gladfelder and Ian Parker for their insightful comments, and to Todd McGowan and Daniela Caselli for being rigorous readers when examining my PhD thesis.

Thank you to the North West Consortium Doctoral Training Partnership and Arts and Humanities Research Council for funding the PhD research which led to this book. Without this support, this work could not have taken place. Thank you also to the School of Arts, Languages and Cultures and the Doctoral Academy at the University of Manchester for supporting research trips where I was able to share my ideas and speak with other scholars.

Thank you to my friends, family and colleagues: Anna Fenemore, Anton Juul, Artemis Christinaki, Emily Pope, Grace Wynne-Wilson, Janelle Hixon, Jess White, Julia, Khoi Nguyen, Martin Thompson, Matt, Mom, Oliver Towarek, Sam Flynn, Sean Burns, Sue, Tasha Pick and Tom Doherty, with particular thanks to Richard Riley, Sabine Sharp, Thomas Grocott and my dad for their thoughtful comments. Thank you to Jenkin van Zyl, for allowing an image from their piece *Looners* (2019) to appear on the cover of this book, and Ryan Trecartin, who generously allowed their work to be reproduced in this book. Thanks also to Sprüth Magers and Morán Morán galleries.

Thank you to Fernanda Negrete and Steven Miller at the Center for the Study of Psychoanalysis and Culture at the University at Buffalo (UB), where I was fortunate enough to spend the Fall 2021 semester. In particular, thanks to the Decolonial Acts in Haitian Vodou, Psychoanalysis, and Art seminar group at UB led by Fernanda. I am also grateful for the opportunities to discuss my work at the Cine-Excess Conference 2019 at Birmingham City University, the British Association of Film, Television and Screen Studies (BAFTSS) Conference 2021 at the University of Southampton, the LACK Conference 2023 at the University of Vermont, the Annual Psychosocial Studies PGR Conference 2023 at the University of Essex, the Association of Adaptation Studies Conference 2023 at the University of Birmingham, the

Screen Conference 2023 at the University of Glasgow, and numerous Film-Philosophy conferences I have attended over the years. Thank you to BAFTSS, Sexuality Summer School and the Centre for the Study of Sexuality and Culture at the University of Manchester, Manchester Psychoanalytic Matrix and the Queer Encounters network. These forums for academic thought and exchange have provided much support during my academic career to date.

Love to my fellow organisers at the Manchester Queer Research Network, Jack Warren, Lois Stone and Sarah-Joy Ford; my fellow readers in the Lacanian Reading Group – Alex, Alexandre, Amanda, Artemis, Bean, Camron, George, Raphael, Richard, Rodrigo and Saskia – which started during the first COVID-19 lockdown and has continued in various configurations; and the Death Drive reading group – Anton, Janelle and Tasha.

Introduction

'Queerness' designates gender and sexual identities that do not conform to the heterosexual and cisgender remit, and the word is often added on to or made synonymous with the LGBT+ acronym. At least, this has become the widely accepted definition in popular culture. Yet 'queer' also problematises the concept of identity, and many works that form the 'queer theory' canon highlight this understanding. Put side by side, two contradictory interpretations of queerness emerge.

While the uptake of 'queer' in liberal mainstream Western society seeks to extend social recognition to its associated sexual and gender minorities, identity increasingly takes on the form of a commodity, and 'queer' is no exception. Increasingly, we can witness how brands regularly integrate the rainbow 'pride flag' symbolising LGBT+ or 'queer' identities into logos and product designs, suggesting an acceptance of such identities while also implicitly acknowledging queer/LGBT+ persons as a consumer base. In this book, this commodification of 'queer' is understood as largely developing out of neoliberal capitalism's complex combination of free-market economics and a supposedly meritocratic individualism. Neoliberalism promotes the idea that anyone, regardless of identity, can rise to the top of the economic chain, while eschewing the long-standing and systemic racism, classism, misogyny and nationalism that continue to make meritocracy a rigged game. Nancy Fraser has termed this "alliance of mainstream currents of new social movements (feminism, anti-racism, multiculturalism, and LGBTQ rights) [...] and high-end 'symbolic' and service-based business sectors (Wall Street, Silicon Valley, and Hollywood)" 'progressive neoliberalism'.[1] Fraser suggests that, in this alliance, historically, fringe social movements have become diluted into 'identity politics', making them more susceptible to neoliberalism's logic of progress, a pillar in the seductive logic of individual choice. However, when one approaches queer as resisting rather than assuming the category of identity, it challenges the political environment that proposes to blend inclusivity with consumerism.

It is specifically queer theory's 'negative turn' that departs from the idea that inclusion into structures that typically serve a conventional heterosexual

DOI: 10.4324/9781003527244-1

majority should be the primary focus for people historically rejected by this culture. Leo Bersani's 1987 seminal essay "Is the Rectum a Grave?" and his 1995 monograph *Homos* introduce queer theory's rejection of social acceptability and are often cited as introducing the 'negative' shift in the canon.[2] Lee Edelman's 2004 book *No Future* continues Bersani's line of enquiry, engaging the psychoanalytic work of Jacques Lacan to situate queerness as a structural outlier to norms rather than a sexual orientation that mainstream culture could or should accept.[3] While this book is indebted to the work of Bersani and Edelman, it extends their work of queerness to ask how a disturbance to regimes and categories of identity might problematise neoliberalism as a particular form of contemporary capitalism.

In response to the ongoing ways that neoliberalism invites queerness to coexist within its logic, *Taking Back Desire* engages a range of film, television and video art texts and reads them with Lacanian psychoanalytic theory to return to a definition of queer that problematises, rather than expands, identity. As 'non-traditional' sexuality and gender positions assimilate into neoliberalism, what might queer resistance look like? By pairing moving image texts with concepts from Lacanian psychoanalysis, queerness is shown to be a 'bone in the throat' of neoliberal capitalism as it works to acknowledge subjectivity as unfixed and unfixable. In this way, it cannot adapt to neoliberalism's regimes of performative diversity or what David Alderson calls the 'diversified dominant', which denotes the seemingly socially progressive tendencies that have arrived with conditions of "neoliberal capitalism and flexible accumulation".[4] Alderson coins this term to describe "the means through which sexually dissident subcultures have been assimilated" into this contemporary political regime, and the diversification that appears to be in play in the cultural sphere.[5] While one can see that those who occupy various roles deemed important by society are made up of a more heterogeneous population, Alderson questions the extent to which this 'diversity' is put into practice across different cultural spaces and national borders.

Popular television series *RuPaul's Drag Race* (2009–; henceforth referred to as *Drag Race*) and *Queer Eye* (2018–) best express how regimes of queerness and neoliberalism have come together in the cultural zeitgeist. RuPaul, along with his long-running series and its numerous spin-offs, has been acknowledged as doing "more than anyone to bring drag to the American mainstream".[6] Following Donald Trump's 2016 presidential election, *Drag Race* has included more overt political messaging. Since season twelve, episodes have concluded with contestants dancing on the stage with placards encouraging people to register to vote. There has also been an emphasis on being 'American', with RuPaul's song of this title featuring in season ten with an upbeat chorus that proclaims, "I am American, American, red, white, and blue [...] I am American, American, just like you too".[7] What does being 'American' mean in this context? It is tempting to suggest that, in uttering such a statement, one does not reinforce the national identification but rather emphasises an underlying fragility that such exclaiming seeks to secure. The song in question situates drag as an expression of patriotism, with drag artists and the associated LGBT+ population united with the presumed 'status quo' under the banner of 'American', while excluding communities and persons who do *not* have access to this citizenship. This patriotism continues a theme established in the show's first season in 2009, where various contestants positioned by national and racial differences navigated United States exceptionalism, as analysed in detail by Matthew Goldmark.[8]

Drag can be rebellious, disrupting that which repudiates the feminine and lauds the typically masculine. By turning towards and celebrating exaggerated femininity, drag situates itself against the machismo that concentrates patriarchal ideas of power and strength. At the same time, there have been numerous critical responses to *Drag Race* that highlight how, while raising the profile of the practice of drag and LGBT+ people, the show's rhetoric of inclusion and care reproduces a neoliberal establishment of the 'self' as the sole agent of one's socio-economic success or failure.[9] In this move, *Drag Race* epitomises how neoliberalism meets queerness in the contemporary moment.

Netflix's *Queer Eye* similarly brings 'queer' into the fold of neoliberalism via the 'makeover' sub-genre of reality television. This reboot of Bravo's *Queer Eye for the Straight Guy* (2003–2007) includes a more racially diverse on-screen team than its predecessor, comprised of Antony Porowski, Bobby Berk, Tan France, Karamo Brown and Jonathan Van Ness, who has come out as non-binary and HIV positive since the show started airing. The "Fab 5", as the show refers to them, enter the life of someone whom a partner, friend or family member has nominated and no longer restrict their nominees to 'straight guys'. Nonetheless, the updated version continues the original's "celebration of gay tastes and the transformative powers of consumption", as characterised by Katherine Sender in her study of the marketing of gay cultures.[10] In each episode, the on-screen experts instruct their new subject on how to dress, groom, cook, and open up emotionally while their house is renovated and wardrobe updated. Like Bravo's original series, *Queer Eye* implicitly and explicitly suggests that "problems [...] result [...] from bad personal decisions, rarely exacerbated by others, societal barriers, or happenstance".[11] With its omission of competition and heightened focus on self-improvement, *Queer Eye* exemplifies the "fashionable embrace" of self-care by "mainstream media and popular psychology" identified by Inna Michaeli.[12]

Recent publications have investigated how self-care has become integral to the neoliberal schema.[13] In this context, it has become severed from its feminist roots, which are distinct from a "privatisation of responsibility" and the "obscuring of the social, economic and political sources of physical, emotional, and spiritual distress and exhaustion".[14] While self-care proclaims to heal the effects of hardship in neoliberal times, it functions more like a *pharmakon* that simultaneously acts as a remedy to and a poison of neoliberal trappings.[15] Miya Tokumitsu summarises how "[c]apitalism will deplete you, while letting you think you have the means to improve your lot. [...] Mindfulness – a state of hyper-awareness tempered with disciplined calm – has become the corporate mantra *du jour*".[16] By inviting us to take an individual approach to 'self-care', Tokumitsu suggests that we do not heed the ways in which it perpetuates an individualistic relationship to structural precarity, thereby allowing inequalities to continue and deepen.

Queer Eye combines 'queerness' with the non-threatening approach of the Fab 5: Their open homosexuality and consequent distance from the typical inscriptions of masculine authority lend an affective softness to the prescriptions given to their weekly clients. The show filters its administration of self-care through the 'queer' personality the Fab 5 embody, which underscores their 'authenticity', a term also frequently ascribed to *Drag Race*.[17]

Resisting the Future

Two contemporary Lacanian thinkers who take temporality as a point of departure and conclusion, Todd McGowan and Edelman, bring together queerness and capitalism in more detail. In a similar formation, McGowan's continued analysis of capitalism contains only the occasional passing reference to queerness, while Edelman's contribution to queer theory in his monograph *No Future* does not directly cite capitalism as the political and economic mode under scrutiny.[18] Nonetheless, an insistence on the impossibility of satiating desire structures both McGowan's intervention into capitalism and Edelman's critique of identity. In both instances, examining desire enables a recognition of why attempts to suture meaning in social reality are always bound to fail. By engaging with the psychoanalytic work of Lacan, embracing the negative dimension of meaning suggests how subjects can sustain a radical reorientation towards loss rather than attempting to extinguish it.

Situating the subject in relation to absence is unpacked across McGowan's and Edelman's work as they endorse two major concepts from Lacan's work. The first is the 'real', which pertains to a structural absence inherent in meaning and forms part of Lacan's interconnected triad along with the imaginary and the symbolic, associated with the specular image and the linguistic signifier, respectively. The second is 'drive', which expresses a psychic repetition of loss. These two concepts become increasingly important in Lacan's middle and later periods, including and following his work on the symbolic order in *The Four Fundamental Concepts of Psycho-Analysis*.[19] Here, Lacan develops the drive as a process of psychic repetition that McGowan and Edelman situate as problematising political imperatives that direct subjects to the fantasy of satiated desire. Both authors stage a confrontation with loss by turning away from the future, a temporal schema that underwrites the appeal of capitalism and identity. Bringing these writers together draws out the close relationship between their respective critiques.

Despite the general omission of queerness in his analyses, McGowan theorises how desire sustains the futurity that characterises capitalism. Though discussed in many of his publications, his 2016 monograph *Capitalism and Desire* best expresses the connection between time and capitalism.[20] Here, McGowan sketches an understanding of capitalism by arguing that its "essence [...] is accumulation", yet the capitalist subject "never has enough and continually seeks more and more".[21] The survival of capitalism rests on a simultaneous promise of satisfaction provided by accumulation and the impossibility of such satisfaction ever being reached. Not only is "the failure to accumulate enough [...] inscribed into the system", but this very failure becomes the "source of satisfaction that the system offers".[22] McGowan reads this paradox of capitalism as an effect of the psychic structure established by the subject's entry into language and the "desire distorted by the signifier" as developed in the work of Lacan.[23] Consequently, McGowan proposes that capitalism is *particularly seductive* for subjects of language without suggesting it is natural, inevitable or necessary.

In his opening chapter, "The Subject of Desire and the Subject of Capitalism", McGowan outlines how the discrepancy between signifier (the word) and signified (that which the word refers to) "introduce[s] a layer of mediation into all the individual's interactions".[24] As Lacan articulates, "[i]t is the world of words that creates the world of things".[25] Symbolic division alters our relationship to objects, transforming them into objects of desire as we seek in them more than they can provide. The deficiency that imbues objects forms the basis for capitalism's promise of fulfilment that commodities represent and the inability of such commodities to satisfy their promise.

Significantly for McGowan, capitalism is not satisfying in terms of the accumulation it encourages. Rather, an enjoyment emerges in the failure to accumulate enough or attain that which would fulfil desire, despite the bombardment of advertising that suggests otherwise.[26] The promise of capitalism rests in an imagined future where our desire will be met, but "[t]his future satisfaction never comes, and obtaining objects brings with it an inevitable disappointment".[27] For this reason, McGowan stresses that capitalism's "promise ensures a sense of dissatisfaction with the present *in relation to the future*".[28] By "invest[ing] oneself in the promise of the future, [...] one accepts the basic rules of the capitalist game".[29] Although this seems counter-intuitive as we expect political projects to strive for a 'better future' (however that may be figured), a future of satisfaction is undone by accepting the impossibility of fulfilment for the subject of language. In this sense, McGowan argues that we must resist capitalism by devaluing the future as a site of promise that structures the logic of accumulation.

McGowan's turn away from futurity as the fulcrum of capitalism's appeal bears similarities to the 'reproductive futurism' that Edelman rejects in his theory of queerness. Because of this joint refusal, the organisation of temporality yokes Edelman's queerness to McGowan's critique of capitalism. Edelman collapses capitalism into political meaning as such, for which the figure of the child consolidates. In the introductory chapter of *No Future*,

Edelman argues that the child "remains the perpetual horizon of every acknowledged politics, the fantasmatic beneficiary of every political intervention".[30] McGowan makes a similar distillation when he suggests that left-wing political thought falls into the trap of capitalism when it continues to affirm the fantasy of a satisfying future. This analysis leads McGowan to posit that the "future-to-come" that leftist politics invests in "must be abandoned": "As long as radical politics operates with the belief that revolution will remove some of the prevailing repression, it accepts the ruling idea of capitalism and buys into the fundamental capitalist fantasy."[31] In this way, McGowan assimilates a range of political positions to the logic of capitalism when the future maintains the hope of resolve.

It is queerness that ruptures the political fabric for Edelman, characterised as those "*not* 'fighting for the children'".[32] Like McGowan's move away from the capitalist promise of satiation, queerness stands in "opposition [...] to the governing fantasy of achieving Symbolic closure through the marriage of identity to futurity in order to realize the social subject".[33] As discussed in *Capitalism and Desire*, the subject's entry into language simultaneously installs lack and introduces the fantasy of its closure. For Edelman, this fantasy maps an investment in identity in the social realm, which he encourages readers to reject along with the promise of its inclusion in the socio-political space. McGowan's and Edelman's refusal to heed the desire for satiation rejects the fantasy of the subject's completion alternately inscribed in the adherence to capitalist accumulation and the shoring up of self-knowledge configured in the paradigm of identity. It is, therefore, Edelman's reading of queer that I support when examining how breaks in the visual-temporal field of moving image texts can disrupt the promise of futurity.

No Future continues the 'negative' or 'anti-social' turn pioneered by Bersani and sustains a focus on the figure of the gay man while maintaining that queerness is not a combination of gendered positions and sexual acts, nor a population that can fold into social acceptability. Instead, queerness forges a structural absence whose exclusion determines the boundaries of political and social meaning. This understanding severs queerness from identity as it "names what resists [...] absorption into the Imaginary identity of the name" and figures "the undoing of the Symbolic, and of the Symbolic subject as well".[34] Edelman situates queerness as that which meaning cannot contain and aligns it with the Lacanian real, the internal limit of the symbolic and imaginary orders. Queerness is always outside what is comprehensible to "the politics of signification (the politics aimed at closing the gap opened by the signifier itself)", which structures the political field.[35] In contrast to Edelman's designation of 'queer', the signification of 'identity' disavows the real kernel of non-knowledge and reorients 'queerness' into that which neoliberalism may incorporate into its regime of acceptable difference.

If the rejection of the future is the point of connection for McGowan's and Edelman's projects, their divergence is distilled in the 'social' as a concept that gets written into their textual practices. For McGowan, the loss that governs the negative content of meaning provides the social link, for what we share is what we do *not* have, rather than what we do. Because the subject of language experiences lack through the division of the signifier/signified, lack creates a commonality that sustains a social dimension. McGowan reflects this sociality in his articulation of ideas that are purposefully accessible and clarifying. His work stabilises Lacan's notoriously confusing seminars and writings, socialising this psychoanalytic tradition by opening it up to a wider audience and putting it into dialogue with Marxism, Hegelian philosophy, and film and literary texts.

Unlike McGowan's social thesis, Edelman maintains queerness as an 'antisocial' position in stark contrast to the inclusion of queerness that series such as *Drag Race* and *Queer Eye* promote. Rather than being connected in our lack, the social link is severed by the queer insistence on negativity that interrupts the coordinates of fantasy which underscore social life. Like McGowan, Edelman writes with a stylistic flair that distils his theoretical position. In a Lacanian spirit replete with sustained wordplay that produces double (or more) meanings, Edelman relishes the fragility of the signifier as the work of punning accentuates language's flexibility. In a departure from McGowan's elucidation, *No Future* does not prioritise accessibility to aid comprehension for new readers of Lacan. Instead, the instability of symbolic meaning performs a turning away from the future, formally glimpsed in the repeated witticisms that underscore the play of language, which emphasises how meaning constantly refers *back* to a network of associations.

Alongside Edelman, *Taking Back Desire* is also influenced by the sustained legacy of Judith Butler's work on gender. In their 1990 monograph *Gender Trouble*, Butler argues that gender develops through social conventions and significations that manifest in unconscious and conscious gestures, producing shifting positions within complex articulations of power.[36] While acknowledging the importance of Butler's work in creating the contemporary field of queer theory, Joan Copjec's critique of Butler in her essay "Sex and the Euthanasia of Reason" brings a pointed Lacanian focus to Butler's analysis.[37] Although Copjec is not considered a figure in the queer theory canon, her work is discussed throughout the following chapters as her rigorous analyses provide provocative enquiries into the meaning ascribed to social reality. Copjec's work bears similarities to McGowan's and Edelman's as she reads Lacan as insisting on the irrevocable alienation and lack that subjects encounter in language. This relationship to the signifier problematises identity as an intelligible, coherent category. Alongside Copjec, other scholars invested in the project of cultural psychoanalysis, who have discussed identity and capitalist ideology without drawing on 'queer' as a mode of problematising knowledge, remain important touchstones in understanding why Lacan's work is crucial for reading queerness against capitalism. As a critical lens, psychoanalysis presents a singularly generative set of coordinates. With the

Lacanian terminology of the real, imaginary and symbolic, we are able to deconstruct the elaborate play of meaning present in, and extinguished from, the representational and 'conscious' planes of texts.

Borders of Inclusion

Neither *Capitalism and Desire* nor *No Future* differentiate between capitalism and the neoliberal capitalism that this book prioritises. However, McGowan's 2004 book *The End of Dissatisfaction?* theorises a transformation from previous forms of "liberal and monopoly capitalism" to the "emergence of global capitalism [...] especially since 1989" and into the 1990s.[38] While McGowan does not employ 'neoliberalism' as a term, this earlier book acknowledges a social-economic and psychic shift during this period, broadly defined by the international expansion of capitalist economics through the deregulation of international markets.

In contrast with McGowan, *Taking Back Desire* insists on naming 'neoliberalism' as a particular form of capitalist modernity that combines free-market economics with an emphasis on individuality to project an image of meritocracy while redistributing wealth upwards. Neoliberalism is often understood to have gained prominence in 1978–1981 with the respective elections of British Prime Minister Margaret Thatcher and President of the United States Ronald Reagan.[39] The appointment of these two figures followed decades of strategic development by economists and think tanks dedicated to proliferating neoliberalism's particular persuasion of economics and its attendant socio-political ideology.[40] This strategy stripped back state funding established through taxation and is vital in the restoration of upper-class power, which David Harvey considers the driving force of the neoliberal project.[41]

Present-day capitalism continues a neoliberal trend that largely supports austerity measures. Such policy includes shrinking national debt by defunding government programs such as those that help create affordable housing, healthcare, public transport, and community centres, among other areas of social infrastructure, while also appealing to a sense of meritocracy and visibility in the cultural arena, including television, film, magazine and advertising media. As suggested by the emergence and popularity of television that celebrates sexual, gendered, and racialised difference, such as the aforementioned *Drag Race* and *Queer Eye*, this form of inclusion disavows the systemic regimes that have shaped long-standing social and financial exclusion. By creating a complex and often confusing set of social and political relationships that differ from earlier forms of capitalism, neoliberalism complicates the definition and situating of queerness in the contemporary moment. Examining how neoliberal discourse opens a narrow regime of social acceptability and the limitations of this approach, *Taking Back Desire* reclaims queerness as a prism to interrogate what it means to be a contemporary political subject.

At the same time that neoliberalism brings some historically marginalised people into a more pronounced media focus, recent years have seen a return to a political discourse that seeks to restore a more overtly segregated capitalist society, which openly discriminates against populations who occupy certain positions of race, class, gender, sexuality and citizenship statuses. The 2016 election of Trump to the American presidential office and his continued presence on the political stage have incentivised racist and anti-feminist attitudes, with an increase in white supremacist demonstrations and violence during his candidacy and assumption of office.[42] Though gaining renewed visibility since Trump's arrival into party politics via the GOP, such groups have a long history in the United States. Joshua Inwood contextualises Trump's political success by considering how American capitalism developed "through technologies and practices [...] rooted in the impulse to control and contain black people in place [...] grounded in plantation logics".[43] Trump's campaign catchphrase, "Make America Great Again", refers to an imagined past of American hegemony. Kehinde Andrews characterises it as exhibiting nostalgia for "a time when the logic of empire was much neater", a time of "[r]acial segregation; no civil rights legislation; respect for law and order; and unchecked United States dominance of the globe".[44] Andrews also identifies a similar yearning in Britain, citing the 2016 Brexit referendum as an intensified point around which such rhetoric gathered.[45] Drawing on the work of Cedric Robinson in *Black Marxism*, Andrews uses the term 'racial capitalism' to highlight the racialised dynamics that have always been present in the capitalist project, from its early development to present-day neoliberalism.[46] Similarly, Gargi Bhattacharyya charts the various ways capitalism has developed "in coincidence with a period of racialised demarcation of the world" and similarly dissolves the distinction between 'racial capitalism' and 'capitalism'.[47] For Fraser, the popularity of Trump, right-wing anti-immigration political parties in Europe and the 2016 socialist Democratic Party candidate Bernie Sanders signal a rejection of what she terms progressive neoliberalism, despite their heterogeneous politics.[48]

The neoliberal 'inclusion' of difference and conservative moralism, which much 'Trumpian' discourse returns to, are seemingly at odds. However, Melinda Cooper gives an overview of how neoliberalism and 'new social conservatism' have come together since the 1970s. Her book *Family Values* maintains the family structure as a privileged site for capitalism's continued functioning.[49] While neoliberalism de-emphasises the nuclear family in favour of, for example, "subsuming the newly liberated labor of former housewives within an expanded market for domestic services", it is also "particularly concerned about the enormous social costs that derive from the breakdown of the stable Fordist family" that may necessitate state support.[50] Tracing different political, economic and social theories developed over the last fifty years, Cooper demonstrates how the family is imbued with value by neoliberal and new conservatism alike and presents a formation that brings together these two "equally constitutive expressions of modern capitalism".[51] Wendy Brown's essay "American Nightmare: Neoliberalism, Neoconservatism, and De-Democratization" is a major influence on Cooper's work. In her essay, Brown provides an in-depth assessment of the differences between these two facets of capitalism before arguing that they have been able to come together to reframe the social subject in the American context.[52] By examining how subjectivity becomes situated in the contemporary moment, *Taking Back Desire* approaches neoliberalism as simultaneously differentiated from more socially conservative forms of capitalism while sustaining the structure of capitalism, which necessarily exploits populations demarcated along racialised and class lines.

Numerous scholars working in the orbit of queer theory have written about LGBT+ personhood in relation to consumer culture and nationalism, including how a strategic acceptance of certain LGBT+ subjects sustains whiteness. Released amid the (second) Iraq war, Jasbir Puar's 2007 book *Terrorist Assemblages* makes the case that America develops a 'sexual exceptionalism' by embracing white male homosexuality. Although "homosexual subjects [...] have limited legal rights within the US civil context", an embodiment of homosexuality sustains notions of democratic freedom when compared with racialised and foreign others whom America establishes as oppressive and 'backward'.[53] Puar terms this gay male figuration as one of "homonationalism". Traces of homonationalism come into operation in the previously cited seasons of *Drag Race*, which, despite the racially diverse casting, maintains an emphasis on American nationalism to secure its mainstream legitimacy and appeal.

Rahul Rao continues Puar's analysis of sexuality by introducing the term 'homocapitalism'.[54] In his book *Out of Time*, Rao cites various examples of how capitalism bridges with LGBT+ rights. These include the World Bank's withholding of a loan for Uganda based on the country's anti-LGBT legislation in 2014, and increased discussions around the financial legitimacy of LGBT+ inclusion in capitalist economies and companies. In line with Puar's thesis, Rao argues that this framing of LGBT+ rights

> perpetuates the homonationalist tropes of cultural backwardness through which the attitudes of ordinary Ugandans are typically viewed, while absolving the Bank and other agents of global capital of complicity in the production of the material conditions in which homophobic moral panics thrive.[55]

As well as geographic and political heterogeneity that influences who is considered deserving of acceptability and tolerance, the pitching of human rights as beneficial to economic growth presents LGBT+ personhood as important to the extent that it can be profitable.[56] For Rao, this "encourages us to forget the many ways in which the pursuit of limitless growth has undermined social justice and the environment" and "obscures the possibility that there might be a specifically queer investment in anti-capitalist critique".[57] Building on key ideas from Puar, Rao suggests ways neoliberalism manoeuvres identities previously considered at odds with capitalist operations into the realm of profitability by aligning them with 'Western' values via financial incentives. In response to this enmeshing of capitalism with the language of LGBT+ and queer identities that Rao identifies in contemporary politics, how can the study of the structures of identity and desire emphasise a pronounced *incompatibility* between neoliberalism and queer?

As well as the influence of economic and national borders, the sustained historical emphasis on racialised difference informs how 'queer' identities are able to enter into social acceptability. While steering away from a focus on identity as such, *No Future* received critiques concerning its presumed whiteness, most notably from José Esteban Muñoz. While acknowledging his "deep [...] sympathy" for Edelman's critical reading of an article by Cornel West and Sylvia Ann Hewitt, Muñoz contends that *No Future* ignores the dimension of race that "is central to the actual editorial" and subsequently reproduces a presumed white gay masculinity in his thesis.[58]

In response to such critical evaluations of his work, Edelman's recent book *Bad Education* directly addresses how women, trans people and people racialised as black are "collectively delegitimated as other than human", while acknowledging "historical differences in lived experiences, socio-economic mobility, degree of precarity, access to power, and positioning in the cultural imaginary" across these social groups.[59] In this move, Edelman resists uplifting identity categories to optimistically recognise such subjects as 'legitimate' in ways that have been traditionally reserved for positions of whiteness, masculinity and heterosexuality. Rather, he reads such historically marginalised figures as "*displacements*" that symbolically determine the category of the human through their very exclusion.[60] Socially rendered as "figures of 'nothing'", Edelman posits a structural similarity between queerness, blackness, transness and womanhood, precisely through examining how such positions and figurations alert us to ontological inconsistency, without making any one specific group responsible for bearing the weight of definitively representing inconsistency itself.[61]

McGowan has also addressed race more directly in recent works. In particular, his 2022 monograph *The Racist Fantasy* interrogates the unconscious enjoyment that, he argues, underpins racism and makes it appealing for subjects who participate (consciously or unconsciously) in its structure of prejudice.[62] In this analysis, McGowan argues that racism is not simply a result of a lack of education and, therefore, cannot be eliminated only by teaching people to be anti-racist. Rather, there is an unconscious psychic appeal to racism that McGowan investigates with careful regard to the structure of fantasy, to consider why racism sustains despite efforts to rehabilitate such attitudes and behaviours.

While remaining attentive to McGowan's and Edelman's analyses of symbolic, imaginary, and real organisation from their earlier works, I highlight the relationship between racism and capitalism to different extents throughout this book. With particular reference to Kalpana Seshadri-Crooks's monograph *Desiring Whiteness* and Sheldon George and Derek Hook's edited collection *Lacan and Race*, a psychoanalytic investigation into the coding of race contributes to my understanding of how neoliberal capitalism disavows 'racial difference' as a historical category and informs the social reproduction of sex.[63] At different points in the following chapters, I ask how racism proposes a system of supposedly optical difference that designates subjects as 'marked' or 'unmarked' by race, and how these regimes contribute to the perception of 'properly' masculine and feminine embodiments. I also ask how race becomes established across practices of inclusion into and exclusion from historical narrativisation and consider examples where scholarly responses affirm racial differentiation, even when the text at hand problematises the 'identification' of persons based on such categories.

Double Exposure

It is temporality that comes to define the cinematic arts and my critique neoliberalism. As well as being fundamental to the moving image form, temporality is often a point of focus in psychoanalytic thinking to understand the psychic hold of capitalism. Elsewhere, I have detailed the unique ways temporality can operate in cinema and the close relationship between temporality and language in Denis Villeneuve's science-fiction film *Arrival* (2016).[64] *Taking Back Desire* elaborates on some of the concerns developed in this earlier work by interrogating the political restrictions and possibilities that time may offer when engaging with different media practices.

Although literature, theatre and music also include time as a formal or narrative feature, they cannot be defined by a specific duration. A film might chronicle decades in two hours or depict a half-hour event from numerous perspectives over the same two-hour duration. While literature and theatre also narrate or enact the passage of time across a book's or play's length, the time it takes to read or perform this varies depending on the reader or performance. In contrast, moving image works are contained in specific temporal boundaries, even if these are interrupted by viewing practices. For example, one could watch a twelve-hour television series in one day or one year, but the time inherent in the duration of the overall work is not subject to change. A music track can be recorded as an audio piece that is otherwise variable during a live recital, thus containing it in a specific duration. However, as McGowan explains, the difference between audio pieces and film hinges on their relationship with the recording process:

Though artists often record music, music is not necessarily recorded in the way that cinema is because music can be recorded live, yet there is no such thing as a live performance of a film. The absence of a live recording of a film – its necessarily recorded status – forces every film to thematize time.[65]

As McGowan emphasises, it is not only that films (and other moving image formats) utilise registers of time; they also *thematise* time owing to the explicit temporal boundaries imposed by the necessity of the recording process. In *Out Of Time*, McGowan explicates some of the ways that temporality complicates typical relationships between desire, accumulation and satiation. By analysing a collection of non-linear films, he argues that atemporal structures repeat loss rather than offer closure in their narrative arrangements, reorientating psychic investments in capitalism.

Time's passage is often (though not always) enhanced by the images on screen that typically represent movement and accentuate the way time affords an understanding of action. However, even when moving image works omit movement by using still images (for example, Chris Marker's *Le Jetée* [1962]), filling the frame with colour (as with Derek Jarman's *Blue* [1993]) or texture and words (such as Len Lye's *A Colour Box* [1935]), they nonetheless maintain temporality as an organising feature. Consequently, McGowan argues that "[e]very film betrays some particular conception of temporality".[66] It is for this reason that, despite their obvious differences, the texts that form the basis of each of the following chapters all negotiate time in particular ways, yet none engage temporality *more* than any other.

Additionally, cinema has a knotted history with psychoanalysis; their dual emergence began in 1895, the year that saw the first projection of the moving image presented by the Lumière brothers and the publication of *Studies in Hysteria* by Joseph Breuer and Sigmund Freud.[67] Despite Freud's personal misgivings about cinema and its relationship with psychoanalysis, the two are "part of the long, uneven history of developments in modern art, science and technology" and present "two powerful ways of seeing and knowing the world", as Vicky Lebeau succinctly summarises when introducing psychoanalysis' influence on the field of film studies.[68] Janet Bergstrom notes that "[i]t would be impossible to construct a comprehensive bibliography of 'psychoanalysis and film theory' today because so much of cinema studies since the 1970s has been permeated with concepts drawn from a Freudian and/or Lacanian framework".[69] So influential was psychoanalysis on film criticism that it was simply dubbed 'theory'. Subsequently, the 'Post-Theory' turn championed by Noël Carroll and David Bordwell typifies a rejection of this tightly bound relationship.[70]

Across the broad sweep of psychoanalytic film theory, psychoanalytic concepts (or 'discoveries') are often read with cinematic practices, genres, eras, forms of representation, themes and specific films. Within this wide-ranging tradition, feminist film studies has brought particular attention to the figure of the woman and the articulation of sexual difference on screen. As an area of film analysis, it has provided a rich exploration and interrogation of social reality that film jointly reflects, maintains, produces and, at times, challenges. The feminist mode of thinking about gender and sexuality on screen is in part due to psychoanalysis' repeated emphasis on women (as established in Freud's writings on hysteria) and the much-debated theory of sexual difference, which Chapter Two of this book takes as its organising concept. As well as these connections brought into the public domain by critics and theorists, psychoanalysis has become a recurring representational feature in film and television.[71]

Lacanian psychoanalysis takes precedence as my conceptual grid to suggest that the moving image refocuses the often-blurred relationship between queerness and neoliberalism. Rather than 'applying' psychoanalytic theory to demonstrate a film's meaning or, conversely, unpacking psychoanalytic concepts by deploying film texts, the following chapters produce a series of synthesised readings that bring text and theory together to generate a political analysis of queerness. Lacanian scholarship establishes how absence is fundamental to the structure of meaning and how queerness and capitalism negotiate absence in ways profoundly antithetical to one another.

Copjec and Lacanian cultural theorist Slavoj Žižek have established a practice of film analysis that emphasises the Lacanian real, which McGowan and Edelman also take up, and which is continued throughout this book.[72] This shift departs from traditional film studies that focus more on the imaginary, as in canonical texts written by Christian Metz and Laura Mulvey.[73] Copjec is particularly important in this move as her 1989 paper "The Orthopsychic Subject: Film Theory and the Reception of Lacan" made a radical intervention in psychoanalytic film theory.[74] As McGowan details, Copjec reinterprets the 'gaze', to which film theory remains indebted following Mulvey's "Visual Pleasure and Narrative Cinema" in *Screen* in 1975, by problematising Mulvey's insistence on mastery of the image and critiquing the alignment of apparatus and the gaze.[75] Following Mulvey, the figure of the woman is largely thought to be constructed by a "panoptic gaze", implying that the social subject becomes defined by the law that collapses knowledge with visibility.[76] According to Copjec, this conflation performs a "'Foucauldization' of Lacanian theory" that understands power as productive, in contrast with the Lacanian position, which "states that that which is produced by a signifying system can never be determinate".[77]

Lacan interrogates the consistency of the visual domain when analysing the role of desire in the scopic field. In his seminar on anxiety, he suggests that we do not encounter the gaze in an image of totality whereby our "castration [...] is [...] elided at the level of desire when it is projected into the image".[78] Rather, the gaze is a disturbing encounter with that which is profoundly unable to present us with a totalised form. When asking "[w]hat gazes at us?", Lacan gives the example of "[t]he white glaze of the blind man's eye".[79] Throughout this seminar, Lacan invites us to consider how approaching the lack that structures desire provokes anxiety. The visual field is "never […] able to grasp any living being" other than as a "*dummy*, a puppet, an appearance", as the regime of the image appears to cover the gap that structures the subject of language.[80] Lacan reiterates that "[t]he reciprocal relationship between desire and anxiety presents itself at this specific [scopic] level in a radically masked form".[81] Importantly, though masked, this gap that organises desire is not eliminated. Copjec points towards this anxiety that troubles the regime of the image by departing from the now popularised use of the 'gaze' in film and cultural theory and returning to Lacan to argue that the gaze is not the "sum of all that appears in the image *and* the point that 'gives' meaning" but the blind eye of Lacan's example, "clouded over and turned back on itself".[82] Unlike the situating of the subject in previous film theory scholarship, Copjec reads the subject as one whose lack is in conflict with law and representation rather than realised or produced by it and gestures towards the impossibility of seeing all.

The upcoming chapters do not reference this essay by Copjec again or debate the finer details of this break with what is termed 'Screen theory' (in reference to the impact of *Screen* journal on film analysis). Nevertheless, my concentration on the Lacanian real and the structure of absence in the moving image is influenced by this significant but often overlooked development in film theory. Indeed, the condition of the unconscious as a radically unknowable psychic dimension sustains the importance of psychoanalysis when theorising what is *not* readily available to be envisioned on screen. As I argue that illusions of neoliberal mastery are maintained or undone in distinctive ways by my chosen texts, Copjec's interrogation of the gaze suggests that there is a staining of the optical field that means we are *not* permitted to see everything. Consequently, this book returns to instances that depart from visual consistency and temporal linearity to develop a theory of queerness as that which refuses to be filled with content and complicates capitalism's fantasies of completion. How is queerness understood as a structural position rather than a regime of representation? Returning to a definition of queer that retreats from identity, how can queerness become apparent in moving image practices and the intersections of visual content and temporality? How does one read a moving image text as querying meaning rather than as producing knowledge? Furthermore, what conventions are implicated and transgressed on screen for queerness to be inferred?

In order to approach these questions, Chapter One opens with a critique of the FX television serial *Pose* (2018–2021) and the intricate ways neoliberalism utilises optical regimes of difference to secure its hegemonic socio-economic structure. *Pose* revisits the late 1980s/early 1990s Harlem ballroom scene as documented in Jennie Livingston's film *Paris Is Burning* (1990) and reimagines this era as an episodic melodrama across its three seasons. As *Pose* is set in the late 1980s and saw its initial release in 2018, it addresses the historical period that witnessed neoliberalism's emergence as the dominant socio-economic and political regime in the United States and offers a vision of this in the contemporary moment.

Importantly, the series' central casting and characterisation of black trans women mark an unprecedented move towards diverse representation and appeal to a sense of inclusivity. However, they do so while disavowing the systemic socio-economic relations that continue to marginalise the very populations the series celebrates on screen. Various media outlets have congratulated *Pose* for its 'authenticity' in its casting, but what does authenticity mean with regard to this show, and how does it come into alignment or tension with neoliberalism's strategies of inclusion, the category of 'realness' as established in ballroom, and the contemporary usage of 'queer'?

In contrast with *Pose, Paris Is Burning* frames embodiment in such a way that it suggests the impossibility of authenticity and, thus, an incompatibility with capitalism's logic. By scrutinising 'realness' as used by interviewees in *Paris Is Burning*, this opening chapter argues that the documentary emphasises the fragility of identity categories, bringing a sense of precarity to the idea of an essential self across time. Near the end of this chapter, I examine the Lacanian 'real' to read the gap in ontological certainty, which *Paris Is Burning* indicates through its display of performance. Departing from the documentary's critical intervention, *Pose*'s emphasis on authenticity secures a dual investment in neoliberal inclusion and futurity, staged by its reconstruction of a past that prioritises visual and temporal consistency. Following the opening chapter, the other works examined complicate rather than affirm identity, as constructions of time and desire are scrutinised to develop a critical definition of queerness. Consequently, the opening chapter is somewhat of an outlier. Rather than focusing on a moving image text that challenges neoliberalism, as Chapters Two, Three and Four do, Chapter One considers how *Pose* merges features of queer identity with neoliberalism and thus becomes a subject of critique.

Chapter Two continues an investigation into televisual renditions of racial and sexual differences by turning to the HBO miniseries *Sharp Objects* (2018) and its extensive use of flashbacks. This neo-noir serial takes place in the fictional town of Wind-Gap, Missouri, which brings together interpersonal tensions and national anxieties surrounding the American Civil War. *Pose* celebrates identarian differences through an updated rendition of the recent past. In a departure from this approach, *Sharp Objects* suggests that the past causes a disturbance to the conventional regimes of temporality and the visual field through themes and formal devices associated with film noir. Chapter Two does not explicitly address queerness. Instead, it turns to Lacan's theory of sexual difference that situates 'masculine' and 'feminine' as symbolic positions to rethink the radical instability of subjectivity.[83] Sexual difference informs an analysis of the series' engagement with noir conventions and its emphasis on the written word as it comes to correspond with atemporality. This meeting of theory and form constructs a psychoanalytic interpretation of how language, race and sex structure political meaning, staged by *Sharp Objects*' narrative organisation that dislodges the subject from linear time and represses the spectres of slavery in America's history while simultaneously exhibiting a nostalgia for the Confederacy and the 1950s post-war period.

The following chapter departs from more conventional media formats to focus on artist Ryan Trecartin's four-channel video and sculptural theatre installation *Priority Innfield*, first exhibited at the fifty-fifth Venice Biennale in 2013 in collaboration with artist Lizzie Fitch. Initially appearing experimental and avant-garde, *Priority Innfield*'s dense audio-visual environments are replete with references to popular media conventions found in music videos, advertisements, online viral videos and, most prominently, reality television. Despite a commitment to recognisable conventions, the intensity of these videos renders the codes of reality television's fast-paced genre uncanny and disturbing. Chapter Three introduces a psychoanalytic interpretation of enjoyment to unpick these seeming contradictions, while the work of media scholars, including Hito Steyerl, Ricardo E. Zulueta and Mark Andrejevic, contextualise the generic tropes that Trecartin employs and subverts. Of particular focus are *Priority Innfield*'s visual over-abundance and its staging of '24/7' temporality and spatial collapse, recognised as features of late capitalism by Jonathan Crary and argued as defining elements of postmodernity by Harvey and Fredric Jameson.[84] Together, this chapter proposes that Trecartin problematises capitalist desire while employing the generic codes that sustain our investment in it, transforming them into a disturbing queer spectacle.

The final chapter turns towards the psychoanalytic theory of the death drive developed by Freud and Lacan, and the use of strobe lighting in Robin Campillo's 2017 narrative feature film *120 BPM*. Examining scenes from this film that feature strobe, Chapter Four investigates how absence on screen distorts movement and temporality. By doing so, the film captures the logic of the drive by creating a discernible blind spot in the field of vision, thus engendering a particular political subjectivity. The mechanism of strobe suggests how queerness and capitalism come into tension on screen through the inclusion of negative space. How does one theorise queerness as having a cinematic or on-screen dimension? This concluding chapter argues that it is at the point that visibility itself falters that we might theorise the joining of queerness and the cinematic.

Noticeably, the selected texts that are brought together here are heterogeneous in format and genre. This decision is in part guided by a desire to discourage queerness from being associated with particular representational codes or being subsumed into the logic of 'depiction'. For example, visible same-sex relationships or the inferred sexuality of a character, such as is staged in Ang Lee's *Brokeback Mountain* (2005) (now an exemplary mainstream representation of 'queer' sexuality and focus of Matthew Tinkcom's book-length introduction to queer film theory), does not translate into the kind of queerness I want to propose.[85] Nor is queerness identified in, say, the homoerotic bonds played out in a specific genre or as emerging in alternative kinships found in children's films, as Jack Halberstam theorises in *The Queer Art of Failure*.[86]

Similarly, I do not critique neoliberalism in ways one may typically expect and which are often associated with overtly political films such as those of British directors Ken Loach and Mike Leigh. For filmmakers such as these, a film's narrative and central characters clearly depict scenarios that draw attention to the material disparity and hardship of working-class people in the UK. For Loach and his long-time collaborator, writer Paul Laverty, a realist aesthetic such as that seen in *I, Daniel Blake* (2016) cements the political commitments of their films. Instead of reproducing images associated with the fantasy and glamour that often endorse capitalism, its aspirational lifestyles and supposed possibilities, Loach's films tend to strip away these presentations. Instead, these works appear grounded in the lives of ordinary people attempting to negotiate and live in a capitalist world built on the exploitation and alienation of working-class labour. While I respect such projects for their political strategies and as cinematic texts, I resist drawing on such examples. This decision is largely informed by the way these texts do not tend to destabilise heteronormative investments or necessarily rethink the psychic imperatives of capitalism. Rather, they make strong alignments with ethical relationships to capital, labour and access to a liveable life in their character-isations, narrative conventions and use of sentimentality.

While I resist 'locating' queerness in character and narrative, in part to maintain the idea that queerness cannot be located as such, there none-theless remains a sense that those who are rendered socially abject take focus in the films, television series and video art under review here. The black and Latino gay and trans ballroom participants in *Paris Is Burning*, the socially outcast woman and the repressed figurations of blackness in *Sharp Objects*, the racially, sexually and gender indeterminate populations of Trecartin's videos, and the HIV/AIDS activists in *120 BPM* come to align with disjuncture in cinematic formalism that threatens the narrative consistency which, as I argue, neoliberalism requires (with *Pose* serving as a practice in assimilation rather than structural disturbance). In this sense, these figures on screen do not offer viewers representations of knowable or secure forms of embodiment but, rather, the opposite: In a capitalist ima-ginary, subjects who threaten the consistency of social reality are those who do not fit in the schema of representation, instead bearing and bringing forth disturbances in the visual, acoustic and temporal field. With this in mind, the selection of texts here not merely is eclectic but hopes to facilitate an argument that cumulatively aims to refresh the project of queerness by combining the critique of identity with the critique of capital. Together, they are able to elaborate on this definition of queerness as a site of non-mean-ing and uncertainty that challenges neoliberalism. They do so through tex-tual perspectives that play with norms and utilise them to a certain extent in order to palpably disturb them.

Further to this, the moving image texts brought together here express a range of temporal negotiations: *Pose* and *120 BPM* reconstruct the past in fictional form; *Paris Is Burning* problematises the notion of stable identities across time by introducing ideas of ontological uncertainty; flashback sequences occur throughout *Sharp Objects; Priority Innfield* presents a spatial and temporal collapse that usurps linear narrative; and the use of flickering lighting techniques distorts regular movement and time in *120 BPM*. These varied inscriptions of time's passage suggest ways temporality can complicate or establish tensions between queerness and neoliberalism that develop – but are not reducible to – genre, format and representational codes. If we follow McGowan's argument that a logic of futurity sustains a psychic investment in capitalism, moving image affords a unique medium to investigate how the political is formally manifested in the cultural sphere.

Notes

1 Nancy Fraser, 'The End of Progressive Neoliberalism', *Dissent Magazine*, 2 January 2017. Available at: https://www.dissentmagazine.org/online_articles/progressive-neoliberalism-reactionary-populism-nancy-fraser/.
2 Leo Bersani, 'Is the Rectum a Grave?' *October* 43 (1987): 197–222, https://doi.org/10.2307/3397574; Leo Bersani, *Homos* (Cambridge: Harvard University Press, 1995); Mari Ruti, *The Ethics of Opting Out: Queer Theory's Defiant Subjects* (New York: Columbia University Press, 2017), 3; Judith Halberstam, 'The Anti-Social Turn in Queer Studies', *Graduate Journal of Social Science* 5, 2 (1 January 2008): 140–156.
3 Lee Edelman, *No Future: Queer Theory and the Death Drive* (Durham: Duke University Press, 2004).
4 David Alderson, *Sex, Needs & Queer Culture: From Liberation to the Post-Gay* (London: Zed Books, 2016), 30.
5 David Alderson, *Sex, Needs & Queer Culture: From Liberation to the Post-Gay* (London: Zed Books, 2016), 30.
6 Spencer Kornhaber, 'Why Drag Is the Ultimate Retort to Trump', *The Atlantic*, June 2017. Available at: https://www.theatlantic.com/magazine/archive/2017/06/rupaul-gets-political/524529/.
7 RuPaul, "American", track 1 on *American*, RuCo, inc., 2017.
8 Matthew Goldmark, 'National Drag: The Language of Inclusion in RuPaul's Drag Race', *GLQ* 21, no. 4 (2015): 501–520, https://doi.org/10.1215/10642684-3123665.
9 Matthew Goldmark, 'National Drag: The Language of Inclusion in RuPaul's Drag Race', *GLQ* 21, no. 4 (2015): 501–520, https://doi.org/10.1215/10642684-3123665; Phoebe Chetwynd, 'Postfeminist Hegemony in a Precarious World: Lessons in Neoliberal Survival from RuPaul's Drag Race', *Journal of International Women's Studies* 21, no. 3 (2020): 22–35; Meredith Heller, 'RuPaul Realness: The Neoliberal Resignification of Ballroom Discourse', *Social Semiotics* 30, no. 1 (1 January 2020): 133–147, https://doi.org/10.1080/10350330.2018.1547490; Landon Sadler, '"If You Can't Love Yourself, How in the Hell You Gonna Love Somebody Else?": Care and Neoliberalism on Queer Eye, RuPaul's Drag Race, and Pose', *Journal of Popular Culture* 55, no. 4 (2022): 799–819, https://doi.org/10.1111/jpcu.13153.
10 Katherine Sender, *Business, Not Politics: The Making of the Gay Market* (New York: Columbia University Press, 2004), 16.
11 Landon Sadler, '"If You Can't Love Yourself, How in the Hell You Gonna Love Somebody Else?": Care and Neoliberalism on Queer Eye, RuPaul's Drag Race,

and Pose', *Journal of Popular Culture* 55, no. 4 (2022): 808, https://doi.org/10.1111/jpcu.13153.

12 Inna Michaeli, 'Self-Care: An Act of Political Warfare or a Neoliberal Trap?', *Development* 60, no. 1 (1 September 2017): 52, https://doi.org/10.1057/s41301-017-0131-8.

13 Inna Michaeli, 'Self-Care: An Act of Political Warfare or a Neoliberal Trap?', *Development* 60, no. 1 (1 September 2017): 53, https://doi.org/10.1057/s41301-017-0131-8; Sarah Badr, 'Re-Imagining Wellness in the Age of Neoliberalism', *New Sociology: Journal of Critical Praxis* 3 (13 June 2022), https://doi.org/10.25071/2563-3694.66; Heidi Rimke, 'Self-Help, Therapeutic Industries, and Neoliberalism', in *The Routledge International Handbook of Global Therapeutic Cultures*, ed. Daniel Nehring (New York: Routledge, 2020), 37–50; Julie A. Wilson, 'The Moods of Enterprise', in *Neoliberalism* (New York: Routledge, 2017), 150–182, https://doi.org/10.4324/9781315623085.

14 Inna Michaeli, 'Self-Care: An Act of Political Warfare or a Neoliberal Trap?', *Development* 60, no. 1 (1 September 2017): 53, https://doi.org/10.1057/s41301-017-0131-8.

15 For a study of the term 'pharmakon', see Jacques Derrida, *Dissemination*, ed. Barbara Johnson (Chicago: Chicago University Press, 1981), 95–117.

16 Miya Tokumitsu, 'Tell Me It's Going to Be OK', *The Baffler*, no. 41 (2018): 9.

17 For an analysis of how 'authenticity' is used in *Drag Race*, see Niall Brennan, 'Contradictions Between the Subversive and the Mainstream: Drag Cultures and RuPaul's Drag Race', in *RuPaul's Drag Race and the Shifting Visibility of Drag Culture*, ed. Niall Brennan and David Gudelunas (Cham: Springer International, 2017), 29–43, https://doi.org/10.1007/978-3-319-50618-0_3.

18 Todd McGowan, *The End of Dissatisfaction?: Jacques Lacan and the Emerging Society of Enjoyment* (Albany: State University of New York Press, 2004); Todd McGowan, *Capitalism and Desire: The Psychic Cost of Free Markets* (New York: Columbia University Press, 2016); Lee Edelman, *No Future: Queer Theory and the Death Drive* (Durham: Duke University Press, 2004).

19 Jacques Lacan, *The Four Fundamental Concepts of Psycho-Analysis*, ed. Jacques-Alain Miller, trans. Alan Sheridan (Harmondsworth: Penguin, 1979).

20 Todd McGowan, *Capitalism and Desire: The Psychic Cost of Free Markets* (New York: Columbia University Press, 2016), 22, 23.

21 Todd McGowan, *Capitalism and Desire: The Psychic Cost of Free Markets* (New York: Columbia University Press, 2016), 21.

22 Todd McGowan, *Capitalism and Desire: The Psychic Cost of Free Markets* (New York: Columbia University Press, 2016), 21.

23 Todd McGowan, *Capitalism and Desire: The Psychic Cost of Free Markets* (New York: Columbia University Press, 2016), 23.

24 Todd McGowan, *Capitalism and Desire: The Psychic Cost of Free Markets* (New York: Columbia University Press, 2016), 23.

25 Jacques Lacan, *Écrits: A Selection*, trans. Alan Sheridan (London: Routledge, 1989), 65.

26 Todd McGowan, *Capitalism and Desire: The Psychic Cost of Free Markets* (New York: Columbia University Press, 2016), 30.

27 Todd McGowan, *Capitalism and Desire: The Psychic Cost of Free Markets* (New York: Columbia University Press, 2016), 33.

28 Todd McGowan, *Capitalism and Desire: The Psychic Cost of Free Markets* (New York: Columbia University Press, 2016), 12, emphasis added.

29 Todd McGowan, *Capitalism and Desire: The Psychic Cost of Free Markets* (New York: Columbia University Press, 2016), 12.

30 Lee Edelman, *No Future: Queer Theory and the Death Drive* (Durham: Duke University Press, 2004), 3.

31 Todd McGowan, *Capitalism and Desire: The Psychic Cost of Free Markets* (New York: Columbia University Press, 2016), 13.

32 Lee Edelman, *No Future: Queer Theory and the Death Drive* (Durham: Duke University Press, 2004), 3, emphasis in original.

33 Lee Edelman, *No Future: Queer Theory and the Death Drive* (Durham: Duke University Press, 2004), 14.

34 Lee Edelman, *No Future: Queer Theory and the Death Drive* (Durham: Duke University Press, 2004), 27.

35 Lee Edelman, *No Future: Queer Theory and the Death Drive* (Durham: Duke University Press, 2004), 27.

36 Judith Butler, *Gender Trouble: Feminism and the Subversion of Identity* (New York: Routledge, 2007).

37 Joan Copjec, 'Sex and the Euthanasia of Reason', in *Read My Desire: Lacan against the Historicists* (Cambridge: MIT Press, 1994), 201–236.

38 Todd McGowan, *The End of Dissatisfaction?: Jacques Lacan and the Emerging Society of Enjoyment* (Albany: State University of New York Press, 2004), 33, 34.

39 David Harvey, *A Brief History of Neoliberalism* (Oxford: Oxford University Press, 2005).

40 Philip Mirowski and Dieter Plehwe, *The Road from Mont Pèlerin: The Making of the Neoliberal Thought Collective* (Cambridge: Harvard University Press, 2009); Nick Srnicek and Alex Williams, 'Why Are They Winning? The Making of Neoliberal Hegemony', in *Inventing The Future: Postcapitalism and a World without Work* (London: Verso, 2016), 51–67.

41 David Harvey, *A Brief History of Neoliberalism* (Oxford: Oxford University Press, 2005).

42 Joshua Inwood, 'White Supremacy, White Counter-Revolutionary Politics, and the Rise of Donald Trump', *Environment and Planning C: Politics and Space* 37, no. 4 (June 2019): 585. https://doi.org/10.1177/2399654418789949. See also Sarah Posner and David Neiwert, 'How Trump Took Hate Groups Mainstream', *Mother Jones*, 14 October 2016. Available at: https://www.motherjones.com/politics/2016/10/donald-trump-hate-groups-neo-nazi-white-supremacist-racism/.

43 Joshua Inwood, 'White Supremacy, White Counter-Revolutionary Politics, and the Rise of Donald Trump', *Environment and Planning C: Politics and Space* 37, no. 4 (June 2019): , 581. https://doi.org/10.1177/2399654418789949.

44 Kehinde Andrews, *The New Age of Empire: How Racism and Colonialism Still Rule the World* (Dublin: Penguin Books, 2022), xvii.

45 Kehinde Andrews, *The New Age of Empire: How Racism and Colonialism Still Rule the World* (Dublin: Penguin Books, 2022), xvii.

46 Cedric J. Robinson, *Black Marxism: The Making of the Black Radical Tradition* (Chapel Hill: The University of North Carolina Press, 2020); Kehinde Andrews, *The New Age of Empire: How Racism and Colonialism Still Rule the World* (Dublin: Penguin Books, 2022), xiv–xvii.

47 Gargi Bhattacharyya, *Rethinking Racial Capitalism: Questions of Reproduction and Survival* (London: Rowman & Littlefield International, 2018), 102.

48 Nancy Fraser, 'The End of Progressive Neoliberalism', *Dissent Magazine*, 2 January 2017. Available at: https://www.dissentmagazine.org/online_articles/progressive-neoliberalism-reactionary-populism-nancy-fraser/.

49 Melinda Cooper, *Family Values: Between Neoliberalism and the New Social Conservatism* (New York: Zone Books, 2017).

50 Melinda Cooper, *Family Values: Between Neoliberalism and the New Social Conservatism* (New York: Zone Books, 2017), 8, 9.
51 Melinda Cooper, *Family Values: Between Neoliberalism and the New Social Conservatism* (New York: Zone Books, 2017), 16.
52 Wendy Brown, 'American Nightmare: Neoliberalism, Neoconservatism, and De-Democratization', *Political Theory* 34, no. 6 (2006): 690–714, https://doi.org/10.1177/0090591706293016.
53 Jasbir K. Puar, *Terrorist Assemblages: Homonationalism in Queer Times* (Durham: Duke University Press, 2017), 3.
54 Rahul Rao, 'Queer in the Time of Homocapitalism', in *Out of Time: The Queer Politics of Postcoloniality* (Oxford: Oxford University Press, 2020), 136–173, https://doi.org/10.1093/oso/9780190865511.003.0005.
55 Rahul Rao, 'Queer in the Time of Homocapitalism', in *Out of Time: The Queer Politics of Postcoloniality* (Oxford: Oxford University Press, 2020), 140. https://doi.org/10.1093/oso/9780190865511.003.0005.
56 Rahul Rao, 'Queer in the Time of Homocapitalism', in *Out of Time: The Queer Politics of Postcoloniality* (Oxford: Oxford University Press, 2020), 146. https://doi.org/10.1093/oso/9780190865511.003.0005.
57 Rahul Rao, 'Queer in the Time of Homocapitalism', in *Out of Time: The Queer Politics of Postcoloniality* (Oxford: Oxford University Press, 2020), 146. https://doi.org/10.1093/oso/9780190865511.003.0005..
58 José Esteban Muñoz, *Cruising Utopia, 10th Anniversary Edition: The Then and There of Queer Futurity.* (New York: New York University Press, 2019), 94; Cornel West and Sylvia Ann Hewitt, 'A Parent's Bill of Rights', *Boston Globe*, 18 September 1998.
59 Lee Edelman, *Bad Education: Why Queer Theory Teaches Us Nothing* (Durham: Duke University Press, 2022), xiv.
60 Lee Edelman, *Bad Education: Why Queer Theory Teaches Us Nothing* (Durham: Duke University Press, 2022), 23, emphasis in original.
61 Lee Edelman, *Bad Education: Why Queer Theory Teaches Us Nothing* (Durham: Duke University Press, 2022), 29.
62 Todd McGowan, *The Racist Fantasy: Unconscious Roots of Hatred* (New York: Bloomsbury Academic, 2022).
63 Kalpana Seshadri-Crooks, *Desiring Whiteness: A Lacanian Analysis of Race* (London: Routledge, 2000); Sheldon George and Derek Hook, *Lacan and Race: Racism, Identity, and Psychoanalytic Theory* (London: Routledge, 2021).
64 James Lawrence Slattery, 'A Matter of Life and Death: Cinematic Necropolitics in "Arrival"', *Free Associations*, no. 79 (August 2020): 121–141.
65 Todd McGowan, *Out of Time: Desire in Atemporal Cinema* (Minneapolis: University of Minnesota Press, 2011), 5.
66 Todd McGowan, *Out of Time: Desire in Atemporal Cinema* (Minneapolis: University of Minnesota Press, 2011), 6.
67 Sigmund Freud, *The Standard Edition of the Complete Psychological Works of Sigmund Freud. Vol. 2 (1893–1895), Studies on Hysteria by Joseph Breuer and Sigmund Freud*, ed. Anna Freud, trans. James Strachey (London: Hogarth Press and the Institute of Psycho-Analysis, 1955); Janet Bergstrom, *Endless Night: Cinema and Psychoanalysis, Parallel Histories* (Berkeley: University of California Press, 1999), 1–2; Vicky Lebeau, *Psychoanalysis and Cinema: The Play of Shadows* (London: Wallflower, 2001), 1–2; Akira Mizuta Lippit, 'Modes of Avisuality: Psychoanalysis – X-Ray – Cinema', in *Atomic Light (Shadow Optics)* (Minneapolis: University of Minnesota, 2005), 35–59; Ben Tyrer, *Out of the Past: Lacan and Film Noir* (Cham: Springer International, 2016), 3.

68 Vicky Lebeau, *Psychoanalysis and Cinema: The Play of Shadows* (London: Wall-flower, 2001), 2.
69 Janet Bergstrom, *Endless Night: Cinema and Psychoanalysis, Parallel Histories* (Berkeley: University of California Press, 1999), 4–5.
70 David Bordwell and Noël Carroll, *Post-Theory: Reconstructing Film Studies* (Madison: University of Wisconsin Press, 1996).
71 See Krin Gabbard and Glen O. Gabbard, *Psychiatry and the Cinema* (Chicago: University of Chicago Press, 1987); Stephen Heath, 'Cinema and Psychoanalysis: Parallel Histories', in *Endless Night: Cinema and Psychoanalysis, Parallel Histories*, ed. Janet Bergstrom (Berkeley: University of California Press, 1999), 25–56; Michael Shortland, 'Screen Memories: Towards a History of Psychiatry and Psychoanalysis in the Movies', *The British Journal for the History of Science* 20, no. 4 (1987): 421–452, https://doi.org/10.1017/S0007087400024213.
72 Outside of film analysis, theorists Patricia Gherovici and Alenka Zupančič are notable for their situating of the real in the field of sexuality. See Patricia Gherovici, *Transgender Psychoanalysis: A Lacanian Perspective on Sexual Difference* (London: Routledge, 2017); Alenka Zupančič, *What Is Sex?* (Cambridge: The MIT Press, 2017).
73 Christian Metz, *Psychoanalysis and Cinema: The Imaginary Signifier*, trans. Celia Britton (London: Macmillan, 1982); Laura Mulvey, 'Visual Pleasure and Narrative Cinema', *Screen (London)* 16, no. 3 (1975): 6–18, https://doi.org/10.1093/screen/16.3.6.
74 Originally published as Joan Copjec, 'The Orthopsychic Subject: Film Theory and the Reception of Lacan', *October* 49 (1989): 53–71, https://doi.org/10.2307/778733.
75 Todd McGowan, 'Psychoanalytic Film Theory', in *Psychoanalytic Film Theory and the Rules of the Game* (London: Bloomsbury, 2018), 17–90; Anthony Ballas, 'Film Theory after Copjec', *Canadian Review of American Studies* 51, no. 1 (2021): 63–81. https://doi.org/10.3138/cras-2019-010.
76 Joan Copjec, 'The Orthopsychic Subject: Film Theory and the Reception of Lacan', in *Read My Desire*, 17.
77 Joan Copjec, 'The Orthopsychic Subject: Film Theory and the Reception of Lacan', in *Read My Desire*, 19, 18.
78 Jacques Lacan, *Anxiety: The Seminar of Jacques Lacan, Book X* (Cambridge: Polity, 2014), 254.
79 Jacques Lacan, *Anxiety: The Seminar of Jacques Lacan, Book X* (Cambridge: Polity, 2014), 254.
80 Jacques Lacan, *Anxiety: The Seminar of Jacques Lacan, Book X* (Cambridge: Polity, 2014), 254, emphasis in original.
81 Jacques Lacan, *Anxiety: The Seminar of Jacques Lacan, Book X* (Cambridge: Polity, 2014), 254.
82 Joan Copjec, 'The Orthopsychic Subject: Film Theory and the Reception of Lacan', in *Read My Desire*, 36.
83 Jacques Lacan, *The Seminar of Jacques Lacan/Book XX, On Feminine Sexuality: The Limits of Love and Knowledge: Encore 1972–1972*, ed. Jacques-Alain Miller, trans. Bruce Fink (New York: Norton, 1999).
84 Jonathan Crary, *24/7: Late Capitalism and the Ends of Sleep* (London: Verso, 2014); David Harvey, *The Condition of Postmodernity: An Enquiry into the Origins of Cultural Change* (Cambridge: Basil Blackwell, 1990); Fredric Jameson, *Postmodernism, or, The Cultural Logic of Late Capitalism* (London: Verso, 1991).
85 Matthew Tinkcom, *Queer Theory and Brokeback Mountain* (London: Bloomsbury, 2018).
86 Jack Halberstam, 'Animating Revolt and Revolting Animation', in *The Queer Art of Failure* (Durham: Duke University Press, 2011), 27–52.

References

Alderson, David. *Sex, Needs and Queer Culture: From Liberation to the Postgay.* London: Zed Books, 2016.

Andrews, Kehinde. *The New Age of Empire: How Racism and Colonialism Still Rule the World.* Dublin: Penguin Books, 2022.

Badr, Sarah. 'Re-Imagining Wellness in the Age of Neoliberalism.' *New Sociology: Journal of Critical Praxis* 3 (13 June2022). https://doi.org/10.25071/2563-3694.66.

Ballas, Anthony. 'Film Theory after Copjec.' *Canadian Review of American Studies* 51, no. 1 (2021): 63–81. https://doi.org/10.3138/cras-2019-010.

Bergstrom, Janet. *Endless Night: Cinema and Psychoanalysis, Parallel Histories.* Berkeley: University of California Press, 1999.

Bersani, Leo. *Homos.* Cambridge: Harvard University Press, 1995.

Bersani, Leo. 'Is the Rectum a Grave?' *October* 43 (1987): 197–222. https://doi.org/10.2307/3397574.

Bhattacharyya, Gargi. *Rethinking Racial Capitalism: Questions of Reproduction and Survival.* London: Rowman & Littlefield International, 2018.

Bordwell, David, and Noël Carroll. *Post-Theory: Reconstructing Film Studies.* Madison: University of Wisconsin Press, 1996.

Brennan, Niall. 'Contradictions Between the Subversive and the Mainstream: Drag Cultures and RuPaul's Drag Race.' In *RuPaul's Drag Race and the Shifting Visibility of Drag Culture*, edited by Niall Brennan and David Gudelunas, 29–43. Cham: Springer International Publishing, 2017. https://doi.org/10.1007/978-3-319-50618-0_3.

Brown, Wendy. 'American Nightmare: Neoliberalism, Neoconservatism, and De-Democratization.' *Political Theory* 34, no. 6 (2006): 690–714. https://doi.org/10.1177/0090591706293016.

Butler, Judith. *Gender Trouble: Feminism and the Subversion of Identity.* New York: Routledge, 2007.

Chetwynd, Phoebe. 'Postfeminist Hegemony in a Precarious World: Lessons in Neoliberal Survival from RuPaul's Drag Race.' *Journal of International Women's Studies* 21, no. 3 (2020): 22–35.

Cooper, Melinda. *Family Values: Between Neoliberalism and the New Social Conservatism.* New York: Zone Books, 2017.

Copjec, Joan. *Read My Desire: Lacan against the Historicists.* Cambridge: MIT Press, 1994.

Copjec, Joan. 'The Orthopsychic Subject: Film Theory and the Reception of Lacan.' *October* 49 (1989): 53–71. https://doi.org/10.2307/778733.

Crary, Jonathan. *24/7: Late Capitalism and the Ends of Sleep.* London: Verso, 2014.

Derrida, Jacques. *Dissemination.* Edited by Barbara Johnson. Chicago: Chicago University Press, 1981.

Edelman, Lee. *Bad Education: Why Queer Theory Teaches Us Nothing.* Durham: Duke University Press, 2022.

Edelman, Lee. *No Future: Queer Theory and the Death Drive.* Durham: Duke University Press, 2004.

Fraser, Nancy. 'The End of Progressive Neoliberalism.' *Dissent Magazine*, 2 January 2017. Available at: https://www.dissentmagazine.org/online_articles/progressive-neoliberalism-reactionary-populism-nancy-fraser/.

Freud, Sigmund. *The Standard Edition of the Complete Psychological Works of Sigmund Freud. Vol. 2 (1893–1895), Studies on Hysteria by Joseph Breuer and*

Sigmund Freud. Edited by Anna Freud. Translated by James Strachey. London: Hogarth Press and the Institute of Psycho-Analysis, 1955.

Gabbard, Krin, and Glen O. Gabbard. *Psychiatry and the Cinema*. Chicago: University of Chicago Press, 1987.

George, Sheldon, and Derek Hook. *Lacan and Race: Racism, Identity, and Psychoanalytic Theory*. London: Routledge, 2021.

Gherovici, Patricia. *Transgender Psychoanalysis: A Lacanian Perspective on Sexual Difference*. London: Routledge, 2017.

Goldmark, Matthew. 'National Drag: The Language of Inclusion in RuPaul's Drag Race.' *GLQ* 21, no. 4 (2015): 501–520. https://doi.org/10.1215/10642684-3123665.

Halberstam, Judith. 'The Anti-Social Turn in Queer Studies.' *Graduate Journal of Social Science* 5, 2 (1 January 2008): 140–156.

Halberstam, Jack. *The Queer Art of Failure*. Durham: Duke University Press, 2011. https://doi.org/10.1515/9780822394358.

Harvey, David. *A Brief History of Neoliberalism*. Oxford: Oxford University Press, 2005.

Harvey, David. *The Condition of Postmodernity: An Enquiry into the Origins of Cultural Change*. Cambridge: Basil Blackwell, 1990.

Heath, Stephen. 'Cinema and Psychoanalysis: Parallel Histories', in *Endless Night: Cinema and Psychoanalysis, Parallel Histories*, ed. Janet Bergstrom (Berkeley: University of California Press, 1999), 25–56.

Heller, Meredith. 'RuPaul Realness: The Neoliberal Resignification of Ballroom Discourse.' *Social Semiotics* 30, no. 1 (1 January2020): 133–147. https://doi.org/10.1080/10350330.2018.1547490.

Inwood, Joshua. 'White Supremacy, White Counter-Revolutionary Politics, and the Rise of Donald Trump.' *Environment and Planning C: Politics and Space* 37, no. 4 (June 2019): 579–596. https://doi.org/10.1177/2399654418789949.

Jameson, Fredric. *Postmodernism, or, The Cultural Logic of Late Capitalism*. London: Verso, 1991.

Kornhaber, Spencer. 'Why Drag Is the Ultimate Retort to Trump.' *The Atlantic*, June 2017. Available at: https://www.theatlantic.com/magazine/archive/2017/06/rupaul-gets-political/524529/.

Lacan, Jacques. *Anxiety: The Seminar of Jacques Lacan, Book X*. Translated by A.R. Price. Cambridge: Polity, 2014.

Lacan, Jacques. *Écrits: A Selection*. Translated by Alan Sheridan. London: Routledge, 1989.

Lacan, Jacques. *The Four Fundamental Concepts of Psycho-Analysis*. Edited by Jacques-Alain Miller. Translated by Alan Sheridan. Harmondsworth: Penguin, 1979.

Lacan, Jacques. *The Seminar of Jacques Lacan/Book XX, On Feminine Sexuality: The Limits of Love and Knowledge: Encore 1972–1972*. Edited by Jacques-Alain Miller. Translated by Bruce Fink. New York: Norton, 1999.

Lebeau, Vicky. *Psychoanalysis and Cinema: The Play of Shadows*. London: Wallflower, 2001.

Lippit, Akira Mizuta. *Atomic Light (Shadow Optics)*. Minneapolis: University of Minnesota, 2005.

McGowan, Todd. *Capitalism and Desire: The Psychic Cost of Free Markets*. New York: Columbia University Press, 2016.

McGowan, Todd. *Out of Time: Desire in Atemporal Cinema*. Minneapolis: University of Minnesota Press, 2011.

McGowan, Todd. *Psychoanalytic Film Theory and the Rules of the Game*. London: Bloomsbury, 2018.

McGowan, Todd. *The End of Dissatisfaction? Jacques Lacan and the Emerging Society of Enjoyment*. Albany: State University of New York Press, 2004.

McGowan, Todd. *The Racist Fantasy: Unconscious Roots of Hatred*. New York: Bloomsbury Academic, 2022.

Metz, Christian. *Psychoanalysis and Cinema: The Imaginary Signifier*. Translated by Celia Britton. London: Macmillan, 1982.

Michaeli, Inna. 'Self-Care: An Act of Political Warfare or a Neoliberal Trap?' *Development* 60, no. 1 (1 September2017): 50–56. https://doi.org/10.1057/s41301-017-0131-8.

Mirowski, Philip, and Dieter Plehwe. *The Road from Mont Pèlerin: The Making of the Neoliberal Thought Collective*. Cambridge: Harvard University Press, 2009.

Mulvey, Laura. 'Visual Pleasure and Narrative Cinema.' *Screen (London)* 16, no. 3 (1975): 6–18. https://doi.org/10.1093/screen/16.3.6.

Muñoz, José Esteban. *Cruising Utopia, 10th Anniversary Edition: The Then and There of Queer Futurity*. New York: New York University Press, 2019.

Posner, Sarah, and David Neiwert. 'How Trump Took Hate Groups Mainstream.' *Mother Jones*, 14 October 2016. Available at: https://www.motherjones.com/politics/2016/10/donald-trump-hate-groups-neo-nazi-white-supremacist-racism/.

Puar, Jasbir K. *Terrorist Assemblages: Homonationalism in Queer Times*. Durham: Duke University Press, 2017.

Rao, Rahul. *Out of Time: The Queer Politics of Postcoloniality*. Oxford: Oxford University Press, 2020.

Rimke, Heidi. 'Self-Help, Therapeutic Industries, and Neoliberalism.' In *The Routledge International Handbook of Global Therapeutic Cultures*. Edited by Daniel Nehring, 37–50. New York: Routledge, 2020.

Robinson, Cedric J. *Black Marxism: The Making of the Black Radical Tradition*. Chapel Hill: The University of North Carolina Press, 2020.

Ruti, Mari. *The Ethics of Opting Out: Queer Theory's Defiant Subjects*. New York: Columbia University Press, 2017.

Sadler, Landon. '"If You Can't Love Yourself, How in the Hell You Gonna Love Somebody Else?": Care and Neoliberalism on Queer Eye, RuPaul's Drag Race, and Pose.' *Journal of Popular Culture* 55, no. 4 (2022): 799–819. https://doi.org/10.1111/jpcu.13153.

Sender, Katherine. *Business, Not Politics: The Making of the Gay Market*. New York: Columbia University Press, 2004. https://doi.org/10.7312/send12734.

Seshadri-Crooks, Kalpana. *Desiring Whiteness: A Lacanian Analysis of Race*. London: Routledge, 2000.

Shortland, Michael. 'Screen Memories: Towards a History of Psychiatry and Psychoanalysis in the Movies.' *The British Journal for the History of Science* 20, no. 4 (1987): 421–452. https://doi.org/10.1017/S0007087400024213.

Slattery, James Lawrence. 'A Matter of Life and Death: Cinematic Necropolitics in "Arrival".' *Free Associations*, no. 79 (August 2020): 121–141.

Srnicek, Nick, and Alex Williams. *Inventing The Future: Postcapitalism and a World without Work*. London: Verso, 2016.

Tinkcom, Matthew. *Queer Theory and Brokeback Mountain*. London: Bloomsbury, 2018.

Tokumitsu, Miya. 'Tell Me It's Going to Be OK.' *The Baffler*, no. 41 (2018): 6–11.

Tyrer, Ben. *Out of the Past: Lacan and Film Noir*. Cham: Springer International, 2016.

West, Cornel, and Sylvia Ann Hewitt. 'A Parent's Bill of Rights.' *Boston Globe*, 18 September 1998.

Wilson, Julie A. 'The Moods of Enterprise.' In *Neoliberalism*, 150–182. New York: Routledge, 2017. https://doi.org/10.4324/9781315623085.

Zupančič, Alenka. *What Is Sex?* Cambridge: The MIT Press, 2017.

Chapter 1

The Real of Realness

Pose, Paris Is Burning and the Limits of Authenticity

Defined as "a posture [...] deliberately adopted and sustained", an artifice is indicated in the assumption of a pose.[1] The body mimics a set of coordinates. In the context of dance, the position is "held without movement", the body contorting into a shape that presumes a genealogy and makes it recognisable as a 'pose': A familiarity with the frozen gesture, a reference to form.[2] The title of the television series *Pose* (2018–2021) refers to vogue dancing, which grew out of the late-1980s and early-1990s black and Latinx gay and trans ballroom culture at the centre of the series.[3] Often, voguing stages a 'battle' between 'houses', the different groups that participate in ballroom. The dance takes its name from the fashion magazine *Vogue*, as the poses mimic those seen on the glossy pages of the publication, staged by models on catwalks, in editorial features, and in advertisements. In ballroom, the dancer will hold a pose momentarily before swiftly transitioning to another, moving between standing, crouching and lying on the floor as they rehearse a visual encyclopaedia of gesture and stance.

Pose references *Vogue* in its 2019 promotional imagery, using the same arrangement of text and image as the magazine's cover. In this recreation, the series' campaign reinforces how inspiration is drawn from such magazines, which often encourage a narrow beauty standard, while positioning itself as a version of the publication along with the cultural capital that this suggests. The posters' graphically rendered black and white portraits of the central cast are set beneath the series title, which borrows *Vogue*'s serifed font. No longer just a signifier for posture, "Pose" is the title of a production that revisits and reimagines a history that was largely unacknowledged by *Vogue* during the 1980s and 1990s when the series is set.

Pose takes much of its inspiration from Jennie Livingston's documentary *Paris Is Burning* (1990). Throughout *Pose*'s three seasons, characters, lines of dialogue and situations are extracted from the film and remixed, repurposed and used as jumping-off points for plotlines. By tracing embellished scenarios back to this source material, one can see how *Pose* poses as *Paris Is Burning* while implicitly critiquing it.[4] For instance, the production team and cast have highlighted the series' inclusivity and 'authenticity' in the media and, in doing so, have drawn attention back to Livingston's whiteness, as scrutinised by bell hooks.[5]

DOI: 10.4324/9781003527244-2

Following establishing shots of New York City in 1987, *Paris Is Burning* introduces Pepper Labeija, who announces himself as the "legendary mother of the House of Labeija". His golden dress is so voluminous that he must turn sideways to enter the ballroom hall. Features and rituals of the Harlem underground ballroom scene, such as 'mopping' and 'reading', are explained by those involved in the documented culture. As well as voguing, ballroom compiles 'categories', which competitors enter and 'walk' before a panel of judges who assess their ability to impersonate a designated identity and its sartorial codes. Those who win trophies are those who embody the category most convincingly, who appear 'real'. The terms 'real' and 'realness' suggest the ability to appear as a 'natural' embodiment of the racial and gendered positions adopted, with special attention paid to how whiteness and a bourgeois socio-economic status structure femininity. Yet, in ballroom, the ability to convincingly 'pass' as these desired subject positions must be achieved by those not already occupying them. As such, 'real', as used by the subjects of *Paris Is Burning*, complicates its conventional associations of a natural or pre-discursive 'reality'.

Ladies' Evening Wear, Military, and Executive Realness are examples of what is competitively approached by the ballroom attendees in *Paris Is Burning*, and such categories speak to versions of personhood held up by the dominant culture of the time. Other categories, such as Butch Queen's First Time in Drags at a Ball, use combinations of gendered tropes that reference performances developed out of ballroom's negotiation with the emulated culture. As the interviewees make clear, categories denote success and privilege found in the 'other' world, the world black and Latinx gay men and trans women cannot access because of anti-black racism and other forms of structural oppression that sustain antagonisms directed towards specific class, sexual orientation and gender expressions.[6]

Instead of the Manhattan streets that introduce *Paris Is Burning*, the pilot episode of *Pose* begins inside the vast room of an apartment. A close-up of a mirror ball fills the opening frame. As it steadily rotates, the camera zooms out. Two arms stretch upwards beneath the reflective sphere, straight but for the wrists cocked inwards at a ninety-degree angle, palms upwards, hands and fingers straightened: The body strikes a pose. The camera continues to recede as the hands rotate from right to left, arms still poised before opening into a horizontal line. With the camera now pulled back into a medium shot, the dancer's body moves through a series of shapes before a series of shots take us around the room, homing in on the cast of characters. They include the mother of the "House of Abundance" Electra Abundance (Dominque Jackson) and her house 'children': Central protagonist Blanca (MJ Rodriguez), Angel (Indya Moore), Lulu (Hailie Sahar), Candy (Angelica Ross), Cubby (Jeremy McClain) and the dancer, Lemar (Jason A. Rodriguez).

The room is made light by its large windows that stretch across the two visible walls. Their rectangular panes are a static grid against which Lemar's voguing arms draw lines of movement and which the disco ball remaps as it bends straight lines to the curvature of its spherical form. The view to the outside world gives the gist of New York City, yet the windows double as a cage of rigid intersecting lines accented by their top arches. The camera sweeps and stills as if voguing. It halts, moves towards, away and across the figures scattered across the room, making vignettes of their flamboyant gestures: Lipstick application, nail-filing, hair-playing, the exaggerated movements of a neck and wrist to emphasise speech, a hand pulling a spoon from a pot of simmering food up towards a mouth.

Later in the pilot, Blanca is diagnosed with HIV at a clinic. After confessing the news to her friend, ballroom emcee Pray-Tell (Billy Porter), she finds and rents an apartment with the hopes of breaking away from the House of Abundance to start her own house, making concrete a connection between ballroom 'house' and the physical site for collective dwelling. By the end of this episode, Blanca has formed the House of Evangelista. This early iteration includes former House of Abundance member Angel, Damon (Ryan Jamaal Swain), who has recently arrived in the city after his parents kicked him out upon discovering he is gay, and a young homeless man called Lil Papi (Angel Bismark Curiel). Houses inform the social spaces and dynamics of *Pose*, structuring kinships and rivalries within the ballroom community. After the series explicitly or implicitly suggests that characters' biological families have rejected them, the house formations become 'chosen families' who live together, with the house mother parenting the 'children'.

Paris Is Burning examines houses and families, but only occasionally are we granted access to their domestic spaces. In contrast, *Pose* creates intimate portraits of family and interpersonal dramas within the home, such as that which opens the series. This emphasis on domestication contributes to the numerous ways the series supplements elements suggested but not detailed in Livingston's film. As such, the reproduction of family performed in *Pose*'s diegesis extends to its textual composition as the series presents a reboot of the documentary, sharing characteristics in a renewed form and functioning as a televisual offspring of its documentary precursor.

Pose was created and produced by Ryan Murphy, an auteur of contemporary American television whom Brenda R. Weber and David Greven credit with being "the most prolific media creator of the new millennium".[7] His films and television work have a distinctively vibrant and polished veneer indicative of their high production value and mainstream appeal. Murphy's productions are often described as 'queer' in the contemporary, popularised usage of the word, which functions as a catch-all for the multiple and expanding identity categories situated outside of heterosexual and cisgender norms. Recently, Murphy's projects have shifted focus from present-day dramas (*Nip/Tuck*, 2003–2010; *Glee*, 2009–2015) to narratives centring LGBT+ characters in different decades of the twentieth century. In addition to *Pose, Hollywood* (2020) is an optimistic reimagining of 1940s Hollywood. It features a diverse cast of characters and versions of historical figures such as Rock Hudson (Jake Picking), Hattie McDaniel (Queen Latifah) and George Cukor (Daniel London). Another example of Murphy's recent turn is *Halston* (2021), based on the life of the eponymous gay fashion designer (Ewan McGregor) between the 1960s and 1980s. *Pose* does not claim a biographical basis like *Halston*, nor is it a dramatically reimagined past like that of *Hollywood*. Instead, a combination of historical moments, fictionalised elements and Murphy's signature aesthetic and affective registers "move us between tragic and joyful" as *Pose* becomes a sanitised rendering of the past that often eschews more troubling aspects of the time.[8]

As well as following the movement of Murphy's production trajectory, the series also coincides with a wider trend in media that takes ballroom as its source material. The long-running drag queen competition show *Ru Paul's Drag Race* (2009–) consistently references *Paris Is Burning* in its script and contestant 'challenges'. The HBO competition show *Legendary* (2020–) stages battles between ballroom houses, while the Vice web series *My House* (2018) and the film *Kiki* (2016) document the contemporary ballroom community in New York City. Meanwhile, the British independent film *Deep in Vogue* (2019) documents the current vogue scene in Manchester, UK. As evidenced by this increase in independent and mainstream productions that take ballroom as a topic of investigation, the 'scene' has transformed from an underground phenomenon into an object for mass visual consumption. In addition to incorporating a renewed interest in ballroom culture, *Pose* is an early example of the recent wave of television reboots centring black, Latinx and Asian LGBT+ actors and characters. These productions have revived series and films from the 1990s through to the 2010s that included minor and predominantly white LGBT+ characters, with an emphasis on LGB rather than trans stories.[9]

This investigation into how *Pose* stages its historical period and subjects begins by surveying how the series draws on a notion of 'authenticity', which underpins its political importance and social impact. But what does 'authenticity' mean when used to describe a fictionalised retelling of a historical period? My examination of this term extends beyond textual analysis to include the extra-textual discursive field that constructs *Pose*'s circulation as a political text, such as coverage of the series in academic journals, popular journalism, and newspaper and magazine interviews with writer, director and producer Janet Mock. Following this, how does *Pose* position LGBT+ identities in its historical setting, and what does this mean at the time of its release? And how does the series' 'positive representation' situate politics as an individual virtue rather than historically contingent? These questions are answered by examining *Pose*'s aesthetic and narrative formula and the ways these features engage neoliberal scripts of meritocracy. Regarding the work of Lauren Berlant, Robyn Wiegman, and co-authors Shani Orgad and Rosalind Gill, this chapter introduces neoliberalism as a political structure and a regime of selfhood, which found an amplified voice during the period of the series' setting.

The following section compares *Pose*'s approach to representation with *Paris Is Burning*'s challenges to concepts of 'naturalised' bodies and subjectivity. The film has been the subject of much discussion, including critiques from hooks and Peggy Phelan, which are read with Judith Butler's and Joan Copjec's theories that question the ontological basis of gender and sex. This combination of scholarship foregrounds a critical enquiry into *Paris Is Burning* and its presentation of racial and sexual difference, contrasted with *Pose*'s staging of subjectivity. In what ways does *Pose* depart from the problematising of identity proposed by *Paris Is Burning*? And how does *Pose*'s connection to 'authenticity' frame understandings of subjectivity in tension with the term 'realness' developed in *Paris Is Burning*? These questions lead to a psychoanalytic reading of subjectivity, where 'queer' is introduced as marking the impossibility of identity rather than a category with which to identify, a shift that I argue problematises neoliberalism. In closing, 'authenticity' and 'realness' are positioned as signifiers that circulate inside and outside the two texts and form distinct approaches to understanding queerness.

Authenticity

Pose has received significant positive attention for its employment practices in front of and behind the camera. The casting of numerous black trans women as central characters whose identities align with those of the actors is remarkable, particularly as *Pose* aired on a mainstream network available to a large audience.[10] Narratives concerning trans people – particularly trans people of colour – are rare in mainstream television and films. On the occasions such characters make an appearance, their stories are often replete with supposedly 'negative' tropes as they are frequently characterised as sex workers, criminals or the victims of violent crime, an issue discussed in detail in the Netflix documentary *Disclosure* (2020).[11] While it is not necessary for actors to play parts that align with their off-screen gender identity, trans characters are understood to provide an occasion for trans actors to 'authentically' inhabit a role. Productions such as *Pose* offer rare job opportunities that resist the discriminatory practices of exclusion that dominate casting procedures. In these circumstances, identity informs a production's textual politics in concert with wider industry debates surrounding hiring and representation. A concern is that many trans actors are not considered for roles – including those that seem to correspond to a lived, bodily reality – which instead get handed to their cis counterparts.

As the majority of Americans do not know an (out) transgender person firsthand, popular media take on a pedagogical responsibility.[12] It is believed that cis actors playing trans characters reinforce misunderstanding. For example, when a cis man plays a trans woman, viewers may be encouraged to think of trans women as men in female attire.[13] Related concerns about casting along the lines of race and sexual orientation have also garnered increased media attention. Notably, Russell T. Davis has discussed casting 'gay as gay' in his miniseries *It's a Sin* (2021), which follows a group of predominantly gay men in London as they navigate the emerging AIDS epidemic in the 1980s.[14] Media 'whitewashing' has also come under renewed scrutiny. Notably, Roland Emmerich's film *Stonewall* (2015) faced a backlash owing to its lack of diversity when depicting the 1969 Stonewall riots and New York City's gay and trans community from that period, and the casting of white actors as Asian characters in recent releases has also been the subject of negative media attention.[15]

As a result of its casting, some have used *Pose* as a marker for progress in trans representation. Actor Laverne Cox described *Pose* as having "changed the game" when asked about how culture has embraced trans people, and writer, producer and actor Jen Richards has invoked the phrase "post-*Pose* world" to indicate the impact the series has had for trans visibility in media.[16] Mock's role as a black trans woman behind the camera is also thought to bring truthfulness and agency to the series. These factors may be understood as fulfilling a reparative function in relation to what has been deemed Livingston's injurious viewpoint in *Paris Is Burning* (located by her white and cisgender perspective, with little attention brought to her lesbian sexuality and Jewish heritage). Michael Cooper writes that "*Pose* is [...] giving cis [...], straight, white America a piece of LGBTQ history and representation that has been absent from the televised zeitgeist in favor of heteronormative stories. That's why it's so important to the LGBTQ community".[17] As a consequence of *Pose*'s employment practices and the attention paid to them by the media, the act of viewing becomes an ethical form of media consumption where audiences can discover a past that contextualises contemporary American LGBT+ rights and, in doing so, become part of that history's legacy.

In an article for the *Los Angeles Review of Books*, Alfred L. Martin Jr. describes how the series follows a trend of inclusivity developed in the 1990s that saw white homosexual characters and storylines find 'quality' audiences and thus advertising revenue, "espousing a neoliberal logic that equates social progress and visibility politics."[18] Because the representation of trans women of colour in the media suffers from a pronounced scarcity, and because of the emphasis *Pose* places on a hiring process that maintains symmetry between actor and character identities, there is a tendency for the actors, characters and texts to "become inextricably linked within audience reception practices. As such, if one expresses disapproval of any of *Pose*'s LGBT characters, it could be constructed as a critique of the actors".[19] This conflation may explain why most reviews, at least during *Pose*'s initial release, focused on casting without scrutinising other areas of the series, including the representation of history, policing, trauma, identity and structural precarity.

In another article, Martin proposes that "scholars have inherited a way to examine images from rights organizations like the National Association for the Advancement of Colored People and GLAAD [Gay & Lesbian Alliance Against Defamation]", which have "sought liberation through the mediated image".[20] Such critiques of representational practices in media highlight specific visible forms of exclusion but can also hinder an understanding of how 'positive' images may assist neoliberal forms of 'inclusion'. For example, films, television and advertisements may encourage identification with those exceptional circumstances where structurally disadvantaged people ascend to positions of power while ignoring the exploited majority who maintain the privileges of the successful few.

Continuing this discussion in "The End of the 'Best Actor' Discourse?", Martin draws from interviews he conducted with *Pose*'s casting director Alexa Fogel and casting associate Kathryn Zamora-Benson.[21] Both women reflect on how they negotiated the industry standard, which purports to hire the 'best actor for the job'. Martin summarises the difficulties with this widely implemented idea, which "elides how casting manoeuvres around preexisting notions of what the best actor for a role resembles, often resulting in heterosexual, cisgender men being cast as trans women", who are then "rewarded for their 'convincing' portrayals [...] with praise and accolades".[22] Commenting on *Pose*'s casting, Zamora-Benson says that "[i]t was a given to be authentic to the story".[23] As this excerpt relays, 'authenticity' was vital when hiring trans actors, "implicitly suggest[ing] that [...] trans representations cast with cis actors are inauthentic" and "fus[ing] actor to role".[24] *Pose* and other Murphy projects have also extended the hiring of trans people, women and people of colour to production roles, which Sarah E.S. Sinwell terms 'showrunning activism'.[25]

Michael Goddard and Christopher Hogg note that, while *Pose* achieves a

"gold standard of representation" at least relative to television's so far low level of achievement, it is difficult to argue the same about its narrative or aesthetic sophistication, which, at times, seems little more than a transposing of the dynamics of *Glee* to the downtown [*sic*] ballroom scene.[26]

Comparing *Pose* to the television show *Transparent* (2014–2019), which cast cis actor Jeffrey Tambour in the lead role of trans woman Maura Pfefferman, Goddard and Hogg acknowledge how

Transparent and *Pose* can be seen as mirror images of each other in which the former is aesthetically sophisticated but representationally compromised, while the latter perhaps has the opposite problem in its lack of an aesthetic adequate to its subject matter.[27]

HBO's series *The Deuce* (2017–2019) invites a similar comparison. Beginning in the 1970s, before moving into the 1980s, *The Deuce* follows characters who operate in the transforming landscape of New York City's Times Square as the porn industry moves sex work from the streets and motels into filmed 'adult entertainment'. *The Deuce* complexly navigates how different lives overlap, including sex workers, pimps, porn producers, law enforcement, nightclub owners, drug dealers and politicians, to map fluctuations of power and social change. Yet, for all its sophisticated interrogation into the intermingling of money, sex and pleasure across borders of race, gender and class, the central leads – Eileen, played by Maggie Gyllenhaal, and twins Vincent and Frankie, played by James Franco – are white, cis and heterosexual, and the series features no prominent trans characters. Other recent examples that introduce racially and sexually diverse casts via a white middle-class lead include the women's prison drama *Orange Is the New Black* (2013–2019), the hospital drama *Grey's Anatomy* (2005–) and the first season of the period drama *Bridgerton* (2020).

In an essay by Debra Ferreday, "From Dorian's Closet to Elektra's Trunk: Visibility, Trauma and Gender Euphoria in *Pose*", 'authenticity' once again becomes a defining term for understanding the series, though the argument takes some unusual turns to defend the use of this term. For Ferreday, *Pose*'s "authenticity is framed, not through claims to documentary realism nor through the privileging of grittiness and trauma, but through fantasy".[28] This reading develops by suggesting that *Pose*'s mode of fantasy presents creativity that emerges from marginalised and trans subjectivity to challenge mainstream media conventions. Besides inviting a confusing combination of terms by arguing that the fantasy spectacle invokes authenticity, Ferreday does not account for the multitude of ways *Pose* rehashes well-established televisual practices. Instead, she maintains that the series engages a "politics of pleasure" generally "missing from mainstream representation" of trans people, citing how the depiction of trans women experiencing painful scenarios has become the norm and highlighting how trans people receive a restricted range of narratives compared with other demographics.[29]

Mock also addresses *Pose*'s departure from typical representations of trauma. In an interview with *Vulture* magazine, she reasons that *Pose* provides positive representations, which produce, as well as accurately depict, the lives of its subjects by drawing on the belief that 'if you can see it, you can be it'. Mock embraces the notion that showing trans women of colour thriving against the odds is empowering and inspiring:

> We've seen images on *Law & Order* [1990–] where we're being brutalized and raped, but we have not seen something where we're gathered together in a space celebrating one another, reading one another, offering encouragement and affirmation. [...] They can say, *This made me feel good, this made me hopeful. This made me feel as if maybe I should go audition for something, and maybe I should go back to school.*[30]

The decision to present *Pose* as something of a modern-day 'fairy tale' (a descriptor evoked by both Mock and Murphy) seeks to empower prospective audience members through uplifting representation, suggesting another marker of its diversity.[31] Nevertheless, characters must be read as good and hard-working to maintain Mock's desire for affirmation, a role epitomised by the character of Blanca. Mari Ruti describes the broad LGBT+ movement as "embracing an ethos of positivity [...] succinctly expressed in the popular 'It Gets Better' campaign", an ethos Mock appears to endorse as she emphasises the importance of positive representation for social reform.[32] As attested to by the fantastical ballroom sequences that lend the series its visual appeal, *Pose* reinforces the myth that "there is no obstacle that cannot be overcome by perseverance; that effort will invariably be rewarded; and that dissatisfaction is merely a temporary state, often just a stepping-stone to satisfaction".[33] As well as gauging success through neoliberal paradigms of acceptability, which I will return to in more depth, the insistence on authenticity is further unsettled as the series departs from the realism this term initially proposes.

Ferreday's argument encounters difficulty as she reads the season three episode "Butterfly/Cocoon" (2021) as an imagined backstory for the dead body that was posthumously discovered in the closet of Dorian Corey, who features in *Paris Is Burning*. Ferreday speculates that the trunk containing a body found in Corey's apartment can be "glimpsed in the foreground during one of Dorian's scenes in [*Paris Is Burning*]", for which there is no evidence, while suggesting that *Pose*'s decision to change the identity of the body "draws out [...] themes of marginality to explore how queer communities operate as a source of solidarity away from the gaze of White heteronormative society". However, it remains unclear how this modification of history pairs with the overarching claims that the series presents authenticity.[34]

The ubiquity of the signifier 'authenticity' in discussions of *Pose* serves to reinforce the idea that the series' version of events is accurate or, if not technically accurate, then touching on experiences that supplement the limited historical accounts of trans lives during this period. One can trace the importance of 'authenticity' in maintaining legitimacy on screen to its use in reality television discourse. This genre, analysed in greater detail in Chapter Three, has been argued as "perhaps *the* central proponent of the authenticity imperative" by Michael Lovelock.[35] This assessment is due to reality television's repeated attempts to ensure that what we are witnessing is unmediated, despite the prevalence of highly produced scenarios curated for maximum dramatic effect. In *Reality TV and Queer Identities*, Lovelock argues that the emphasis on authenticity generated by reality television, in combination with the relatively large presence of LGBT+ persons in such shows, has had a significant "impact upon how queer sexualities and gender identities have come to be made sense of in contemporary Anglo-American popular thought".[36] Reality television relies on surveillance to generate action and intrigue. Based on the assumption that subjects are heterosexual and cisgender unless explicitly described otherwise, Lovelock contends that the revelation of someone's LGBT+ identity tends to manifest in a confessional mode, situating it as a truth one must disclose.[37]

Lovelock's assessment builds on Sarah Banet-Weiser's argument that authenticity is historically understood as residing "in the inner self" with "the outer self [...] merely an expression, a performance, [...] often corrupted by material things".[38] While Banet-Weiser does not make the same connections with LGBT + identities, she studies how a sense of authenticity supports the "complex process of branding", aiding the "making and selling of immaterial things – feelings and affects, personalities and values – rather than actual goods".[39] Banet-Weiser goes on to examine how the distinction between authentic and commercial has eroded in neoliberalism. As such, one might read the insistence on *Pose*'s authenticity as part of its branding strategy, which corresponds to a growing commercial inclusion and framing of LGBT+ subjects.

Pose's corral of authenticity through casting and engagement with *Paris Is Burning* for numerous plotlines promotes a sense of bodily and historical accuracy despite the series' theatrical scripting, *mise-en-scène* and "over-the-top performative sensibility".[40] As attested to by the volume of publications that include the word, 'authenticity' has become a master-signifier which secures meaning in *Pose* even as it arrives outside the main body of the series in the form of reviews, academic responses and industry interviews.[41] In psychoanalytic discourse, a master-signifier is a signifier that organises meaning and is "typically [...] those oft-repeated or affectively-loaded terms which function to ground a given system of references".[42] For Jacques Lacan, "[e]verything radiates out from and is organized around this signifier. [...] It's the point of convergence that enables everything that happens in this discourse to be situated retroactively and prospectively".[43] We can see the retroactive and prospective dimensions of the master-signifier at work as the responses to *Pose* have been articulated post-production and release, yet their emphasis on authenticity has structured an understanding of the series. Derek Hook and Stijn Vanheule present a lucid study of the function of the master-signifier, which they characterise as "a temporary point of fixity [in signification]; [master-signifiers] ground a point of belief and/or authority" and function to "'button down' meaning and ensure the smooth exchange of signifiers".[44] The instantiation of 'authenticity' naturalises *Pose*'s combination of references and revisions to history by securing its fabulous rendition of the past into an understanding that its rehearsal of ballroom and black and Latinx trans feminine embodiment is truthful.

Fabulation

Across its narratives and characters, *Pose* performs fabulation based on instances from *Paris Is Burning*. Saidiya Hartman defines fabulation as the

> rearranging [of] the basic elements of the story, by re-presenting the
> sequence of events in divergent stories and from contested points of view,

[...] to displace the received or authorized account, and to imagine what might have happened or might have been said or might have been done.[45]

We can see this process at work at the end of *Pose*'s season two finale when Blanca meets two young runaways outside the ballroom and invites them into her care. These two children are reminiscent of the young boys briefly featured in *Paris Is Burning*, with whom they share corresponding outfits (one in white, the other in blue) and ages (in *Pose*, the children are fourteen, and, in *Paris Is Burning*, one is thirteen and the other fifteen). The boys in *Paris Is Burning* are filmed hanging out on the street, arms hung around one another in casual intimacy as they talk offhandedly about their precarious lives with smiling ease. As with most in the film, there is no follow-up to their stories.

In *Pose*, Blanca is sitting in a wheelchair she must temporarily use since becoming unwell owing to an HIV-related illness. She clutches her recently won trophy from the ballroom in her hands, awarded for the category "Mother of the Year". As if to emphasise her worthiness of this title, Blanca beckons the two children over. As they approach and begin speaking, non-diegetic string music underscores the emotional weight of the scene. The framing moves from a series of medium and close-up shots to tighter shot-reverse shots, staging a developing connection by placing the camera deeper within the action. When Pray-Tell joins Blanca, he greets the children. As he stands next to Blanca, his blue outfit and her white jacket mirror the clothing worn by the children, reflecting them in adult form, before all four leave together as a family. By taking in these youths, otherwise at a loss, Blanca becomes reminiscent of Silvia Rivera and Marsha P. Johnson, who started the STAR house (Street Transvestite Action Revolutionaries) in the 1970s following the Stonewall riots and who are now celebrated pioneers of gay and trans liberation.[46] This anachronistic reference brings figures from the decade preceding *Pose*'s 1980s setting into its present moment by drawing on STAR's work, which provided a relatively safe domestic space for vulnerable trans youth. Collapsing activist and ballroom history, Blanca becomes a representation and representative of a historical trans woman of colour in America; she is framed as a figure of the time while also standing in for an overlooked part of LGBT+ history.[47]

This scene is indicative of *Pose*'s return to *Paris Is Burning*'s archive and its fabulation that fills gaps the documentary leaves open. In "Posing as Normal?", Lynne Joyrich reflects on how the series engages with and departs from the mainstream appeal of heteronormative 'futurity' across its televisual formatting and diegetic action.[48] Joyrich suggests that the televisual format is itself reliant upon "a kind of endless generative productivity (whether a text generates storylines via series' internal repetitions or serials' expanding reverberations) [...] designed to yield profit for the industry via consuming/ commodifying pleasure for viewers".[49] By utilising the television format, creators such as Murphy are perceived as "undoing the force of disruption and negativity" associated with queerness. At the same time, such shows potentially make television "more queer" as they introduce a diverse set of characters who remake the nuclear family.[50]

Joyrich's assessment of *Pose* and Murphy's impact on mainstream television resonates with Richard Dyer, who considers how Hollywood entertainment is "produced for profit [...] with the [...] aim of providing pleasure".[51] However, it "does not simply 'give the people what they want' (since it actually defines those wants)" and, thus, "does not simply reproduce unproblematically patriarchal-capitalist ideology".[52] Pointing to cinema's reflection and creation of norms and their transgressions, Dyer contends that it is on show business' ability to "achieve both these often opposed functions simultaneously that its survival largely depends".[53] This combination is also suggested by Annette Kuhn when reflecting on melodrama and soap operas as 'women's genres'. Responding to the notion that these genres "raise the possibility of female desire and female point of view" in a "society whose representations are otherwise governed by the masculine", Kuhn asks how "popular narrative art [can] itself be regarded as transgressive?"[54] Echoing Dyer's recognition of show business' negotiations with mainstream appeal, Kuhn suggests that

> [b]ecause texts do not operate in isolation from contexts, any answer [...] must take into account the ways in which popular narratives are read, the conditions under which they are produced, consumed, and the ends to which they are appropriated.[55]

It is this tension between a desire to break away from mainstream constraints and a desire to retain their appeal that Joyrich reads as a defining characteristic of *Pose* and other Murphy projects.

Pose simultaneously confirms and rethinks the possibilities of mainstream programming by reimagining family formations outside of biological ties. On the one hand, Joyrich acknowledges that *Pose* enacts a "standard, neoliberal, pull-oneself-up-by-one's-bootstraps success story", which contributes to its mainstream appeal.[56] On the other hand, she reads the celebration of family, which season two's closing scene exemplifies, as "differently figured".[57] This assessment is primarily due to the idea that the houses, "for all their familial discourse and routines, [...] are explicitly contrasted to 'traditional' American families" as they develop "mutual support made possible through multiracial queer community".[58] Joyrich admits that *Pose* does not align with queer's 'negative turn', whereby queer stands outside the demand for 'reproductive futurism', as defined in Lee Edelman.[59] Nonetheless, she maintains that the series produces "a different kind of sentimentality, [...] if not of the Child" – the figure for Edelman's regime of normativity – "then certainly of the 'Future Legendary Children'", the ballroom vernacular for new arrivals on the scene.[60] Notwithstanding the divergent kinship the series celebrates, *Pose* provides closure in the narrative, affective and visual field by offering the family as a remedy for structural hardships and sutures the gaps in history that *Paris Is Burning* does not (or is unable to) offer solutions for.[61]

Looking Forward

Berlant's 'cruel optimism', designated as a relation to "something you desire [that] is actually an obstacle to your flourishing", contextualises *Pose*'s commitment to closure and the socio-political effects of this strategy.[62] Berlant's definition opens their book *Cruel Optimism*, which examines numerous film and literary texts that struggle with an investment in the 'good life' developed in capitalist schemes of subjectivity. Optimism is highly seductive, yet the capitalism that promotes it also bars most people from its promises. *Pose* does not query optimism, repeatedly delivering good life fantasies that are historically (and often continue to be) enabled by exploiting those it thrusts into success. In its depiction of 1980s New York, *Pose* adopts the conceit that the opportunity to attain the good life is available to anyone as long as they demonstrate hard work and courage. Situating their 2011 study, Berlant traces the "precariousness in the present" in "decades of class bifurcation, downward mobility, and environmental, political, and social brittleness that have increased progressively since the [Ronald] Reagan era", the era of *Pose* and a concentrated period for understanding the economic and social organisation often referred to as neoliberalism.[63]

David Harvey opens his history of neoliberalism by citing 1978–1980 as "a revolutionary turning point in the world's socioeconomic history".[64] The importance of these years is primarily due to political and economic changes in China, the United States and the UK.[65] The year 1980, seven years before season one of *Pose* is set, saw the election of Reagan as president of the United States. During his presidency, Reagan introduced "policies to curb the power of labour, deregulate industry, agriculture, and resource extraction, and liberate the powers of finance both internally and on the world stage".[66] Consequently, the United States saw a lowering in taxation, disruption to union organising and cuts in government spending while promoting deregulation in trade and finance that dissolved barriers to international commerce, contributing to the 'globalisation' of capitalism.[67] Following these changes, new embodiments of wealth became apparent, particularly in financial capitals such as New York City. The reduction in state assets and the increase in money flowing through financial trading and private corporations redistributed wealth upwards, widening the income gap and creating ultra-affluent individuals. Todd McGowan cites this era as promoting a "society of enjoyment", an idea returned to in Chapter Three, as globalisation seemingly reduced obstacles to the enjoyment associated with consumption through the deregulation of markets and the expansion of capitalist economics.[68]

A growing emphasis on individual choice and the seductive appeal of *nouveau riche* luxuries helped render the devaluation of the state appealing, even to those who would face increasing material hardship in its wake. Investment bankers and 'titans of business' emerged as icons of this neoliberal shift, concentrated in the figure of Donald Trump, who lingers as an invisible but named presence in *Pose*'s first season. Judith Williamson identifies a range of films concerned with business and finance from the 1980s, including *Baby Boom* (1987), *Big* (1998), *Big Business* (1988), *Empire State* (1987), *The Secret of My Success* (1987), *Trading Places* (1983), *Wall Street* (1987) and *Working Girl* (1988). Although many of these films initially indicate ethical difficulties in the business world of the 1980s, Williamson shows how these issues are resolved by savvy, moral individual characters who transform from 'outsiders' or the 'little guy' to successful 'insiders', thus validating the business world as a space where anyone can thrive.[69]

Pose introduces the emergent affluent class of the 1980s during the pilot episode via Stan Bowes (Evan Peters), who has an extra-marital romance with Angel throughout season one. In the first episode, Stan attends an interview at Trump Tower. His soon-to-be boss, Matt (James Van Der Beek), represents a Trumpian enjoyment of excessive wealth and is energised by his own lavish behaviour. Matt exemplifies the cultural figure of monetary plenitude that finds its most brutal embodiment in Wall Street banker and serial killer Patrick Bateman, the narrator of Bret Easton Ellis's 1991 novel *American Psycho*.[70] Matt exclaims, "for the first time in American history, it's considered a good thing to flaunt your success". He then snorts cocaine and lists an array of his extravagant possessions before punctuating the end of the scene with "God bless Ronald Reagan", shoring up the historical and political significance of his behaviour.

The reframing of the subject through the language of agency and meritocracy was a strategic mission in the conceptualisation of neoliberalism. The Mont Pelerin Society, formed by economist Friedrich von Hayek in 1947, developed a "novel structure of intellectual discourse [...] designed to advance and integrate various types of specialized knowledge within and across the confines of philosophy, academic research in economics, history, sociology, and applied policy knowledge in its various forms".[71] This approach was similarly enacted by think tanks developed in the 1970s, such as the Institute of Economic Affairs and the Heritage Foundation. Purposeful moves made by neoliberal organisations promoted "[i]ndividual success or failure [...] in terms of entrepreneurial virtues or personal failings (such as not investing significantly enough in one's own human capital through education) rather than being attributed to any systemic property".[72] Because of the range of strategies encouraging neoliberalism's economic and social transformation, Philip Mirowski and Dieter Plehwe argue that it is "both political philosophy and political practice".[73] As state funding dries up, the psychic and economic burden on the individual replaces historically contingent inequalities with personal motivation. To make the 'playing field' equal, everyone would begin from the same place, yet the neoliberal turn has increasingly implemented the opposite. It is, therefore, important to highlight the struggle between capitalism's reliance on hierarchies of race, gender and class for concentrating wealth and the rhetoric that promotes neoliberalism as supposedly indifferent to such social positions.

The fantasy of neoliberal meritocracy is clearly reproduced by *Pose* in season three when the series depicts its four central women as having achieved the good life. The series finale acknowledges their success in its visual and spoken references to their entry into mainstream appeal. As Blanca, Electra, Lulu and Angel walk down the street before sitting around a table in a high-end bar to have some drinks, they appear as versions of Carrie (Sarah Jessica Parker), Miranda (Cynthia Nixon), Samantha (Kim Cattrall) and Charlotte (Kristin Davis), the iconic foursome of the HBO series *Sex and the City* (1998–2004). This popular show has started airing in the diegetic present of *Pose*, causing Lulu to remark on the "*Sex and the City* effect" when they observe numerous groups of women sitting at nearby tables, while Blanca comments on the show's overwhelming whiteness. Instead of the cosmopolitan cocktails (the drink famously consumed in *Sex and the City*) knowingly suggested by the waiter, Electra orders them all whisky, stating that she refuses "to let some TV show about white girls define how we eat, drink and gather as girlfriends".

In this scene, *Pose* conforms to the mainstream while simultaneously departing from it, a recurring textual practice for the series. We may recall the cruel treatment of black trans women in a now infamous episode of *Sex and the City*, "Cock-a-Doodle-Do" (2000). This episode sees Samantha complain about and harass the 'noisy' sex workers operating in the area she has recently moved to, with her arrival signalling and perpetuating the gentrification of previously undesirable Manhattan neighbourhoods. By making an intertextual reference to *Sex and the City, Pose* positions itself as critical of its predecessor while also becoming an updated version that goes beyond its visible narrowness, much like its promotional campaign that references and updates the *Vogue* cover format.

Electra speaks of how *Sex and the City* does not define them as the scene plays on its well-established conventions, inviting the audience to designate the *Pose* women as versions of the "white girls" they explicitly acknowledge. This scene involves what Berlant describes as "one of optimism's ordinary pleasures[, which] is to induce conventionality, that place where appetites find a shape in the predictable comforts of the good-life genres that a person or a world has seen fit to formulate".[74] By emulating the conventions of the women's comedy-drama, for which *Sex and the City* is definitive, the appetites of Blanca, Electra, Angel, and Lulu fit into this genre with the swapping of cosmopolitans for Johnnie Walker. The political shift taking place in this mimesis is motioned through the transposition of femininity from white and cisgender to black, Latinx and trans, as *Pose*'s women have now entered into regimes of femininity more palatable for mainstream conventions: Blanca is working as a nurse, Lulu as an accountant, and Angel is married and a full-time

mother to Papi's biological child, of whom he has recently gained legal cus-
tody. Electra is still somewhat of an outlier, as season three sees her amass
extreme wealth from her phone and webcam sex work businesses that launder
money for the mafia. Although this entanglement with criminality is not
reducible to conventional femininity, it draws on tropes associated with the
self-made success of entrepreneurialism and the popular gangster genre, both
of which often elicit a perception of individual rigour in combination with a
sense of familial duty.

The upward mobility of characters throughout *Pose* functions to show a
wider community 'what is possible', presenting individual perseverance as the
route to success, a narrative widely taken up in popular media and the political arena. Often, *Pose* addresses inequalities but does not suggest how to
implement structural change. Instead, characters overwhelmingly navigate
discrimination by appealing to or circumventing specific individuals. Berlant
asks why "people stay attached to conventional good-life fantasies – say, of
enduring reciprocity in couples, families, political systems, institutions, markets, and at work – when the evidence of their instability, fragility, and dear
cost abounds?"[75] Unlike the texts Berlant examines that call into question the
good life, *Pose* suggests one can overcome the costs of capitalism to enter its
world of fulfilment.

In season three, Angel and Papi decide to marry. This plotline calls attention
to a major point of contention in mainstream LGBT+ activism and acceptability that has long centred marriage equality. Although Angel's passport says
she is male, making her marriage to Papi illegal, Papi successfully distracts the
woman at the registry office, causing her to mistakenly sign their marriage cer-
tificate. Their union becomes an event that gives the trans community hope of
attaining legal partnership. As Blanca explains to Papi in episode five,

> all those girls […] get to watch one of their own walk down a real aisle, in
> a real wedding dress, not for some plastic trophy, but to marry a real man
> who loves her. They will then realise they can do it, too.

Hyperbolising the already highly valued form of partnership, Electra gifts all
the trans women who attend the wedding a bridal gown. Following a dinner
with Angel's friends, Electra exhibits a vast array of white dresses she has
stolen from a bridal shop with the help of her mafia business partners after
Angel, Electra, Blanca and Lulu are subjected to transphobic abuse while
helping Angel shop for a dress.

Ruti takes "gays and lesbians [extended in this case to trans people] who
hang their political hopes on marriage" as prime examples of Berlant's 'cruel
optimism' as they "hope that the heteronormative, patriarchal, and state-
controlled institution of marriage will somehow make up for the legacies of
gay and lesbian abjection".[76] As with the reference to *Sex and the City*, the
signifiers of heterosexual marriage are transplanted into the hands of the

trans community, proposing that, if there was a transfer of consumption and traditional forms of partnership, one could remain faithful to the good life the American dream offers. Following her refusal to let the *Sex and the City* women dictate their tastes, Electra speaks of how "we've always made our own rules and we ain't stopping now", yet their commitment to the good life fantasy persists.

In these narrative conceits, *Pose* engages a temporal framework that underpins narratives of normativity and reproduction. In her book *Time Binds*, Elizabeth Freeman characterises the temporal regimes of heterosexual conventions as "schemes of events or strategies for living such as marriage, accumulation of health and wealth for the future, reproduction, childrearing, and death and its attendant rituals".[77] According to Freeman, these standards reproduce subjects into "chrononormativity", a word signifying the temporality that binds "naked flesh [...] into socially meaningful embodiment" in order to organise it "toward maximum productivity".[78] Freeman identifies queer modes of temporality in film and literary texts that diverge from regulatory time. *Pose*, however, translates its marginalised subjects, often written under the identity category of 'queer', into forms of Freeman's chrononormativity.

As well as engaging with temporal structures of normativity, *Pose* supports emerging social norms concerning confidence and self-love. Orgad and Gill name this recent phenomenon "confidence culture" and argue that the imperatives to "love yourself" and "love your body" found in "postfeminist", "postracial" and "postqueer" discourses imply that society has "'moved on' from painful historical power relations" and the need for feminist, anti-racist and queer critique.[79] In its place emerges "a situation in which individual psychological change is required rather than social transformation".[80] Orgad and Gill argue that the insistence on individual agency "has become part of a cultural, discursive, and affective scaffolding of neoliberalism".[81] Drawing on advertising campaigns by beauty brands Dove and L'Oréal, the authors demonstrate how confidence culture "*selectively* draws on the significance of race and remakes it in a highly specific fashion" where it is "flexibly dissociated from the continuing power of historical structures and material resources [...] to offer 'inclusion' or 'visibility' within resolutely neoliberal paradigms".[82] Here, the authors describe how the use of black bodies in marketing often disavows racist structures that permeate capitalism and infuse the production and selling of such commodities.

Importantly, *Pose* does tackle some of the ways black and Latinx gay and trans people are disproportionately affected by systemic prejudice, which hinders access to secure jobs and healthcare. For example, during season two, Blanca opens a nail salon only to find it shut down when the landlord, Frederica (Patti LuPone), realises she is a trans woman. AIDS and the activist group ACT UP also become points of narrative focus throughout this season. *Pose*'s overt engagement with political action has been praised in numerous responses to the series and demonstrates a concern with capitalism's privileging of whiteness, masculinity, cisgenderism and middle- and upper-class lives.[83] These aspects bring political reflections into mainstream programming and operate alongside the rehearsal of individualism and neo-liberal dictates of success that drive character development and overarching storylines. There is a sense that injustice occurs when capitalism excludes certain people from participating in its structure of labour and profit rather than examining how injustice may be central to its functioning, even if it appears more inclusive.

In part because Blanca's journey guides the narrative, in conjunction with the emphasis on characterisation and casting, representation becomes the central vehicle for *Pose*'s critique of the social world. Orgad and Gill describe contemporary culture as rendering visibility "an end in itself – a marker of progress and inclusion, which signifies nothing has to change, since the politics *is* visibility".[84] *Pose*'s specific period envisions a lineage of black and Latinx trans history. In this way, it avoids a 'postracial' discourse that promotes 'colour-blind' casting, a process that may include racially diverse people without interrogating how race is socially informed. Yet, even though the series does not negate how racialized, sexual and gendered differences affect one's ability to operate in society, the series consistently deploys confidence messaging to situate change as an individual praxis.

Pose's impulse to represent black and Latinx trans women as successful in attaining stable housing, jobs and romantic relationships contrasts with *Paris Is Burning*, which does not organise its recurring interviewees and clearly defined segments into an overarching individual trajectory. Rather, the film stitches moments together, including events centring specific persons, explanations of rituals, and footage from inside and outside the balls. Many ballroom attendees desire to occupy femininity, understood as a white and bourgeois position. In this way, they conform to 'normative' renditions of womanhood as inscribed in capitalist hegemony. The talking-head format constructs time, place and culture through personal accounts and oral history. However, there are no conclusive narratives demonstrating the rules that would allow subjects to attain success according to capitalist demands within and beyond the ballroom. Even as figures such as Willie Ninja establish themselves in areas of mainstream culture, the documentary does not correlate success with sheer personal motivation and avoids reproducing the individual as a figure of mastery.

However, it is worth noting that, although *Pose*'s central characters move up the economic ladder and expand their family networks, several deaths indicative of systemic violence haunt their success. For instance, season three sees the HIV-related deaths of Cubby and Pray-Tell. HIV becomes a defining dimension of *Pose*'s era as the series chronicles the effects of the disease on the LGBT+ community, something *Paris Is Burning* does not explicitly address. Nonetheless, *Pose* presents HIV as a narrative fulcrum for self-development through selflessness. As is established in the pilot episode,

Blanca desires a family to traverse the loss of her futurity, cut short by the prospect of death announced with her HIV diagnosis. With her corporeal precarity brought to her attention, she explicitly describes her desire to start a house to ensure her legacy after she is gone. In this act, Blanca quells the discovery of her vulnerable body by transforming the traumatic emergence of AIDS into a noble cause that can save others. Viewers likely assume she contracted HIV through sexual contact, but the series never confirms this, allowing her to remain saintly, a woman who sacrifices herself for her children and whose sickness allows this sacrifice to come into being. In a similar vein, a young dancer named Ricky (Dyllon Burnside) is diagnosed with HIV near the end of season two, which becomes a point of connection between him and Pray-Tell and sparks their romantic and sexual relationship. Later, Pray-Tell dies after giving Ricky his life-saving drugs from a new trial for which Ricky did not qualify.

Another poignant death in the series is that of Candy, a member of the House of Abundance. One of the most striking scenes demonstrating *Pose*'s commitment to resolving what *Paris Is Burning* cannot occurs during season two, episode four, "Never Knew Love Like This Before". In this episode, a maid finds Candy's murdered body in a hotel room closet, a scenario based on the death of Venus Extravaganza detailed in *Paris Is Burning*. In the doc-umentary, Angie Extravaganza recounts Venus's murder near the end of the film. The violent attack, which left Venus dead in a motel room for several days before the discovery of her body, follows several interviews with Venus. Con-sequently, we learn about Venus's desires – to be a "spoiled rich white girl" – and insights into how sex and money operate in gendered dynamics across class boundaries before being told of her death. *Pose* reimagines Venus's nar-rative far beyond *Paris Is Burning*. Following the news of Candy's murder, the central characters of *Pose* plan and attend her funeral. But, rather than a solemn reflection, this scene becomes a fantastical sequence as an apparition of Candy reappears to provide individual characters with a sense of closure unique to their relationship before performing a lip sync to a packed ballroom.

While acknowledging a host of ways that discrimination affects black, gay and trans lives, *Pose* demonstrates a sense that, if allowed, marginalised people could achieve the same American dream society largely reserves for white affluence. Like Orgad and Gill, Wiegman considers how visibility becomes politics. In her book *American Anatomies*, she cites the 1980s as a time when representation underwent a pronounced transformation. In this era, overtly racist caricatures – "the bug-eyed, large-lipped faces gracing kitchen wares" of the previous decades – gave way to "cinema, television, and video [...] [which served] up bodies as narrative commodities, detached from the old economy of corporeal enslavement".[85] As neoliberalism intensifies personal agency, identity becomes enmeshed with commodification. In mining economic and social value, financial markets and branding strategies embrace visible 'difference' to draw in potential consumer bases. Bodies become "situated [...] in the panoply of signs, texts, and images through which the discourse of race functions now to affirm the referential illusion of an organic real".[86] As a concentration on personal agency underplayed systemic positioning, identity increasingly entered into commercial visual circulation.

Pose displays the upward trajectories of identities typically excluded from socio-economic success. However, its arrangements of representation do not account for how entry into the hegemonic system of capitalism is "triumphant in its ability to mask deep disparity on the one hand, and yet thoroughly rigid in its maintenance of naïve individualism and rhetorical democracy".[87] Instead, the series structures political progress in affective, visual and narrative modes that do not encourage spectators to be cognizant of the ways white supremacy and patriarchy prop up capitalism.

Investigating coverage of trans figures in the mainstream press, C. Riley Snorton considers how ideas of American exceptionalism and freedom become bound up with trans persons entering celebrity or notoriety.[88] Snorton turns to Christine Jorgensen, a Danish-American ex-GI who garnered media attention as they transitioned socially and medically in the early 1950s. Snorton argues that Jorgensen was able to connect to a "peculiar emblem of national freedom" in part because her image was reminiscent of the 'blonde bombshell' who figured appropriate femininity at the time.[89] Though Jorgensen's association with this notion of freedom moved between varying degrees of 'success', it manifested in the press as "a spectacular story about personal triumph, scientific transformation, and confessional ideality".[90] But whereas Jorgensen's "media figuration came to represent a form of freedom", Snorton suggests that "it also signified upon the various kinds of unfreedom that marked and continue to animate black and trans temporalities".[91] Snorton goes on to study black trans lives and the scrutiny they were placed under in different media publications in the years surrounding Jorgensen's celebrity, detailing the ways trans "shifts in relation to racial blackness".[92] In a complex series of ongoing negotiations, the figures studied by Snorton "shed light on the negativity of value, exposing how the notion is produced in an alchemy of black criminalization, violence, disappearance, and death" as well as "other ways to be trans".[93] But how does *Pose* reframe subjectivity at the meeting of blackness and trans embodiment in the United States, both in its 1980s setting and 2018–2021 release period? Moving forward over fifty years from Snorton's case studies, *Pose* invites us to read the potential for the historically subjugated figure of difference and 'negative value' as able to ascend to the levels of social capital previously bestowed upon only the narrow figuration of trans that Jorgensen supposed, and, even then, with a wavering public reception.

Departing from an engagement with black trans existence that served to prop up a meeting of exceptionalism, whiteness and femininity through modes of disavowal, *Pose* invites us to read characters such as Blanca as able to reframe trans embodiment and racial blackness under the banner of American patriotism. For instance, before taking in the two young homeless children at the end of season two, Blanca performs a sincere rendition of the American national anthem in the ballroom while sitting in her wheelchair. As this patriotic act suggests, *Pose* does not seek to critique America but "partakes in the very meaning of 'America': that rhetoric of nation, narrative of origin, and abstracted locus of supposedly equal entitlements", which Wiegman identifies in the "interracial buddy narratives" that gained popularity in the 1980s.[94] Examining this cinematic trope, Wiegman argues that, by securing the idea of the nation through reformed social relations, the "racial dissonance" of the 1960s has been absorbed "into a reconstructed mythology of U.S. cultural relations", which disavows the country's imperialist legacies.[95] Disenfranchisement takes the position of an obstacle one must overcome as, to borrow Weigman's phrasing, *Pose*'s "historically constructed differences are [...] recast as a function of capitalist attainment, and the spectacle of middle-class life" that, one might argue, Jorgensen's femininity and racialised whiteness were somewhat able to achieve in the 1950s.[96]

The series reimagines a period of recent American history to include scenes of acceptance without envisioning a transformation or overhaul of capitalism. Instead, its reformist image partakes in an endorsement of difference that neoliberalism inconsistently extends to certain racialised and gendered positions. Its representation includes a range of identities that enter the capitalist imaginary while suppressing the continual structural inequality that falls across lines of race, gender, class and disability within the United States, the wider Western world and the global labour infrastructure that services capitalist demands. Despite being the primary source material that *Pose* draws from, *Paris Is Burning*'s staging of embodiment problematises *Pose*'s understanding of subjectivity by refusing to locate an 'authentic' self. In doing so, it challenges the neoliberal promise of closure for those across the class spectrum, in and out of ballroom.

Realness

The best-known critical reading of *Paris Is Burning* comes from hooks's essay "Is Paris Burning?".[97] Here, hooks argues that the film reproduces Western white patriarchy by focusing on the fantasised spectacle of femininity the predominantly black and Latinx ballroom participants reproduce. According to hooks, their aspirations show a "longing to be in the position of the ruling-class woman" and, thus, "a desire to act in partnership with the ruling-white male", reinforcing the chain that links gender to sexuality, whereby the woman is recognised by her proximity to the man in the heterosexual couple.[98] Following this, hooks dissects how Livingston is constructed as absent from the documentary (though we do, on occasion, hear her voice), giving the viewers the false impression of watching an "ethnographic film documenting the life of black gay 'natives'".[99] She suggests that this choice is part of a larger tradition of the colonial gaze presenting knowledge of the 'other' in a manner that pertains to be objective. hooks extends her concern with whiteness as an invisible position by considering other situations where white people take on the role of passive spectators looking at black culture to remind readers that there is no equivalent where a black subject would be able to document a white phenomenon and retain the illusion of neutrality.[100]

In a similar vein to hooks, Phelan contends that, in using ethnographic aspects (intertitles and explanations of rituals), the world of ballroom becomes fetishized as a knowable entity, transformed from enigmatic to comprehensible by the camera's relay of information. In her essay "The Golden Apple", Phelan argues that the explanatory power of the film frames Livingston as having "mastered [the ballroom participants'] drama, their pain, their art".[101] Livingston's position is complicated, however, by the fetishization of the fetishization of woman, which "motivates the drag performance itself".[102] By looking at the act of looking, *Paris Is Burning* suggests that the category of woman is approached yet never reached, a position that "cannot be said to exist" as Lacan claims, because it is constructed as a symptom of man's fantasy.[103] While initially drawing upon the visual conceit of 'transparency' that shows a world in the reportage stylings of documentary filmmaking, *Paris Is Burning* plays with the visual language of truthfulness on screen.

Butler likewise reads *Paris Is Burning*'s politics as ambiguous.[104] Recognising that the subjectivity idolised at the balls aligns with norms steeped in racism and misogyny, Butler contemplates how injurious terms that mark subjects can be rehearsed and reinvented in ways that generate agency and resistance. Drag's emphasis on imitation is central to this ambivalence, which informs how the rehearsal of gendered meaning produces the very thing it is supposedly replicating. Butler argues that drag is "subversive to the extent that it reflects on the imitative structure by which hegemonic gender is itself produced and disputes heterosexuality's claim on naturalness and originality".[105] The film destabilises norms by suggesting that they are themselves performed, even as the performers desire specific articulations of race, gender and class. Granted, *Paris Is Burning* does not directly discuss how these idealisations reinforce femininity as a racialised category that is accentuated by proximity to whiteness and, in turn, perpetuates violence towards 'difference'. In part, this is because the documentary does not locate this dual process of racial and gendered manifestation within a longer historical emergence but situates it as part of then-contemporary 1980s America. Despite not probing the historical contexts that have supported the merging of whiteness with femininity, *Paris Is Burning* presents a longing for this dominant version of femininity while subsequently drawing attention to the acceptability and prestige that often go unnoticed in the standardised notion of personhood.

The film's scepticism of identity is best observed when the film turns from ballroom participants consciously imitating versions of masculinity and femininity to the aspirational subjects walking around Manhattan and the magazines and adverts that (re)produce the desire to inhabit these positions.

Through the juxtaposition of images of the 'imitation' next to the supposed 'real thing', viewers are invited to consider how signifiers such as clothing and gesture convey class, race and gender. As the film introduces ballroom before showing us the affluent white New Yorkers, the latter appear to accomplish identity by utilising signifiers and not because they possess an authenticity that precedes inscription.

Paris Is Burning's emphasis on the construction of embodiment is suggestive of Butler's earlier thesis in *Gender Trouble*, where "*fabrications* manufactured and sustained through corporeal signs and other discursive signs" are understood to constitute gendered meaning.[106] For Butler, "to qualify as a substantive identity is an arduous task, for such appearances are rule-generated, ones which rely on the *consistent and repeated* invocation of rules".[107] *Paris Is Burning* indicates how circulated conventions constitute identity by framing the performances in ballroom as simulacra – "the generation by models of a real without origin or reality" – thus drawing attention to the requirement of repetition in the practice of signification.[108]

The emphasis on repetition signals a temporality that rethinks gender and disputes the 'authenticity' upon which *Pose* capitalises. Whereas repetition indicates the need for the constant refreshing of signification to give the appearance of identity across time, the notion of an authentic embodiment suggests a kernel or essence that is unwavering in both the span of someone's life and a broader timeline, which serves to secure conceptions of gender and identity more generally. In this sense, 'authenticity' operates in terms of what Ruti defines as "the fantasy of an 'essential,' inviolable inner core [that] obscures our ontological void, offering us the comforting illusion of a flawlessly integrated psychic life".[109] Although *Pose* explicitly supports trans embodiment through its celebratory humanising of subjects who occupy this position, 'authenticity' and the sense that someone should be 'true to oneself' rely upon a notion of temporal security, a stability of self that is *not* subject to fluctuation. Butler's proposal that repetition produces gender as a signifying system "reveal[s] its fundamentally phantasmatic status" that underpins claims to 'naturalness' which are implicitly maintained by the insistence of 'authenticity' in *Pose*'s articulation of subjectivity.[110]

'Realness', as used in *Paris Is Burning*, continues to complicate the presumed ability to inhabit identity. During the clips of the white bourgeois public, Cheryl Lynn's 1978 song "Got to Be Real" plays as the film leads into its section dedicated to "Realness". In voice-over, interviewee Corey introduces realness as the ability to "blend", to "pass the untrained eye, or even the trained eye, and not give away the fact that you're gay, that's what's realness. [...] You erase all the [...] giveaways to make your illusion perfect". During this explanation, we see footage of ballroom participants walking categories pertaining to straight masculinity and femininity. As Corey continues, we also discern the necessity of realness for avoiding danger: "When they're undetectable, when they can walk out of that ballroom into the sunlight and [...] get home and still have all their clothes and no blood running off their bodies, those are the femme realness queens". This closing point becomes especially poignant as it plays over a series of close-ups that introduce Venus Extravaganza styling her hair, whose brutal murder later in the documentary retroactively brings a tragic weight to the stakes described by Corey. Consequently, it is worth noting that the normative modes of gender imitated by the subjects of *Paris Is Burning* and depicted in *Pose* are life-saving devices that protect the ballroom participants.

As Corey's definition indicates, the basis of realness is emulation, the ability to 'pass' as a formation of sexuality and gender. However, the element that would confer identity – and transform performing into being – cannot be located, even when the camera turns to those the ballroom participants imitate. As Phelan argues, "realness becomes such a fluid term that these heterosexual white couples seem exceptionally artificial".[111] The 'thing' that would confer an 'authentic', natural or pre-discursive embodiment is perpetually lost as the performance of identity continually orbits this absence, even for those imagined as possessing it. The film seeks to represent the world of ballroom by examining how idealised embodiments operating 'outside' exclude people owing to the "forces of class, racism, and homophobia [that] conspire to make their political-social exclusion seem ontological".[112] Being 'real' is introduced as alluring at the point that it is barred from the subjects, held at an irrecuperable distance by how "falsely narrow the white heterosexual 'real' is".[113] The camera shapes this perspective as it turns towards the 'unmarked' persons who appear enmeshed within, yet unaware of, their rehearsal of certain social mandates.

Paris Is Burning's problematising of subjectivity differs from *Pose*. In *Pose*, trans is framed as an identity, yet *Paris Is Burning* invites us to read identity itself as a construction, which the ballroom participants – knowingly or unknowingly – reveal. In their book *Hatred of Sex*, Oliver Davis and Tim Dean describe identities as attempting to "forge coherence out of disorder and alterity".[114] Such disorder re-emerges, however, when our desires do not conform to our identities. We may want things that we 'shouldn't', things that undermine the very identities we associate with. As such, identities are "misleading because they conceal from me my own incoherence, my constitutive dividedness, and those aspects of me with which I cannot readily identify or sympathize".[115] As attested to by the creators' pledge to 'authenticity', part of *Pose*'s mission is to uphold trans as a valid identity by portraying bodies and characters in a way that elicits sympathy and acceptance, legitimating trans subjects as equal to those who do not bear the same weight of scrutiny. *Paris Is Burning* also frames the ballroom participants in ways that highlight their humanity and charisma, encouraging us to read them as smart, witty and beautiful. Yet it also challenges identity itself by highlighting its construction, an approach that chimes with recent scholarship that develops 'trans' not as an identity but as a relationship to embodiment.

In *Transgender Psychoanalysis*, clinician and theorist Patricia Gherovici positions trans not as a category "opposed to normative gendered bodies" but rather as an "experience" that "shows us that there is a disjunction between how subjects experience their bodies and the given corporeal contours of their flesh".[116] Unlike understanding trans as opposite to cis-embodiment, Gherovici invites readers to consider trans as articulating a disjunction that "is not pathological but universal".[117] Given that everybody has to negotiate "a process of embodiment", disjunction "will be at play for everyone who tries to bridge the gap and embody their carnal reality in order to flesh out subjectivity".[118] Rather than trans being an identity, Gherovici suggests that trans expresses a difficulty with embodiment that all subjects experience, whether that challenge is registered in the domain of gender or not.

A similar move to universality is staged by Andrea Long Chu, whose polemical text *Females* boldly claims that "[e]veryone is female, and everyone hates it", with female being defined as "any psychic operation in which the self is sacrificed to make room for the desire of another".[119] While not explicitly engaging with the category of trans here, Chu nonetheless signals a disjuncture (to borrow Gherovici's term) between 'self' and 'desire', designated under a provocative signifier – 'female'. Thus, 'trans' for Gherovici and 'female' for Chu do not describe gender identities but rather troubled relationships to embodiment and desire, which are experienced by all.

We can see this move from particular identity to universal experience play out in *Paris Is Burning*. While some ballroom participants are trans and others are not, the construction of 'regular' (white, affluent and cis) personhood is informed by the explicit performances we see from within the balls. Rather than reading these two populations as holding opposing identities, the disjuncture in embodiment pervades those who are, as Phelan distinguishes, both 'marked' and 'unmarked'. Where *Paris Is Burning* dissolves a fundamental distinction between the world inside and outside the balls, without undermining that lived experiences differ greatly, *Pose* motivates identity to explore its wider political field. In doing so, it departs from *Paris Is Burning*'s alienating staging of New York City's privileged population and instead brings white affluence into direct contact with ballroom via Stan and Angel's romantic relationship in season one. By having Stan as a recurring central character throughout the first season, *Pose* actively engages with the world of white upwardly mobile personhood. *Paris Is Burning* interviews ballroom attendees and shares intimate footage of their lives but keeps the bourgeois Manhattanites at a distance and Livingston herself out of the frame. In contrast, *Pose* gives voice to this dominant culture in a way that creates narrative overlap while emphasising difference.

During *Pose*'s pilot episode, Stan visits the piers where Angel operates as a sex worker. He picks her up and they go to a hotel room, marking the beginning of their explicitly transactional and romantic relationship. In what might be part of its strategy of 'positive' representation, *Pose* departs from

Paris Is Burning's admiration of white femininity as discussed candidly – but not necessarily uncritically – by the interviewed subjects. hooks conflates this idealisation of white femininity espoused by the interviewees with the film more generally, stating that *Paris Is Burning* celebrates a "brutal imperial ruling-class capitalist patriarchal whiteness that presents itself – its way of life – as the only meaningful life there is".[120] Many from ballroom have absorbed the cultural mandate to recognise 'legitimate' femininity through the prism of race and class. However, the camera's alienating look, directed at those whom ballroom culture idolises, complicates the film's supposed complicity in this fantasy of racialised gender. *Pose* omits this idealisation in as much as its characters do not vocalise a desire to be specifically white women, and Stan does not return after season one. Yet the progress narratives that many of the characters follow do not disrupt the normative aspirations associated with 1980s neoliberalism.

Instead of being held as a model to attain, *Pose* portrays Stan as the unfulfilled, unsatisfied and inauthentic character who produces Angel as 'authentic' and 'real'. After arriving at a hotel room, Angel removes her underwear at Stan's request and euphemistically explains that she is saving up to have her 'little friend' removed. She comments that Stan must have parts of his body that he does not like too, "that [he] would love to have go away", to which he responds, "mine are all on the inside, though". Stan's dissatisfaction is re-emphasised in the following episode when he takes Angel to a diner after finding her performing at a coin-operated peep show. Over the table, Angel asks what Stan's 'deal is', observing that his type is usually gay and closeted or straight but unable to ask their wives to "stick a finger up their behind". After stating that he is neither of these 'types', Stan gives a lengthier response:

> I'm no one. I want what I'm supposed to want, I wear what I'm supposed to wear, and I work where I'm supposed to work. I stand for nothing, [...] I don't live, I don't believe, I accumulate. I'm a brand, a middle-class white guy. But you are who you are, even though the price you pay for it is being disinvited from the rest of the world. I'm the one playing dress-up. Is it wrong to want to be with one of the few people in the world who isn't? To have one person in my life who I know is real?

Stan's shallow adherence to convention contrasts with how the ballroom participants in *Paris Is Burning* imbue white middle-class subjects with a fulfilment to which they aspire and which provides entry into 'unmarked' safety. *Pose* reverses this dynamic by having the white middle-class man position the trans subject as possessing an authenticity he is unable to achieve. The way Angel and Stan are mutually situated refutes the idea that trans people are imitating gender not 'authentic' to bodily reality, instead framing the privileged cis person as the one 'playing dress-up'. This staging goes against narratives that devalue trans embodiment and hinder trans people's access to

various services and spaces by reducing their experiences to sartorial imita-
tions of the so-called 'opposite sex'. However, Stan's confession also suggests
that the trans subject is able to be 'real' and 'authentic'. *Paris Is Burning*
problematises this idea by showing ballroom participants *and* those they
idealise as caught in knots of imitation, which are never fully tightened.
Rather than approaching realness as a persistent deadlock that disturbs identity and embodiment, *Pose* depicts lack as individual and specific as it locates
the potential to be 'real' in the cultural 'other'.

It is through his romantic and erotic encounter with Angel, sustained by a
monetary arrangement, that Stan can be 'honest' about his own perceived
emptiness, brought into relief by Angel's struggle. Their exchange rebalances
their markedly unequal access to social and monetary currency. Angel's virtue
of being 'true to oneself', which emerges at the point of structural dis-
advantage, is thought to compensate for her social inferiority. Stan, who
conveys his identity as absent, lacks the spiritual enjoyment Angel supposedly
possesses. Yet the 'gap' where his identity would or should be suggests that he
is without signifiers, disavowing whiteness as a racialised position and allowing him to remain 'unmarked'.[121] In contrast, *Paris Is Burning*'s juxtaposition
of ballroom with the 'outside' de-naturalises the invisibility of signification
across clothing, gesture and other racial, gender and class markers. Figures
from ballroom and those they are emulating inform each other's signification,
yet both are implicated by a loss that underwrites their embodiment. Traversing the fantasy of a pre-discursive self indicates how social reality inscribes
the body in service of identification, yet this inscription can never deliver a
subject who is transparent to their signification.

For Butler, there is "no ontological status apart from the various acts which
constitute its reality"; that is, signifying acts generate an ontological status
rather than reflect one.[122] Drawing out the psychoanalytic dimension of Butler's work, Dean and Cynthia Dyess argue that Butler reads gender in Lacan's
symbolic and imaginary registers. The symbolic designates the realm of language, which "is something we all share, but none of us creates", whereas the
imaginary is the order into which reality is consigned, with reality designating
the "social norms and practices to which we are supposed to adapt".[123] As
Dean and Dyess recap, for Butler, "there is no viable distinction between the
concept or discourse of gender and gender itself".[124] Rather than being pre-
discursive subjects who enter or opt out of social norms, we establish gender
by how we consciously and unconsciously adopt discursive practices, which
constitute what we understand as 'reality'.

Returning to *Paris Is Burning*, Phelan grapples with her position as a
viewer and her desire for Livingston's film to be 'real', to be a "perfect
unbiased record of the [ballroom] performances", which she knows it cannot
be.[125] Presumably, like the white upwardly mobile types Livingston candidly
records, Phelan proposes that "[w]hite women like myself have been encouraged to mistake performance for ontology[,] to believe that the role is real,

and thus sufficient to constitute an identity, a sense of purpose, a reason for being".[126] Mistaking social norms and their attendant performances for the nature of one's being and value has also been absorbed by those excluded from aspirational personhood; hence, the ballroom participants long to occupy specific positions. Ruti articulates how "we routinely resort to social fantasies that blind us to the possibility that the big Other might be plagued by exactly the same kind of internal fractures as we ourselves belabor under".[127] In *Paris Is Burning*, we may assume the ballroom participants follow the cultural norm that imbues the bourgeois elites with a fulfilment that they, in turn, do not possess. Yet the film itself does not offer the same guarantee.

Phelan considers how "the only way to see if performance is an adequate substitute for ontology is through the staging of performances".[128] *Paris Is Burning* questions whether performance can generate identity by examining both ballroom performances and the surrounding discourse generated by the film's interviews. However, whereas Butler reads ontology *as* constituted through performative acts, Phelan separates ontology from gesture and signification: "In that enactment, however, we make conscious again the *difference between performance and ontology*: precisely what motivates the performance is that which ontology – the questions of being itself – will not and cannot answer."[129] As Corey explains in the documentary, realness is an ability to create a compelling illusion, but one cannot find the point where illusion ceases. Nor do the images of aspirational subjects dissuade us from the need for performance in sustaining legibility. As such, *Paris Is Burning* frames ontology as a locus of unknowability veiled by the performance process that those inside and outside of ballroom sustain. It presents performance as covering the absence of ontology but, by doing so, it cannot help but expose a fundamental gap. Rather than being what signification fails to cover, this gap is the failure of signification as such. Realness – as a category of meaning in ballroom – designates not transparency between signification and embodiment but the difficulty installed in the very process of signification.

Copjec shares Phelan's resistance to reading ontology-as-performance in her essay "Sex and the Euthanasia of Reason".[130] Here, Copjec challenges Butler's theory of gender by introducing the Lacanian order of the 'real', defined by Dean and Dyess as that which "resists assimilation to any imaginary or symbolic mode".[131] Significantly, this use of the word 'real' departs from "its colloquial connotations" as "the real has nothing to do with what we understand by 'reality'".[132] Copjec brings the real to the fore when situating sex, which occupies a position adjacent to Butler's 'gender'. Instead of locating sex as an effect of signification, Copjec argues that sex is "the stumbling block of sense", a negativity devoid of content that is made apparent by inscriptions' repeated failure to foreclose meaning.[133] Copjec is not suggesting that sex is "something that is beyond language. Something that language forever fails to grasp".[134] Rather, sex "coincides with this *failure*"; it is the "impossibility of completing meaning".[135] Although Phelan does not explicitly refer to the Lacanian real, her challenge to the collapse of performance and ontology brings out the real in 'realness'.

One of *Paris Is Burning*'s greatest achievements is not that it invites us to speculate on how manufactured rich white people are. Rather, it is the sense that no amount or version of signification would ever confer an immutable position of man or woman. In contradistinction, *Pose* proposes what Berlant terms "fantasies of unconflicted subjectivity" by closing *Paris Is Burning*'s critical fissure, opened up by the missing signifier between performance and identity that bars authenticity's establishment.[136] In doing so, *Paris Is Burning* denies the regime of identity that underwrites the neoliberal construction of success and validity, redeployed by *Pose*'s optimistic reimagining of subjects entering the American dream. The promise of the good life that *Pose* reiterates rests on a belief that, against the odds, one can attain the social placement and consequent psychic fulfilment typically reserved for those occupying specific intersections of race, class and gender that go unnamed in the conceit of meritocracy.

Conclusion

Between *Pose* and *Paris Is Burning*, two understandings of 'queerness' emerge through their heterogeneous framing of identity which bear relation to the signifiers 'authenticity' and 'realness'. *Pose* presents identity as a legible conglomerate of characteristics through its rehearsal of coherent subjects. The series does not utter 'queer' or 'authentic' in its diegesis. However, it employs tropes widely associated with these terms, which then circulate in its surrounding literature and media. The discourse of 'authenticity' suggests that the gay male and transgender experiences represented in *Pose* partake in the idea that it is important to be 'true to oneself' and live according to one's 'own rules'. In media responses, 'authenticity' has become a signifier that elevates previously erased LGBT+ identities into the realm of naturalism that white masculinity has not historically had to justify. 'Queer' is embraced as a catch-all word for LGBT+ identities, designating sexual and gender divergence from assumed heterosexual cisgender embodiment. Though queer-as-identity denotes difference, it does not delegitimise the idea of a pre-discursive body or an essential self. Instead, the hegemonic position of the 'unmarked' subject is called upon to accommodate an expanded range of identities that may make similar claims to naturalism.

Despite its obvious fictionalisation, *Pose* has taken the position of being a more 'authentic' depiction of the ballroom culture and community than its documentary predecessor. Its images of success, uplifting affect and spectacular set pieces that transform the balls into dazzling events have not appeared to undermine the idea of authentic representation. Rather, its mode of fabulation puts marginalised figures into a formula that typically centres white, cis and heteronormative persons. For Linda Williams, "the contemporary form of [American] serial television that has recently out-produced and, for many, out-classed Hollywood is fundamentally melo-drama".[137] Williams traces the rising popularity of this combination of genre and format, demonstrating how melodrama is apt for the long-form narrative structure now commonplace in television programming. *Pose* employs this popular form of on-screen storytelling, making its affective and narrative cues easy to read. It is not necessarily that *Pose*'s characters and narratives are more authentic than those of other mainstream projects. It is rather that *Pose* presents its characters via well-established practices. Because the representation of black and Latinx trans women is undeniably rare in mainstream television (especially when *Pose* first aired in 2018), the series *feels* like a radical departure from the norm. Mainstream programming does not typically present audiences with characters such as Blanca, Electra or Pray-Tell as persons with whom we are encouraged to identify, marked as they are by their racial and gendered particularity as opposed to the white masculinity that historically situates a supposedly universal subject.

In expressing queerness using the language of authenticity, characters and the past are rendered sensible as *Pose* seeks to heal the wounds of history and the gap in ontology that can never be sutured. With its revised retelling of the late 1980s into the 1990s, the series positions itself as shining a light on a vital but overlooked part of LGBT+ history. Positivity and overcoming adversity structure its narrative threads and maintain the increasingly ubiquitous connection between LGBT+ politics and a sense of 'pride', a noun that has evolved from the increasingly commercial 'gay pride parade' tradition to become a stand-in for a more generalised affect associated with LGBT+ identities.[138] This shift in discourse departs from that of *Paris Is Burning*, where the invocation of 'realness' suggests an inability to render identity comprehensible and where gestures are always an imitation of something out of reach. 'Authenticity' and 'realness' initially seem to call to a similar sense of unmediated access to the self. However, they stand disjointed as the former disavows what the latter indicates through the inability to foreclose the meaning of signification – a persistent gap, designated here by the Lacanian real.

Rather than seeking to legitimate a multiplicity of identities, 'realness' evokes a reading of queerness as that which undermines identity's conventional securing. This definition initially appears counter-intuitive, considering that the subjects of *Paris Is Burning* express a desire to assimilate into the mainstream personifications of gender. However, although this longing is more explicit in *Paris Is Burning* than in *Pose*, the film maintains that 'beneath' the performative enactments of identity, one does not find an original. This philosophical move rethinks subjectivity as discursively produced and alters the psychic investment in the fiction of meritocratic individualism. In neoliberalism, the emphasis on meritocracy sustains its economic proliferation by disavowing the intersecting forms of systemic discrimination required for its functioning.

Beyond the parameters of *Paris Is Burning*'s specific context, queer as an intervention in the construction of identity destabilises capitalism's promise of the good life. Queerness contributes to this political intervention by recognising how traditional embodiments of concentrated power do not possess that piece of the 'real' that would confer an inherent or accumulated value. Instead, queer is a position that alienates the signifying processes that wed aspiration to coordinated identity markers and which engage the paradigm of naturalism to reaffirm the hegemony of white bourgeois personhood. This intervention that queerness makes does not in itself alleviate the entrenched material and social hierarchies that situate us as social beings. However, it can problematise the neoliberal scripts of success that seductively fold us into a (cruel) optimism that sustains its psychic hold despite the pervasive lack of deliverance to the good life promised.

Notes

1 'Pose, n.6, Sense 2.a' (Oxford: Oxford University Press, July 2023), *Oxford English Dictionary*, https://doi.org/10.1093/OED/5014973257.
2 'Pose, n.6, Sense 2.b', *Oxford English Dictionary*, https://doi.org/10.1093/OED/4516862784.
3 *Pose* is created by Ryan Murphy, along with Brad Falchuk and Steven Canals, for FX studio, a subsidiary of the Disney entertainment conglomerate.
4 Jennie Livingston also directed an episode of *Pose*: S2E7, "Blow" (2019).
5 bell hooks, *Reel to Real: Race, Sex, and Class at the Movies* (London: Routledge, 1996), 275–90.
6 In *Paris Is Burning*, the trans subjects are referred to (by themselves and others) as transsexuals. Although this language is carried over into *Pose*, the language surrounding the television series (articles, interviews, etc.) uses 'transgender'. This chapter uses the contemporary term 'trans', which designates a range of non-cisgender positions including transsexual and transgender.
7 Brenda R. Weber and David Greven, 'Introduction: Touching Queerness: Ryan Murphy's Queer America', in *Ryan Murphy's Queer America*, ed. Brenda R. Weber and David Greven (London: Routledge, 2022), 1, https://doi.org/10.4324/9781003170358-1.
8 Lynne Joyrich, 'Posing as Normal?', in *Ryan Murphy's Queer America*, by Brenda R. Weber and David Greven (London: Routledge, 2022), 36. https://doi.org/10.4324/9781003170358-3.
9 Examples of updated versions of previous productions include *Gossip Girl* (rebooted 2021–, original series 2007–2021), *Queer as Folk* (rebooted 2022, original series 1999–2001), *A League of Their Own* (rebooted as a series 2022–, original film 1992), *L Word: Generation Q* (rebooted 2019–, original series [*The L Word*] 2004–2009), *And Just Like That* (rebooted 2021–, original series [*Sex and the City*] 1998–2004), *Queer Eye* (rebooted 2018–, original series [*Queer Eye for the Straight Guy*] 2003–2007), *Tales of the City* (rebooted 2019, original series 1993) and *Heartbreak High* (rebooted 2022–, original series 1994–1999). The sheer (and growing) number of updated series indicates a significant demand for mainstream shows that introduce and focus on a more diverse cast of characters.
10 Leslie Goldberg, 'Ryan Murphy Makes History with Largest Cast of Transgender Actors for FX's "Pose"', *The Hollywood Reporter*, 25 October 2017; Rhyannon Styles, 'Why, to a Transgender Woman, New TV Series Pose Seems So

Incredible', *Elle*, 7 March 2019, https://www.elle.com/uk/life-and-culture/elle-voices/a26745725/pose-tv-show-importance-transgender-community/; Jon Bernstein, '"Nothing Like This Has Ever Happened": How TV Drama Pose Breaks New Ground', *The Guardian*, 1 June 2018, online edition, https://www.theguardian.com/tv-and-radio/2018/jun/01/pose-ryan-murphy-transgender-actors-groundbreaking-new-show.

11 Other recent television shows have employed trans actors to play trans roles, such as Candis Cayne in *Dirty Sexy Money* (2007–2008), Laverne Cox in *Orange is the New Black* (2013–2019) and Alexandra Billings and Trace Lysette in *Transparent* (2014–2019). However, these examples are of supporting roles, while central trans roles are overwhelmingly played by cis actors. Recent examples of this casting include Jeffrey Tambour in *Transparent*, Felicity Huffman in *Transamerica* (2005), Jared Leto in *Dallas Buyers Club* (2013) and Eddie Redmayne in *The Danish Girl* (2015). For longer lists of cis actors appearing as trans characters in television and film, see Mary Grace Lewis, '23 Cisgender Actors Who Played Transgender in Movies', *Advocate*, no date, https://www.advocate.com/arts-entertainment/2018/7/10/23-cisgender-actors-who-played-trangender-movies#media-gallery-media-1.

12 'GLAAD Works with Hollywood to Shape Transgender Stories and Help Cast Trans Actors', GLAAD.org, 12 May 2020, https://www.glaad.org/blog/glaad-works-hollywood-shape-transgender-stories-and-help-cast-trans-actors.

13 See Nina Metz, 'Why Trans Actors Should Be Cast in Trans Roles', *Chicago Tribune*, 13 July 2018, online edition, https://www.chicagotribune.com/entertainment/movies/ct-mov-trans-actors-for-trans-roles-0713-story.html.

14 See Jake Kanter, 'Russell T Davies on How the Queer Casting Rule on HBO Max's "It's a Sin" Proved a Triumph', *Deadline*, 2 March 2021, online, deadline.com/2021/03/russell-t-davies-omari-douglas-its-a-sin-interview-gay-casting-1234699738/; Nick Levine and Russell T. David, 'It's a Sin Creator Russell T Davies: "Cast Gay as Gay"', *AnOther Magazine*, 20 January 2021, online, https://www.anothermag.com/design-living/13057/its-a-sin-creator-russell-t-davies-channel-4-cast-trailer-review-interview.

15 Richard Lawson, 'Stonewall Is Terribly Offensive, and Offensively Terrible', *Vanity Fair*, 22 September 2015; Mark Segal, 'I Was at the Stonewall Riots. The Movie "Stonewall" Gets Everything Wrong', PBS News Hour, 23 September 2015, https://www.pbs.org/newshour/arts/stonewall-movie; Maya Stanton, '"Stonewall": EW Review', *Entertainment Weekly*, 28 September 2015, https://ew.com/article/2015/09/28/stonewall-ew-review/; David C. Oh, *Whitewashing the Movies: Asian Erasure and White Subjectivity in U.S. Film Culture* (New Jersey: Rutgers University Press, 2021), https://doi.org/10.36019/9781978808669.

16 Variety's Transgender in Hollywood Roundtable, YouTube video, 7 August 2018, https://www.youtube.com/watch?v=6_oqeXz7vbc.

17 Michael Cooper, 'Why Pose Is the Most Groundbreaking LGBTQ TV Show Ever', *LA Weekly*, 19 July 2018. See also Treye Green, '"It Made My Walk a Little Taller": The Inspiring LBGTQ Legacy of Pose', *The Guardian*, 8 July 2021, online edition, https://www.theguardian.com/tv-and-radio/2021/jun/08/pose-tv-show-fx-lgbtq-legacy.

18 Alfred L. Martin Jr., 'Pose(r): Ryan Murphy, Trans and Queer of Color Labor, and the Politics of Representation', *Los Angeles Review of Books*, 2 August 2018.

19 Alfred L. Martin Jr., 'Pose(r): Ryan Murphy, Trans and Queer of Color Labor, and the Politics of Representation', *Los Angeles Review of Books*, 2 August 2018.

20 Alfred L. Martin, 'For Scholars … When Studying the Queer of Color Image Alone Isn't Enough', *Communication and Critical/Cultural Studies* 17, no. 1 (2 January 2020): 70, https://doi.org/10.1080/14791420.2020.1723797.

21 Alfred L. Martin, 'The End of the "Best Actor" Discourse?', in *Ryan Murphy's Queer America*, by Brenda R. Weber and David Greven (London: Routledge, 2022), 213–226. https://doi.org/10.4324/9781003170358-18.

22 Alfred L. Martin, 'The End of the "Best Actor" Discourse?', in *Ryan Murphy's Queer America*, by Brenda R. Weber and David Greven (London: Routledge, 2022), 215. https://doi.org/10.4324/9781003170358-18.

23 Alfred L. Martin, 'The End of the "Best Actor" Discourse?', in *Ryan Murphy's Queer America*, by Brenda R. Weber and David Greven (London: Routledge, 2022), 221. https://doi.org/10.4324/9781003170358-18.

24 Alfred L. Martin, 'The End of the "Best Actor" Discourse?', in *Ryan Murphy's Queer America*, by Brenda R. Weber and David Greven (London: Routledge, 2022), 221. https://doi.org/10.4324/9781003170358-18.

25 Sarah E.S. Sinwell, 'Showrunning Activism', in *Ryan Murphy's Queer America*, by Brenda R. Weber and David Greven (London: Routledge, 2022), 241–253, https://doi.org/10.4324/9781003170358-20.

26 Michael Goddard and Christopher Hogg, 'Introduction: Trans TV Dossier, III: Trans TV Re-Evaluated, Part 2', *Critical Studies in Television* 15, no. 3 (2020): 261, https://doi.org/10.1177/1749602020937566.

27 Michael Goddard and Christopher Hogg, 'Introduction: Trans TV Dossier, III: Trans TV Re-Evaluated, Part 2', *Critical Studies in Television* 15, no. 3 (2020): 261, https://doi.org/10.1177/1749602020937566.

28 Debra Ferreday, 'From Dorian's Closet to Elektra's Trunk: Visibility, Trauma and Gender Euphoria in Pose', *Queer Studies in Media & Popular Culture* 7, issue 1 (June 2022): 9–25. https://doi.org/10.1386/qsmpc_00065_1, 11.

29 Debra Ferreday, 'From Dorian's Closet to Elektra's Trunk: Visibility, Trauma and Gender Euphoria in Pose', *Queer Studies in Media & Popular Culture* 7, issue 1 (June 2022): 9–25. https://doi.org/10.1386/qsmpc_00065_1, 12.

30 E. Alex Jung, '"We Did Something Revolutionary": Janet Mock on the First Season of FX's Pose, Challenging Ryan Murphy, and the Politics of Desire', *Vulture*, no date, emphasis in original.

31 E. Alex Jung, '"We Did Something Revolutionary": Janet Mock on the First Season of FX's Pose, Challenging Ryan Murphy, and the Politics of Desire', *Vulture*, no date; Phillip Galanas, 'Ryan Murphy and Janet Mock on "Pose," Diversity and Netflix', *The New York Times*, 23 May 2018, online edition, https://www.nytimes.com/2018/05/23/arts/television/pose-ryan-murphy-janet-mock.html.

32 Mari Ruti, *The Ethics of Opting Out: Queer Theory's Defiant Subjects* (New York: Columbia University Press, 2017), 2.

33 Mari Ruti, *The Ethics of Opting Out: Queer Theory's Defiant Subjects* (New York: Columbia University Press, 2017), 2.

34 Debra Ferreday, 'From Dorian's Closet to Elektra's Trunk: Visibility, Trauma and Gender Euphoria in Pose', *Queer Studies in Media & Popular Culture* 7, issue 1 (June 2022): 9–25. https://doi.org/10.1386/qsmpc_00065_1, 18.

35 Michael Lovelock, *Reality TV and Queer Identities: Sexuality, Authenticity, Celebrity* (Cham: Palgrave Macmillan, Springer International, 2019), 8.

36 Michael Lovelock, *Reality TV and Queer Identities: Sexuality, Authenticity, Celebrity* (Cham: Palgrave Macmillan, Springer International, 2019), 8.

37 Lovelock, 'Queerness as Authenticity in Reality TV', in *Reality TV and Queer Identities*, 63–92.

38 Sarah Banet-Weiser, *Authentic TM: The Politics and Ambivalence in a Brand Culture* (New York: New York University Press, 2012), 10.

39 Sarah Banet-Weiser, *Authentic TM: The Politics and Ambivalence in a Brand Culture* (New York: New York University Press, 2012), 7.

40 Lynne Joyrich, 'Posing as Normal?', in *Ryan Murphy's Queer America*, by Brenda R. Weber and David Greven (London: Routledge, 2022), 36. https://doi.org/10.4324/9781003170358-3.

41 For examples see Leslie Goldberg, 'Ryan Murphy Makes History with Largest Cast of Transgender Actors for FX's "Pose"', *The Hollywood Reporter*, 25 October 2017; Michael Cooper, 'Why Pose Is the Most Groundbreaking LGBTQ TV Show Ever', *LA Weekly*, 19 July 2018; Meredith James, '"Nobody Wants to See That Fuckhead": Ball Culture and Donald Trump in FX's Pose', in *Trump Fiction: Essays on Donald Trump in Literature, Film, and Television*, ed. Stephen Hock (Lanham: Rowman & Littlefield, 2019), 213–224; Rhyannon Styles, 'Why, to a Transgender Woman, New TV Series Pose Seems So Incredible', *Elle*, 7 March 2019, https://www.elle.com/uk/life-and-culture/elle-voices/a26745725/pose-tv-show-importance-transgender-community/; Treye Green, '"It Made My Walk a Little Taller": The Inspiring LBGTQ Legacy of Pose', *The Guardian*, 8 July 2021, online edition, https://www.theguardian.com/tv-and-radio/2021/jun/08/pose-tv-show-fx-lgbtq-legacy; Debra Ferreday, 'From Dorian's Closet to Elektra's Trunk: Visibility, Trauma and Gender Euphoria in Pose', *Queer Studies in Media & Popular Culture* 7, issue 1 (June 2022): 9–25. https://doi.org/10.1386/qsmpc_00065_1; Alfred L. Martin, 'The End of the "Best Actor" Discourse?', in *Ryan Murphy's Queer America*, by Brenda R. Weber and David Greven (London: Routledge, 2022), 221. https://doi.org/10.4324/9781003170358-18.

42 Derek Hook and Stijn Vanheule, 'Revisiting the Master-Signifier, or, Mandela and Repression', *Frontiers in Psychology* 6 (19 January 2016): 2, https://doi.org/10.3389/fpsyg.2015.02028. See also Slavoj Žižek, The Sublime Object of Ideology (London: Verso, 2008), 113.

43 Jacques Lacan, *The Seminar of Jacques Lacan. Book 3, The Psychoses, 1955–1956*, ed. Jacques-Alain Miller, trans. Russell Grigg (London: Routledge, 1993), 268.

44 Derek Hook and Stijn Vanheule, 'Revisiting the Master-Signifier, or, Mandela and Repression', *Frontiers in Psychology* 6 (19 January 2016): 2, https://doi.org/10.3389/fpsyg.2015.02028.

45 Saidiya Hartman, 'Venus in Two Acts', *Small Axe: A Journal of Criticism* 12, no. 2 (2008): 11, https://doi.org/10.1215/-12-2-1.

46 Susan Stryker, *Transgender History: The Roots of Today's Revolution* (New York: Seal Press, 2017), 110–111.

47 Gayatri Chakravorty Spivak discusses these two different modes of representation in 'Can the Subaltern Speak?' in Gayatri Chakravorty Spivak, *Can the Subaltern Speak: Reflections on the History of an Idea*, ed. Rosalind C. Morris (New York: Columbia University Press, 2010), 28.

48 Lynne Joyrich, 'Posing as Normal?', in *Ryan Murphy's Queer America*, by Brenda R. Weber and David Greven (London: Routledge, 2022), 36. https://doi.org/10.4324/9781003170358-3.

49 Lynne Joyrich, 'Posing as Normal?', in *Ryan Murphy's Queer America*, by Brenda R. Weber and David Greven (London: Routledge, 2022), 29. https://doi.org/10.4324/9781003170358-3.

50 Lynne Joyrich, 'Posing as Normal?', in *Ryan Murphy's Queer America*, by Brenda R. Weber and David Greven (London: Routledge, 2022), 28. https://doi.org/10.4324/9781003170358-3.

51 Richard Dyer, *Only Entertainment* (New York: Routledge, 2002), 19.

52 Richard Dyer, *Only Entertainment* (New York: Routledge, 2002), 20.

53 Richard Dyer, *Only Entertainment* (New York: Routledge, 2002), 20.

54 Annette Kuhn, 'Women's Genres: Melodrama, Soap Opera, and Theory', in *Feminist Television Criticism: A Reader*, ed. Charlotte Brunsdon, Julie D'Acci and Lynn Spigel (Oxford: Clarendon, 1997), 153.

55 Annette Kuhn, 'Women's Genres: Melodrama, Soap Opera, and Theory', in *Feminist Television Criticism: A Reader*, ed. Charlotte Brunsdon, Julie D'Acci and Lynn Spigel (Oxford: Clarendon, 1997), 153.

56 Lynne Joyrich, 'Posing as Normal?', in *Ryan Murphy's Queer America*, by Brenda R. Weber and David Greven (London: Routledge, 2022), 34. https://doi.org/10.4324/9781003170358-3.

57 Lynne Joyrich, 'Posing as Normal?', in *Ryan Murphy's Queer America*, by Brenda R. Weber and David Greven (London: Routledge, 2022), 35. https://doi.org/10.4324/9781003170358-3.

58 Lynne Joyrich, 'Posing as Normal?', in *Ryan Murphy's Queer America*, by Brenda R. Weber and David Greven (London: Routledge, 2022), 35. https://doi.org/10.4324/9781003170358-3.

59 Lee Edelman, *No Future: Queer Theory and the Death Drive* (Durham: Duke University Press, 2004).

60 Lynne Joyrich, 'Posing as Normal?', in *Ryan Murphy's Queer America*, by Brenda R. Weber and David Greven (London: Routledge, 2022), 39. https://doi.org/10.4324/9781003170358-3.

61 In addition to this regeneration of family that closes season two, the development of Blanca's House of Evangelista throughout the series and Angel and Papi's family in season three reinforce the importance of family for establishing happiness and success in capitalist society.

62 Lauren Berlant, *Cruel Optimism* (Durham: Duke University Press, 2011), 1.

63 Lauren Berlant, *Cruel Optimism* (Durham: Duke University Press, 2011), 10–11.

64 David Harvey, *A Brief History of Neoliberalism* (Oxford: Oxford University Press, 2005), 1.

65 David Harvey, *A Brief History of Neoliberalism* (Oxford: Oxford University Press, 2005), 1.

66 David Harvey, *A Brief History of Neoliberalism* (Oxford: Oxford University Press, 2005), 1.

67 David Harvey, *A Brief History of Neoliberalism* (Oxford: Oxford University Press, 2005), 5–38.

68 Todd McGowan, *The End of Dissatisfaction?: Jacques Lacan and the Emerging Society of Enjoyment* (Albany: State University of New York Press, 2004), 34.

69 Judith Williamson, '"Up Where You Belong": Hollywood Images of Big Business in the 1980s', in John Corner and Sylvia Harvey, *Enterprise and Heritage: Crosscurrents of National Culture* (London: Routledge, 1991), 147–156.

70 Bret Easton Ellis, *American Psycho* (London: Picador, 1991); film adaptation directed by Mary Harron, *American Psycho* (2000).

71 Philip Mirowski and Dieter Plehwe, *The Road from Mont Pèlerin: The Making of the Neoliberal Thought Collective* (Cambridge: Harvard University Press, 2009), 5.

72 David Harvey, *A Brief History of Neoliberalism* (Oxford: Oxford University Press, 2005), 65–66.

73 Philip Mirowski and Dieter Plehwe, *The Road from Mont Pèlerin: The Making of the Neoliberal Thought Collective* (Cambridge: Harvard University Press, 2009), 2.

74 Lauren Berlant, *Cruel Optimism* (Durham: Duke University Press, 2011), 2.

75 Lauren Berlant, *Cruel Optimism* (Durham: Duke University Press, 2011), 2.

76 Mari Ruti, *The Ethics of Opting Out: Queer Theory's Defiant Subjects* (New York: Columbia University Press, 2017), 16.

77 Elizabeth Freeman, *Time Binds: Queer Temporalities, Queer Histories* (Durham: Duke University Press, 2010), 4.

78 Elizabeth Freeman, *Time Binds: Queer Temporalities, Queer Histories* (Durham: Duke University Press, 2010), 6.

79 Shani Orgad and Rosalind Gill, *Confidence Culture* (Duke University Press, 2022), 7.

80 Shani Orgad and Rosalind Gill, *Confidence Culture* (Duke University Press, 2022), 7.

81 Shani Orgad and Rosalind Gill, *Confidence Culture* (Duke University Press, 2022), 17.

82 Shani Orgad and Rosalind Gill, *Confidence Culture* (Duke University Press, 2022), 40–41, emphasis in original.

83 See Debra Ferreday, 'From Dorian's Closet to Elektra's Trunk: Visibility, Trauma and Gender Euphoria in Pose', *Queer Studies in Media & Popular Culture* 7, issue 1 (June 2022): 9–25. https://doi.org/10.1386/qsmpc_00065_1, 15; Lynne Joyrich, 'Posing as Normal?', in *Ryan Murphy's Queer America*, by Brenda R. Weber and David Greven (London: Routledge, 2022), 36. https://doi.org/10.4324/9781003170358-3.

84 Shani Orgad and Rosalind Gill, *Confidence Culture* (Duke University Press, 2022), 41.

85 Robyn Wiegman, *American Anatomies: Theorizing Race and Gender* (Durham: Duke University Press, 1995), 41.

86 Robyn Wiegman, *American Anatomies: Theorizing Race and Gender* (Durham: Duke University Press, 1995), 41.

87 Robyn Wiegman, *American Anatomies: Theorizing Race and Gender* (Durham: Duke University Press, 1995), 42.

88 C. Riley Snorton, 'A Nightmarish Silhouette: Racialization and the Long Exposure of Transition' in *Black on Both Sides: A Racial History of Trans Identity* (Minneapolis: University of Minnesota Press, 2017), 139–175.

89 C. Riley Snorton, 'A Nightmarish Silhouette: Racialization and the Long Exposure of Transition' in *Black on Both Sides: A Racial History of Trans Identity* (Minneapolis: University of Minnesota Press, 2017), 142.

90 C. Riley Snorton, 'A Nightmarish Silhouette: Racialization and the Long Exposure of Transition' in *Black on Both Sides: A Racial History of Trans Identity* (Minneapolis: University of Minnesota Press, 2017), 139

91 C. Riley Snorton, 'A Nightmarish Silhouette: Racialization and the Long Exposure of Transition' in *Black on Both Sides: A Racial History of Trans Identity* (Minneapolis: University of Minnesota Press, 2017), 142.

92 Snorton studies coverage of Lucy Hicks Anderson, Georgia Black, Carlett Brown, James McHarris/Annie Lee Grant and Ava Betty Brown; C. Riley Snorton, 'A Nightmarish Silhouette: Racialization and the Long Exposure of Transition' in *Black on Both Sides: A Racial History of Trans Identity* (Minneapolis: University of Minnesota Press, 2017), 175.

93 C. Riley Snorton, 'A Nightmarish Silhouette: Racialization and the Long Exposure of Transition' in *Black on Both Sides: A Racial History of Trans Identity* (Minneapolis: University of Minnesota Press, 2017), 175.

94 Robyn Wiegman, *American Anatomies: Theorizing Race and Gender* (Durham: Duke University Press, 1995), 131.

95 Robyn Wiegman, *American Anatomies: Theorizing Race and Gender* (Durham: Duke University Press, 1995), 133.

96   Robyn Wiegman, *American Anatomies: Theorizing Race and Gender* (Durham: Duke University Press, 1995), 140.

97   bell hooks, 'Is Paris Burning?', in *Reel to Real: Race, Sex, and Class at the Movies* (London: Routledge, 1996), 275–290.

98   bell hooks, 'Is Paris Burning?', in *Reel to Real: Race, Sex, and Class at the Movies* (London: Routledge, 1996), 279.

99   bell hooks, 'Is Paris Burning?', in *Reel to Real: Race, Sex, and Class at the Movies* (London: Routledge, 1996), 283.

100   bell hooks, 'Is Paris Burning?', in *Reel to Real: Race, Sex, and Class at the Movies* (London: Routledge, 1996), 284–287.

101   Peggy Phelan, 'The Golden Apple: Jennie Livingston's Paris Is Burning', in *Unmarked: The Politics of Performance* (London: Routledge, 1993), 94.

102   Peggy Phelan, 'The Golden Apple: Jennie Livingston's Paris Is Burning', in *Unmarked: The Politics of Performance* (London: Routledge, 1993), 94.

103   Jacques Lacan, *The Seminar of Jacques Lacan/Book XX, On Feminine Sexuality: The Limits of Love and Knowledge: Encore 1972–1972*, ed. Jacques-Alain Miller, trans. Bruce Fink (New York: Norton, 1999), 7.

104   Judith Butler, *Bodies That Matter: On the Discursive Limits of 'Sex'* (Abingdon: Routledge, 2011), 81–97.

105   Judith Butler, *Bodies That Matter: On the Discursive Limits of 'Sex'* (Abingdon: Routledge, 2011), 85.

106   Judith Butler, *Gender Trouble: Feminism and the Subversion of Identity* (New York: Routledge, 2007), 185, emphasis in original.

107   Judith Butler, *Gender Trouble: Feminism and the Subversion of Identity* (New York: Routledge, 2007), 198, emphasis added.

108   Jean Baudrillard, *Simulacra and Simulation*, trans. Sheila Faria Glaser (Ann Arbor: University of Michigan Press, 1994), 1.

109   Mari Ruti, *The Singularity of Being: Lacan and the Immortal Within* (New York: Fordham University Press, 2012), 37–38.

110   Judith Butler, *Gender Trouble: Feminism and the Subversion of Identity* (New York: Routledge, 2007), 200.

111   Peggy Phelan, 'The Golden Apple: Jennie Livingston's Paris Is Burning', in *Unmarked: The Politics of Performance* (London: Routledge, 1993), 103.

112   Peggy Phelan, 'The Golden Apple: Jennie Livingston's Paris Is Burning', in *Unmarked: The Politics of Performance* (London: Routledge, 1993), 104.

113   Peggy Phelan, 'The Golden Apple: Jennie Livingston's Paris Is Burning', in *Unmarked: The Politics of Performance* (London: Routledge, 1993), 104.

114   Oliver Davis and Tim Dean, *Hatred of Sex* (Lincoln: University of Nebraska Press, 2022), 31.

115   Oliver Davis and Tim Dean, *Hatred of Sex* (Lincoln: University of Nebraska Press, 2022), 31.

116   Patricia Gherovici, *Transgender Psychoanalysis: A Lacanian Perspective on Sexual Difference* (London: Routledge, 2017), 103.

117   Patricia Gherovici, *Transgender Psychoanalysis: A Lacanian Perspective on Sexual Difference* (London: Routledge, 2017), 103.

118   Patricia Gherovici, *Transgender Psychoanalysis: A Lacanian Perspective on Sexual Difference* (London: Routledge, 2017), 103.

119   Andrea Long Chu, *Females* (London: Verso, 2019), 12.

120   bell hooks, 'Is Paris Burning?', in *Reel to Real: Race, Sex, and Class at the Movies* (London: Routledge, 1996), 281.

121 See Richard Dyer, 'The Matter of Whiteness', in *White: Essays on Race and Culture* (London: Routledge, 2013), 1–40. Whiteness as a racial and historical category is explored further in the second chapter of this book.
122 Judith Butler, *Gender Trouble: Feminism and the Subversion of Identity* (New York: Routledge, 2007), 185.
123 Cynthia Dyess and Tim Dean, 'Gender: The Impossibility of Meaning', *Psychoanalytic Dialogues* 10, no. 5 (15 September 2000): 740. https://doi.org/10.1080/10481881009348579.
124 Cynthia Dyess and Tim Dean, 'Gender: The Impossibility of Meaning', *Psychoanalytic Dialogues* 10, no. 5 (15 September 2000): 746. https://doi.org/10.1080/10481881009348579.
125 Peggy Phelan, 'The Golden Apple: Jennie Livingston's Paris Is Burning', in *Unmarked: The Politics of Performance* (London: Routledge, 1993), 104.
126 Peggy Phelan, 'The Golden Apple: Jennie Livingston's Paris Is Burning', in *Unmarked: The Politics of Performance* (London: Routledge, 1993), 105.
127 Mari Ruti, *The Singularity of Being: Lacan and the Immortal Within* (New York: Fordham University Press, 2012), 38.
128 Peggy Phelan, 'The Golden Apple: Jennie Livingston's Paris Is Burning', in *Unmarked: The Politics of Performance* (London: Routledge, 1993), 105.
129 Peggy Phelan, 'The Golden Apple: Jennie Livingston's Paris Is Burning', in *Unmarked: The Politics of Performance* (London: Routledge, 1993), 105, emphasis added.
130 Joan Copjec, 'Sex and the Euthanasia of Reason', in *Read My Desire: Lacan against the Historicists* (Cambridge: MIT Press, 1994), 201–236.
131 Cynthia Dyess and Tim Dean, 'Gender: The Impossibility of Meaning', *Psychoanalytic Dialogues* 10, no. 5 (15 September 2000): 742. https://doi.org/10.1080/10481881009348579.
132 Cynthia Dyess and Tim Dean, 'Gender: The Impossibility of Meaning', *Psychoanalytic Dialogues* 10, no. 5 (15 September 2000): 738. https://doi.org/10.1080/10481881009348579.
133 Joan Copjec, 'Sex and the Euthanasia of Reason', in *Read My Desire: Lacan against the Historicists* (Cambridge: MIT Press, 1994), 204.
134 Joan Copjec, 'Sex and the Euthanasia of Reason', in *Read My Desire: Lacan against the Historicists* (Cambridge: MIT Press, 1994), 206.
135 Joan Copjec, 'Sex and the Euthanasia of Reason', in *Read My Desire: Lacan against the Historicists* (Cambridge: MIT Press, 1994), 206, emphasis in original.
136 Lauren Berlant, *The Female Complaint: The Unfinished Business of Sentimentality in American Culture* (Durham: Duke University Press, 2008), 35.
137 Linda Williams, 'World and Time: Serial Television Melodrama in America', in *Melodrama Unbound: Across History, Media, and National Cultures*, ed. Christine Gledhill and Linda Williams (New York: Columbia University Press, 2018), 169.
138 For an analysis of the history of pride and its increased commercialisation, see Jodie Taylor, 'Festivalizing Sexualities: Discourses of "Pride", Counter-Discourses of "Shame"', in *The Festivalization of Culture*, ed. Andy Bennett and Jodie Taylor (London: Routledge, 2016), 27–48, https://doi.org/10.4324/9781315558189.

References

Banet-Weiser, Sarah. *Authentic TM: The Politics and Ambivalence in a Brand Culture.* New York: New York University Press, 2012.

Baudrillard, Jean. *Simulacra and Simulation*. Translated by Sheila Faria Glaser. Ann Arbor: University of Michigan Press, 1994.

Berlant, Lauren. *Cruel Optimism*. Durham: Duke University Press, 2011.

Berlant, Lauren. *The Female Complaint: The Unfinished Business of Sentimentality in American Culture*. Durham: Duke University Press, 2008.

Bernstein, Jon. '"Nothing like This Has Ever Happened": How TV Drama Pose Breaks New Ground.' *The Guardian*, 1 June 2018. Available at: https://www.theguardian.com/tv-and-radio/2018/jun/01/pose-ryan-murphy-transgender-actors-groundbreaking-new-show.

Butler, Judith. *Bodies That Matter: On the Discursive Limits of 'Sex'*. Abingdon: Routledge, 2011.

Butler, Judith. *Gender Trouble: Feminism and the Subversion of Identity*. New York: Routledge, 2007.

Chu, Andrea Long. *Females*. London: Verso, 2019.

Cooper, Michael. 'Why Pose Is the Most Groundbreaking LGBTQ TV Show Ever.' *LA Weekly*, 19 July 2018.

Copjec, Joan. *Read My Desire: Lacan against the Historicists*. Cambridge: MIT Press, 1994.

Davis, Oliver, and Tim Dean. *Hatred of Sex*. Lincoln: University of Nebraska Press, 2022.

Dyer, Richard. *Only Entertainment*. New York: Routledge, 2002.

Dyer, Richard. *White: Essays on Race and Culture*. London: Routledge, 2013.

Dyess, Cynthia, and Tim Dean. 'Gender: The Impossibility of Meaning.' *Psychoanalytic Dialogues* 10, no. 5 (15 September 2000): 738–746. https://doi.org/10.1080/10481881009348579.

Easton Ellis, Bret. *American Psycho*. London: Picador, 1991.

Edelman, Lee. *No Future: Queer Theory and the Death Drive*. Durham: Duke University Press, 2004.

Ferreday, Debra. 'From Dorian's Closet to Elektra's Trunk: Visibility, Trauma, and Gender Euphoria in Pose.' *Queer Studies in Media & Popular Culture* 7, no. 1 (June 2022): 9–25. https://doi.org/10.1386/qsmpc_00065_1.

Freeman, Elizabeth. *Time Binds: Queer Temporalities, Queer Histories*. Durham: Duke University Press, 2010.

Galanas, Phillip. 'Ryan Murphy and Janet Mock on "Pose," Diversity and Netflix', *The New York Times*, 23 May 2018. Available at: https://www.nytimes.com/2018/05/23/arts/television/pose-ryan-murphy-janet-mock.html.

Gherovici, Patricia. *Transgender Psychoanalysis: A Lacanian Perspective on Sexual Difference*. London: Routledge, 2017.

Goddard, Michael, and Christopher Hogg. 'Introduction: Trans TV Dossier, III: Trans TV Re-Evaluated, Part 2.' *Critical Studies in Television* 15, no. 3 (2020): 261–263. https://doi.org/10.1177/1749602020937566.

Goldberg, Leslie. 'Ryan Murphy Makes History with Largest Cast of Transgender Actors for FX's Pose.' *The Hollywood Reporter*, 25 October 2017.

Green, Treye. '"It Made My Walk a Little Taller": The Inspiring LBGTQ Legacy of Pose.' *The Guardian*, July 8, 2021. Available at: https://www.theguardian.com/tv-and-radio/2021/jul/08/pose-tv-show-fx-lgbtq-legacy.

Hartman, Saidiya. 'Venus in Two Acts', *Small Axe: A Journal of Criticism* 12, no. 2 (2008): 11. https://doi.org/10.1215/-12-2-1.

Harvey, David. *A Brief History of Neoliberalism*. Oxford: Oxford University Press, 2005.

Hook, Derek, and Stijn Vanheule. 'Revisiting the Master-Signifier, or, Mandela and Repression.' *Frontiers in Psychology* 6 (19 January 2016): 2–5. https://doi.org/10.3389/fpsyg.2015.02028.

hooks, bell. *Reel to Real: Race, Sex, and Class at the Movies*. London: Routledge, 1996.

James, Meredith. '"Nobody Wants to See That Fuckhead": Ball Culture and Donald Trump in FX's Pose.' In *Trump Fiction: Essays on Donald Trump in Literature, Film, and Television*, edited by Stephen Hock, 213–224. Lanham: Rowman & Littlefield, 2019.

Joyrich, Lynne. 'Posing as Normal?' In *Ryan Murphy's Queer America*, edited by Brenda R. Weber and David Greven, 28–36. London: Routledge, 2022. https://doi.org/10.4324/9781003170358-3.

Jung, E. Alex. '"We Did Something Revolutionary": Janet Mock on the First Season of FX's Pose, Challenging Ryan Murphy, and the Politics of Desire', *Vulture*, no date.

Kanter, Jake. 'Russell T Davies on How the Queer Casting Rule on HBO Max's *It's a Sin* Proved a Triumph.' *Deadline*, 2 March 2021. Available at: https://deadline.com/2021/03/russell-t-davies-omari-douglas-its-a-sin-interview-gay-casting-1234699738/.

Kuhn, Annette. 'Women's Genres: Melodrama, Soap Opera, and Theory.' In *Feminist Television Criticism: A Reader*, ed. Charlotte Brunsdon, Julie D'Acci and Lynn Spigel, 153. Oxford: Clarendon, 1997.

Lacan, Jacques. *The Seminar of Jacques Lacan. Book 3, The Psychoses, 1955–1956*. Edited by Jacques-Alain Miller. Translated by Russell Grigg. London: Routledge, 1993.

Lacan, Jacques. *The Seminar of Jacques Lacan/Book XX, On Feminine Sexuality: The Limits of Love and Knowledge: Encore 1972–1972*. Edited by Jacques-Alain Miller. Translated by Bruce Fink. New York: Norton, 1999.

Lawson, Richard. 'Stonewall Is Terribly Offensive, and Offensively Terrible.' *Vanity Fair*, 22 September 2015.

Levine, Nick, and Russell T. David, 'It's A Sin Creator Russell T Davies: "Cast Gay as Gay"', *AnOther Magazine*, 20 January 2021. Available at: https://www.anothermag.com/design-living/13057/its-a-sin-creator-russell-t-davies-channel-4-cast-trailer-review-interview.

Lewis, Mary Grace. '23 Cisgender Actors Who Played Transgender in Movies', *Advocate*, no date. Available at: https://www.advocate.com/arts-entertainment/2018/7/10/23-cisgender-actors-who-played-trangender-movies#media-gallery-media-1.

Lovelock, Michael. *Reality TV and Queer Identities: Sexuality, Authenticity, Celebrity*. Cham: Palgrave Macmillan, Springer International, 2019.

Martin, Alfred L. Jr. 'For Scholars … When Studying the Queer of Color Image Alone Isn't Enough.' *Communication and Critical/Cultural Studies* 17, no. 1 (2 January 2020): 70–76. https://doi.org/10.1080/14791420.2020.1723797.

Martin, Alfred L. Jr. 'Pose(r): Ryan Murphy, Trans and Queer of Color Labor, and the Politics of Representation.' *Los Angeles Review of Books*, 2 August 2018.

Martin, Alfred L. Jr. 'The End of the "Best Actor" Discourse?' In *Ryan Murphy's Queer America*, by Brenda R. Weber and David Greven, 213–226. London: Routledge, 2022. https://doi.org/10.4324/9781003170358-18.

McGowan, Todd. *The End of Dissatisfaction?: Jacques Lacan and the Emerging Society of Enjoyment*. Albany: State University of New York Press, 2004.

Metz, Nina. 'Why Trans Actors Should Be Cast in Trans Roles.' *Chicago Tribune*, 13 July 2018. Available at: https://www.chicagotribune.com/entertainment/movies/ct-m ov-trans-actors-for-trans-roles-0713-story.html.

Mirowski, Philip, and Dieter Plehwe. *The Road from Mont Pèlerin: The Making of the Neoliberal Thought Collective.* Cambridge: Harvard University Press, 2009.

Oh, David C. *Whitewashing the Movies: Asian Erasure and White Subjectivity in U.S. Film Culture.* New Brunswick, NJ: Rutgers University Press, 2021. https://doi.org/10.36019/9781978808669.

Orgad, Shani, and Rosalind Gill. *Confidence Culture.* Durham: Duke University Press, 2022.

Phelan, Peggy. *Unmarked: The Politics of Performance.* London: Routledge, 1993.

Ruti, Mari. *The Ethics of Opting Out: Queer Theory's Defiant Subjects.* New York: Columbia University Press, 2017.

Ruti, Mari. *The Singularity of Being: Lacan and the Immortal Within.* New York: Fordham University Press, 2012.

Segal, Mark. 'I Was at the Stonewall Riots. The Movie "Stonewall" Gets Everything Wrong.' PBS News Hour, 23 September 2015. Available at: https://www.pbs.org/newshour/arts/stonewall-movie.

Sinwell, Sarah E.S. 'Showrunning Activism.' In *Ryan Murphy's Queer America*, by Brenda R. Weber and David Greven, 241–253. London: Routledge, 2022. https://doi.org/10.4324/9781003170358-20.

Snorton, C. Riley. *Black on Both Sides: A Racial History of Trans Identity.* Minneapolis: University of Minnesota Press, 2017.

Spivak, Gayatri Chakravorty. 'Can the Subaltern Speak?' In Gayatri Chakravorty Spivak, *Can the Subaltern Speak?: Reflections on the History of an Idea*, edited by Rosalind C. Morris. New York: Columbia University Press, 2010.

Stanton, Maya. '"Stonewall": EW Review.' *Entertainment Weekly*, 28 September 2015. Available at: https://ew.com/article/2015/09/28/stonewall-ew-review/.

Stryker, Susan. *Transgender History: The Roots of Today's Revolution.* New York: Seal Press, 2017.

Styles, Rhyannon. 'Why, to a Transgender Woman, New TV Series Pose Seems So Incredible.' *Elle*, 7 March 2019. Available at: https://www.elle.com/uk/life-and-cul ture/elle-voices/a26745725/pose-tv-show-importance-transgender-community/.

Taylor, Jodie. 'Festivalizing Sexualities: Discourses of "Pride", Counter-Discourses of "Shame".' In *The Festivalization of Culture*, edited by Andy Bennett and Jodie Taylor, 27–48. London: Routledge, 2016. https://doi.org/10.4324/9781315558189.

Weber, Brenda R., and David Greven. *Ryan Murphy's Queer America.* London: Routledge, 2022.

Wiegman, Robyn. *American Anatomies: Theorizing Race and Gender.* Durham: Duke University Press, 1995.

Williams, Linda. 'World and Time: Serial Television Melodrama in America.' In *Melodrama Unbound: Across History, Media, and National Cultures*, edited by Christine Gledhill and Linda Williams. New York: Columbia University Press, 2018.

Williamson, Judith. '"Up Where You Belong": Hollywood Images of Big Business in the 1980s.' In *Enterprise and Heritage: Crosscurrents of National Culture*, edited by John Corner and Sylvia Harvey, 147–156. London: Routledge, 1991.

Žižek, Slavoj. *The Sublime Object of Ideology.* London: Verso, 2008.

Chapter 2

The Feminine Shadow
Sexual Difference, Race and Noir in *Sharp Objects*

Sharp Objects (2018) opens with the camera travelling through an American town in slow motion, panning around like a neck twisting to glance at features before they are passed by.[1] American flags sprout from every lamp post, the many trees are green and the parked cars and empty streets are still. Moving through the space, we see men sitting outside a barber shop, a butcher's, a candy store, staples of a small town that has retained old-fashioned shop fronts with traditional signage. Continuing, we encounter a series of 1950s-style painted advertisements adorning the sides of buildings, worn and chipped. Wind-Gap appears picturesque, but this initial impression is complicated as the murals of America's Eisenhower-era consumerism suffer from deterioration and the large white faces peer through decay, pasted over with Clinton–Gore and Bush–Quayle 1992 presidential candidate posters and scrawls of graffiti. "Welcome to Wind-Gap" is painted in white letters across a decorative train carriage, caught in time and going nowhere, as a distant figure in white moves into its dark inside.

The roads are wide. Two girls, whom we can retroactively identify as the teenage protagonist Camille Preaker (Sophia Lillis) and her younger sister Marian (Lulu Wilson), glide down the asphalt on roller skates. The space between them shrinks till their arms reach out and their fingers touch. Near their home, they pull off their roller skates, clamber around a large gate and traverse the verdant ground that leads towards their grand house. They sneak through the door, light on their feet so their mother, Adora Crellin (Patricia Clarkson), will not notice they have been out.

Viewers come to understand this opening sequence as part memory, part dream. The girls move through their house before seamlessly stepping into the modern day, where the adult Camille (Amy Adams) sleeps in her apartment in St. Louis, Missouri. The teenage Camille takes a paper clip from the bedside table and presses it into the adult Camille's sleeping hand, causing her to wake with a startle. Here, the past bridges to the present, a past designated by Camille's younger self moving through an environment replete with ageing American nostalgia. History is not a time departed from in *Sharp Objects* but persists and intrudes upon Camille's life in the contemporary day of the

DOI: 10.4324/9781003527244-3

diegesis. The insistence on history is most palpable in the use of analepsis, or 'flashbacks', where the chronological narrative is interrupted by moments from the past. These disturbances reveal moments from Camille's life – brief, enigmatic interjections that relate to words Camille has cut into her body during (unseen) acts of self-harm and from which the episodes take their titles: "Vanish", "Dirt", "Fix", "Ripe", "Closer", "Cherry", "Falling", "Milk".

Following the opening dream sequence, we see Camille at work in the offices of the *St. Louis Chronicle*. Early in episode one, "Vanish", Camille's editor Frank (Miguel Sandoval) insists she travels to her hometown of Wind-Gap to cover the recent murders of two local girls, Natalie Keen (Jessica Treska) and Ann Nash (Kaegan Baron), and the ongoing investigation into finding their killer. Despite her resistance, Frank convinces Camille that her personal connection to the town presents a unique opportunity for her to write a compelling piece. It is only in scenes where we see Frank conversing with his wife Eileen (Barbara Eve Harris) that we realise his ulterior motive: That returning home will encourage Camille to confront and perhaps resolve her troubled past that Frank believes is contributing to her barely disguised drinking problem.

When Camille arrives in Wind-Gap, Ann's body has already been discovered in the town's woodland area and, at the end of the first episode, Natalie is found in the middle of town, propped up on a windowsill in an alleyway. Both corpses have had their teeth removed. During her extended visit, Camille stays with her mother, Adora, sister, Amma Crellin (Eliza Scanlan), and stepfather, Alan Crellin (Henry Czerny). As the investigation catalyses Camille's return to Wind-Gap, its unfolding occurs with viewers learning about her life via flashbacks and interactions with various Wind-Gap residents. Camille also serves as a conduit for Wind-Gap's history and its broader political implications as the series reveals her family's Confederate ties.

The theme of a returning past is woven through the series and echoes a key feature of *noir*, a debated 'canon' and set of conventions that *Sharp Objects* employs and, at times, subverts. Typically, noir designates the 'film noir' genre and its associated visual iconography, such as a detective or private investigator, a gun, a femme fatale, chiaroscuro lighting and a nocturnal urban environment. Other recurring components considered central to noir include confessions (often the protagonist's) that open into extended flashback sequences and the Hollywood production period of the 1940s–1950s.[2] However, numerous scholars contest even these more recognisable noir tropes when attempting to identify a coherent group of noir productions, making it "easier to recognise a film noir than to define the term".[3] Some understand noir as a historical period of cinema, a genre like the Western or the gangster film, others as a stylistic and thematic movement that continues into contemporary film and television.

The term 'film noir' was designated as a category by French film critics in the mid-1940s and not created by the Hollywood studio system, hence the

French, rather than English, designation.[4] As well as being a cinematic category, noir has strong affiliations with the British and American detective
novels that frequently served as source material for noir films.[5] Notable in this
literary canon are Dashiell Hammett's *The Maltese Falcon* and Raymond
Chandler's *The Big Sleep*, which were adapted into two of the most famous
film noirs.[6] Because of debates concerning what constitutes noir, some film
scholars have taken ambiguity as one of its elements, proposing uncertainty as
a feature that contributes to its coding while simultaneously problematising
noir as a coherent category.[7] As such, *Sharp Objects*' inconsistent play with
noir elements can be recognised as part of its resonance with noir, even as it
departs from some of its familiar iconography.

In the first book-length study of film noir, Raymond Borde and Etienne
Chaumeton argue that "the presence of crime [...] gives film noir its most
distinctive stamp".[8] However, noir does not remain on the side of the law that
looks upon the criminal world from a distance but is set "in the criminal
milieu itself", with the favoured private detective figure serving as a "midway
point between order and crime".[9] In keeping with this tradition, the investigation into the local murders in Wind-Gap becomes the narrative spine of
Sharp Objects, situating crime and its uncovering as central to its development. Though not a private detective, Camille's occupation as a journalist
allows her to move between the realm of the official investigation, led by local
police Chief Bill Vickery (Matt Craven) and out-of-town Detective Richard
Willis (Chris Messina), and the informal gossip of the town's inhabitants,
many of whom she grew up with. In episode two, "Dirt", Camille exchanges
her local knowledge for Richard's insights that act as official comments in her
reporting. Camille thus draws together the police perspective that searches for
hard evidence and the colloquial chatter of the town that an outsider such as
Richard would not be able to access. The two meet in the local bar and
negotiate this arrangement, with Camille summarising the town's attitude as a
guise of pleasantry that masks its more brutal resentment: "If someone says
'bless your heart', what they really mean is 'fuck you'". Early on, Richard
develops a romantic and sexual interest in Camille and suggests that their
foray into the woodland area where they later trade information is a 'date'.

Viewers' impression of Wind-Gap must negotiate its quaint outward
appearance and Camille's flashbacks, which are initially indeterminate and
out of focus. Accompanying these memories, figures from the past also
intrude in the present moment. For instance, there are repeated glimpses of a
young woman in Camille's immediate surroundings, later revealed to be Alice
(Sydney Sweeney), with whom Camille shared a room in a rehabilitation
facility after a suicide attempt. Camille's little sister, Marian, is also periodi-
cally seen in the family home or the nearby woods, uncanny and visible only
for a split second.

Experiences from Camille's past are written into her body, as the words
with which she has self-harmed seem enigmatically related to her flashbacks,

tethering her corporeality to these movements across time. As inscrutable images repeat throughout episodes and the overall series, we are given a sense of repetition and return, a circling of fragmented memories that indicate moments of trauma, in part because they are unable to be relayed in a sensible form. For instance, during the first episode, we briefly glimpse a blurry red shape and a shot of a trolley filled with cleaning products that are only contextualised by the end of episode three, "Fix", when we also see the only example of Camille cutting the titular word into her arm.

For Paul Kerr, film noir places great importance on "such fragmented narrative structures as the flashback", and Ben Tyrer names noir a "retroactive category" with "narrative structures [...] often concerned with the production of knowledge ex post facto".[10] In *Sharp Objects*, flashbacks create an anachronic order in which the narrative unfolds, obscuring the central investigation into the local murders with which they are not obviously associated. As the town's name, Wind-Gap, suggests, there is always a gap in meaning, and the series formally acknowledges this by continually refusing narrative and visual completion.

As the analepses introduce confusion, *Sharp Objects* differs from classical noir films that often include extended flashback sequences to contextualise the present day.[11] However, some critics suggest that purposeful confusion is a noir sensibility. Along with their situating of crime, Borde and Chaumeton cite confusion as being at "the very heart of the oneiric quality" of noir, where "components of noir style [...] disorient the spectators, who no longer encounter their customary frames of reference".[12] Camille does not suffer from amnesia like some noir protagonists, but the memories we see are fragmented and splintered, inconclusive and disjointed.[13] As Georges Sadoul suggests, interjecting flashbacks cause "the story [to] remain opaque, like a nightmare, or the ramblings of a drunk".[14] Sadoul's description resonates with *Sharp Objects*, particularly as there are numerous disconcerting dream sequences and Camille's behaviour is made erratic by her compulsive drinking, established in episode one as she ritualistically decants vodka into water bottles to sip undetected.

Conversely, Joan Copjec complicates the identification of confusion as a noir component. In her introduction to *Shades of Noir*, Copjec agrees that noir is a contested term that films have been included in or excluded from over time. However, she then interrogates the difficulty in establishing noir, inviting readers to question the ambiguity or "absent cause" that noir organises around.[15] For Copjec, Sadoul's definition cited above "will no longer suffice".[16] Instead, she suggests that "[w]e now want to know why we have become sensible to these nightmares and why these drunks submit to the frustrations of their incomprehension".[17] Rather than tussling with the uncertain darkness of noir, Copjec enquires into the cause of this turn to darkness that paradoxically cannot be forged out of noir's inconsistency. Richard Dyer notes that "[u]ncertainty is built into noir's central narrative organisation", which continually undermines its categorisation.[18] *Sharp Objects* invokes noir's ambiguous quasi-category by toying with its aesthetic conventions and themes. Through its double-play of reference and subversion, *Sharp Objects* elicits uncertainty by introducing absence across the visual and temporal arena. Noir informs the series' problematising of knowledge, first concerning Camille and, later, the United States, which she comes to partially represent.

This chapter begins by examining how Camille functions in relation to the series' diegetic and formal coordinates and how her interruptive flashbacks rework noir's chiaroscuro lighting technique. Part of the visual iconography of classical film noir, chiaroscuro casts long, dark shadows, often through slatted blinds. Drawing on Hugh S. Manon's interrogation of the chiaroscuro technique in film noir, Camille's flashbacks are situated as bridging a disturbing past with the present-day – complicating the public image of Wind-Gap as foregrounded in the opening sequence – and the visual spectacle to Americana that represses a violent legacy.[19]

This prototypical image of America and Camille's disturbance of this image are developed through the paradigm of 'sexual difference', understood in its Lacanian designation, where 'masculine' and 'feminine' are positions that relate to signification. Against their typical definitions, masculine and feminine in the Lacanian tradition have no biological grounding and refuse the idea of two compatible opposites that would join to make a whole, as the fantasy of heterosexual coupledom promises. Sexual difference, or 'sexuation' as it is also referred to, is central to Jacques Lacan's "Seminar XX", *Encore*.[20] In a companion to this seminar, Suzanne Barnard comments on the complexity and particular difficulty of this work, noting that Lacan's designations of "man" and "woman" have often been misunderstood, partly because interpretations have overlooked the function of the real.[21]

As Barnard summarises, masculine/man and feminine/woman are often read as corresponding with "dominant discourses of sex and gender in the United States [...] framed in terms of either natural science, phenomenology, or forms of sociohistorical analysis and cultural studies".[22] In these fields, sexual difference becomes subsumed by "constructs such as gender identity and embodiment (i.e., the 'lived body') and the symbolic aspects of the body and sexuality that are 'socially constructed'".[23] This reading, however, misconstrues Lacan's formulation. In an early section of *Encore*, Lacan suggests that "[w]hat constitutes the basis of life [...] [is] to do with the relations between men and women, what is called collectivity, it's not working out".[24] At first, this quote seems to rehearse the idea that men and women are two stable categories that cannot 'get along'. Thinking such as this foregrounds the pop psychology that posits ideas such as 'men are from Mars, women are from Venus'.[25] However, Lacan then proposes that these positions "mean [...] nothing qua prediscursive reality. Men, women, and children are but signifiers".[26] In this passage, Lacan rethinks categories typically understood as relying on physical characteristics as purely discursive. He repeatedly argues that subjectivity develops through the signifier and its (barred) relation to the signified. As such, sexual difference is arranged by how speaking beings relate to the signifier – not only what the signifier 'says', but also the gap that emerges with it, and how this relates to knowledge.

With reference to sexual difference, Camille can be read as occupying the feminine position. As her flashbacks depart from linearity and lucidity, the text refuses a comprehensible insight into her past, forging Camille as a limit to sense-making. Regarding Lacan's formula of sexuation, how do Camille, non-linear temporality and noir interrogate the conquest of knowledge in the series? It is the feminine that comes to articulate the radical instability of the subject, and this in turn becomes a way to recognise the role of temporality and the linguistic signifier as they manifest on screen. To better comprehend how *Sharp Objects* ties temporality to Camille's body, other cinematic and scholarly works that usurp textual conventions are brought into conversation with the series. These include Nicolas Roeg's film *Bad Timing* (1980), as analysed by Theresa de Lauretis, and Mary Ann Doane's work on the femme fatale in film noir.[27] As the linguistic markings on Camille's body are subjected to repeated visual and narrative focus, an interrogation of the symbolic order informs how language may undo, rather than stabilise, meaning across time.

After establishing Camille as a figure of feminine disruption, this chapter brings Wind-Gap into sharpened focus. Located in Missouri, the town contains tensions relating to the American Civil War when the state straddled the Mason–Dixon line, marking the border between the American North and South. During this period, Missouri was governed by both the Union and the Confederacy. The series directly addresses Civil War history in the mid-point episode, "Closer", which centres on the annual "Calhoun Day" festival hosted by Adora on her family's land. How does the noir theme of a returning past contextualise Camille's flashbacks, the legacy of the American Civil War and whiteness? How do these interconnected histories produce a political reading of the recent murders in Wind-Gap? Reading Scott Loren's study of noir's persistence of history, Sheldon George's and Kalpana Seshadri-Crooks's analyses of racial difference, Kaja Silverman's theory of 'historical trauma', and scholarship focusing on race in film noir, the second half of this chapter addresses these questions to interrogate how *Sharp Objects* critically stages national and racial identity.

Camille's scarred body indicates a traumatic personal history that cannot be told. As the series progresses, we also discern the larger historical trauma of American slavery as that which cannot be seen or heard but lurks beneath the town's Confederate insignia and Camille's Civil War-era family home. *Sharp Objects* meditates on Wind-Gap's nostalgic yearnings, established by the town's painted billboards and founding Confederate myth. By analysing *Sharp Objects* through Lacan's theory of sexual difference and the conventions of film noir, temporality becomes a point of critical intervention into the naturalised hegemony of whiteness and masculinity in the service of American capitalism.

X-Ray Time

The days are bright, and the heat is oppressive in Wind-Gap. Amma and her two friends, Kelsey (Violet Brinson) and Jodes (April Brinson), roller-skate in denim shorts and vest tops. Sweat patches form on the back of Richard's and Chief Vickery's blue shirts. Fans are perpetually rotating, their circular movement appearing in almost every interior. Despite the heat, Camille wears dark, long-sleeved tops and jeans. We first see her self-harm at the end of episode one when she eases into a bath after arriving at the family home, her skin a plain of textured scar tissue forming the words across her body. Viewers are privy to this scripture, yet this is not the case for most characters in the series, as Camille has no visible scars on her hands, neck or face, enabling her to hide these marks by covering herself in public.

The prominence of daytime scenes most obviously sets *Sharp Objects* apart from the visual tradition of noir's night-time settings. Chiaroscuro lighting's graphic shadows cause silhouettes to stretch from ominous figures, and slatted blinds stripe peering eyes and interior walls under the blanket of dark skies. For Manon, this lighting indicates a rupturing of everyday normalcy. In a departure from understanding this play of light and shadows as indicative of characters' "psychological imprisonment while creating an atmosphere of claustrophobia and duplicity", Manon argues that chiaroscuro "schemes frequently resemble a medical X-ray".[28] This technique suggests an ability to see beyond the illusory social order and into the criminal 'beneath', just as an X-ray can look at the skeletal body that otherwise goes unseen by the naked eye. While *Sharp Objects* is visually distinct from classical noir, the analeptic and hallucinatory flickers that signal Camille's intrusive memories refigure the effect of noir's lighting as Manon understands it.

Numerous theorists and critics have argued that noir departs from the "unveiling of narrative enigma" generally seen in thrillers, gangster films and "classical detective whodunits".[29] For Manon, chiaroscuro transforms quotidian environments as dynamic shadows reconfigure spatiality, "as if our most banal assumptions about everyday locality have been X-rayed to reveal a dark and undetectable disease".[30] In *Sharp Objects*, appearances are deceiving as Camille's flashbacks create a schism in the surface of the American town. On her drive to Wind-Gap from St. Louis, Camille remembers a cabin in the woodland area, decorated with distressed pornographic images. Finding this cabin seems to frighten and arouse Camille as a teenager and as an adult remembering this moment. Her adolescent eyes tentatively move around the space, looking at the magazine snippets, intercut with close-ups of Camille's face as she masturbates in the motel room she is staying in to break up her journey. Upon her arrival in Wind-Gap, Camille makes her way to this same woodland area visited in her memory. People have gathered to search for the newly missing girl, Natalie. Later, the family house triggers memories of Camille's younger sister, Marian, whose room has remained unchanged since she died. In flashback, we see the sisters lying in bed, staring at the ceiling and finding shapes in the plaster and cracks before Marian suddenly has a seizure and, shortly after, dies. Although the town's murders demonstrate palpable violence in the present day, Camille's memories foreground a lurking sense of loss and perversion across the outdoor and interior spaces.

Manon suggests that the chiaroscuro technique communicates "the point of interface between the criminal and the legitimate that the general public fails to recognize as such" by shining light through architectural space to suggest an uncanny distortion in interior environments.[31] Citing the "classic *noir* point-of-view shot in which a character peers out of a window" through blinds, Manon describes how the perspective moves from the interior to the exterior, "disallow [ing] the possibility of the look being returned".[32] The iconic horizontal sha-dows passing through slatted Venetian blinds become a privileged example of chiaroscuro's X-ray aesthetic as the window becomes a screen between public and private. With its flickering editing, *Sharp Objects* slides between the 'normal' present-day appearances of Wind-Gap and Camille's personal recol-lections of violence that indicate a "deception at the very surface of things – a carefully managed artificial reality that the public sees but fails to detect".[33] As a result of this technique, *Sharp Objects* aligns viewers with Camille's ambig-uous memories that penetrate the appearance of Wind-Gap.

As well as introducing visual confusion, flashbacks and apparitions disorganise the chronology of the murder investigation that provides the overarching linear timeline of the series. The anachronic structure associated with Camille's bodily *cuts* is produced by the jarring editorial *cuts* that erratically move through time and space. Chiaroscuro lighting points to a "third-person perspective" that "envelops both the films' criminals and their potential discoverers"[34] as it indicates a "semi-permeability of spatial divides" by emphasising light passing *through* barriers in the creation of graphic shadows.[35] In this respect, *Sharp Objects*' ana-lepses depart from Manon's treatment of chiaroscuro by re-integrating obscured past events with the public illusion of decency from the perspective of Camille, rather than the "barrier-defying, horizontal trajectory" of chiaroscuro that is not associated with a particular character's viewpoint.

Manon's understanding of chiaroscuro hinges on its ability to create "a Moebius strip-like arrangement in which the underworld dovetails [...] with our own".[36] Camille's flashbacks rework this effect by producing unnerving visual links between the diegetic present and the town's public face. Classical noir suggests that, "in the modern world, the spheres of criminal and legit-imate activity interpenetrate" through the staging of graphic lighting.[37] In *Sharp Objects*, flashbacks bridge the public or 'surface' presentation of Wind-Gap with its violent past which, like noir, "confronts viewers with the impossibility of clearly dividing the world into 'places of innocence' and 'places of deceit'".[38] *Sharp Objects* brings the noir trope of public and private worlds meeting into contact with the theme of the returning past, with Camille designating the point of narrative disorganisation.

As well as evoking a temporal and visual disturbance, the cutting of the body in *Sharp Objects* complicates Manon's extension of chiaroscuro's X-ray quality to the everyday appearances of noir's social realms that he associates with skin: Because X-rays penetrate the skin to reveal otherwise undetectable issues, noir's chiaroscuro scheme "resembles an X-ray because both an X-ray and the noir narrative infiltrate an otherwise sealed interior while insisting that the skin remains unruptured".[39] In this argument, the outward appearances of civilised society are connected to and contrast with the criminality at work behind closed doors as "a skin-defying X-ray view [...] is most needed in cases where outwardly no symptoms appear", emphasised by chiaroscuro as its graphic shadows pass through and accentuate architectural features.[40] In *Sharp Objects*, skin – taken as a metaphor for "a commonplace site of unsuspicion" by Manon – becomes the location that complicates the small American town as Camille's past is written into her flesh while her return to Wind-Gap introduces her as a figure from the past who reappears. As such, Camille's skin becomes part of how the 'X-ray' of Wind-Gap takes place and contributes to her visual distinction instead of maintaining an appearance of normality.

Although there are numerous female characters in *Sharp Objects*, Camille maintains a singular alignment with the feminine that disrupts the series' intelligibility. Turning to Roeg's *Bad Timing* illuminates how the feminine functions as a structural position rather than a representation of what is typically associated with the social category of 'woman'. In this film, Milena (Theresa Russell) bears similarities to Camille as she articulates temporal misalignment through her association with the film's anachronic cutting across time. With reference to de Lauretis's essay, "Now and Nowhere: Roeg's *Bad Timing*", the parallels between Camille and Milena are emphasised to illustrate the particular feminine mode of *syuzhet* construction that both texts engage, whereby the central women correspond with the interference of linearity, a linearity here associated with Lacan's masculine 'side' of sexual difference and the ascription of knowledge with regard to law.[41]

Bad Timing's anachronic structure fragments a love story gone wrong. Shortly after the opening scene, we see Milena in an ambulance. Tubes are stuck into her mouth as a flurry of paramedics try to revive her from a coma, while Inspector Netusil (Harvey Keitel) questions her lover, Alex (Art Garfunkel), about the preceding events. Set in Vienna during the Cold War, the film begins with a close-up detail of native artist Gustav Klimt's painting *The Kiss* (1907–1908), hung in the national gallery Milena and Alex are visiting. The woman in the painting, cloaked in squares of golden hues, her face and arms peering from beneath the decorated sheet, will come to contrast with Milena's body as it is stripped and penetrated throughout the film by both Alex and surgical instruments. The recurring scenes of medical procedures attempting to revive her, intercut with Netusil's investigation into how Milena came to be in this state, invite us to consider how the body of the woman may contain the answer to the very enigma she introduces. The unknown moment that Netusil tries to excavate from Alex as a confession – what happened during the time between Alex going to Milena's apartment and calling the ambulance – is not admitted by Alex but is, near the end of the film, revealed to the audience during a sequence where Alex rapes Milena as she lies unconscious from a drug overdose. Although *Sharp Objects* does not ultimately 'reveal' Camille's traumatic past or detail the murders of Ann and Natalie, *Bad Timing* and *Sharp Objects* share a temporal mapping that corresponds to the axis of sexual difference.

Bad Timing's disorientation occurs through the collision of Alex's and Netusil's embodiment of the law and Milena's usurping of this law. Alex, a research psychoanalyst, and Netusil, a police inspector, represent an investigative law and take Milena as their object of interest. In contrast, Milena represents "the time of her desire [that] is in another register altogether, not congruent and commensurate with Alex's time, which leads forward to possession as marriage and backward to fetishistic possession."[42] Milena pronounces this contrast when she exclaims, following Alex's marriage proposal, "what about my time?", "what about now?". During the scene where this exchange occurs, Alex seeks to establish romantic norms that Milena rejects. Her questions vocalise a sense of time that departs from Alex's as the film performs an anachronic relay of events, suggesting that the syuzhet construction enacts Milena's desire in the film's temporal schema. This strategy of disorder also undermines Netusil's desire to reconstruct the night in question and render the past sensible and coherent. De Lauretis reads Alex's time as travelling along a "linear dimension [...] in the unified trajectory of phallic desire" where "marriage and love can only 'mean' in his way and Milena's 'now' has no place".[43] Like Milena, Camille does not present a 'different version of events' or the 'other side to a story' that would demonstrate an alternative narrative to give a complete account of what happened from multiple perspectives. Instead, she aligns with that which bears upon the text as uncertainty, a departure from the overarching linear narrative driven by Chief Vickery and Richard. Like *Bad Timing*'s Alex and Netusil, these two men represent the law as they attempt to make sense of events in the diegesis.

Though de Lauretis sets up her analysis with reference to Michel Foucault, she takes a Lacanian turn when suggesting how phallic desire associated with the masculine appears complete and coherent, in contrast to the feminine that refuses such containment. De Lauretis characterises this difference, though not opposition, by suggesting that "[l]inear time" functions as the "logic of identity and non-contradiction", "a necessary condition of all investigation and of all narrative".[44] This reading of temporal disorganisation of narrative consistency chimes with Ellie Ragland's clarifying articulation of Lacan's masculine position, which identifies

> with a master signifier or the reality principle. The effect produced by
> identification with a symbolic order position is a belief in, or considerable

certainty about, the knowledge one takes as reality. [...] From the masculine position, language is spoken in the imperative and in the declara-
tive modes. Feminine identification bears on the question; that is, it
unveils impasses in the knowledge that bases its claims on certainty.[45]

Here, Ragland emphasises the disjuncture between masculine and feminine,
unlike a 'binary' distinction of man and woman where woman complements
man through a designation of lack to reassert his supposed totality. In *Sharp
Objects* and *Bad Timing*, the investigative drive – directed by figures of the
law – cannot organise Camille and Milena into a linear narrative. The women
embody the feminine not because they occupy the social position of 'woman'
but because they undermine the consistency of the diegetic fabulation associated with the masculine position without becoming its complementary
opposite. In both texts, law enforcement's attempts to construct linearity in
the service of narrativity hinge on discovering the 'missing piece': Who killed
Natalie and Ann? What did Alex do before he called the ambulance? If this
fragment is found, it is presumed that the 'whole' of knowledge could be
restored. Camille and Milena disavow this fantasy of resolve: There is no
'missing piece', no completion that precedes or proceeds their intervention. In
Sharp Objects, the more we see Camille's past, the less we understand the
events of her life and what structures her desire.

To stress the distinction between women and the feminine, *Sharp Objects*
includes female characters who do not problematise the fantasy of men and
women as complementary opposites. This version of womanhood is pronounced in episode six, "Cherry", when Camille reconnects with women from
the town with whom she was on the cheerleading team as a teenager. When
Camille spends time with this group at the house of one of them, they collectively express that a woman's purpose is to be a wife and mother. In this
declaration, the women do not challenge, but rather reinforce, traditional
ideals of sexual union, aligning with the masculine rather than the feminine
position of sexual difference, despite clearly being coded as women. During
their conversation, Camille's Wind-Gap peers conform to what Elizabeth
Freeman describes as 'chrononormativity', a temporality that sutures bodies
into patterns of reproduction, or what Lee Edelman typifies as 'futurity', the
temporal structure characterised by the figure of the child and its need for
protection.[46] For both Freeman and Edelman, traditional structures of family,
which these women of Wind-Gap exemplify, sustain norms that contribute to
understandings of legitimate personhood.

In the closing moments of *Bad Timing*, we see a final encounter between
Alex and Milena – "the only one in which Milena is shown not in flashback
but in a diegetic time subsequent to her hospitalization".[47] As Alex walks out
of a building and on to a New York City street, Milena exits a taxi. They do
not see one another at first but, as Alex gets into the car Milena has just
exited, she turns to him. This encounter is punctuated by a startling shot that

zooms into an extreme close-up of Milena's neck, which now bears a scar caused by the incision into her throat during the procedure that saved her life following her overdose and the rape. Like the scar that closes Milena's wounded body, this closing moment also sutures the narrative, allowing us to step into the diegetic 'present' that becomes an epilogue to all that came before. The now-healed cut recalls the film's cutting that makes anachronic structuring possible as the site of Milena's desire, who, like Camille, bears the 'cut' as a visible sign.

As agents of narrative disruption, Milena and Camille evoke and complicate the noir femme fatale, described by Mary Ann Doane as a "figure of a certain discursive unease, a potential epistemological trauma".[48] In Doane's analysis of the film noir *Gilda* (1946), the movement of the camera (the body of the film) and the movement of the titular woman played by Rita Hayworth (the body of the woman) inform one another. *Gilda* opens with "a slow tilt upwards by the camera", a shot "[l]ater [...] paralleled by the shot which introduces Gilda herself", where Gilda enters an empty frame by moving into it from below.[49] In examining the introduction to the film *Gilda* and the character Gilda, Doane demonstrates how "the movement upward to fill the frame with a content is displaced from the camera to Gilda", relating the cinematic apparatus to the femme fatale.[50] Following her introduction in the film, Gilda's recent husband, Ballen (George Macready), describes her to Johnny (Glenn Ford) as "not coming under the category of woman" despite "the immediate recognizability of Gilda as woman", to which Johnny retorts: "I could have been mistaken".[51] Here, the femme fatale is articulated as a non-subject "within a phallocentric discourse" even as her visual spectacle structures the cinematic movement as she "fill[s] [...] the frame and narrative with a content".[52] Building on Doane's reading, the figure of the femme fatale casts a shadow on Camille as she becomes the object of Richard's sexual and romantic attention while upending the linearity with which he comes to be associated, structuring narrative focus and temporal (dis)order.

The Feminine Cut

The words written across Camille's corporeal surface further complicate *Sharp Objects'* dynamic overlapping of the body, the cut and temporality. The body's scripture informs how we read Camille, yet its meaning is opaque and extends beyond the specificity of her flesh. The title of each episode emphasises a particular word, seen as a scar or spoken by a character, most often Adora, within an episode. For example, in episode six, "Cherry", we do not witness Camille cut this titular word but, during a flashback, Adora remarks that Camille looks like a cherry in a coded reference to her sexuality. At other times, an episode's title and an instance of self-harm resonate with a scenario in the diegetic present. Episode five's title, "Closer", references Camille and Richard getting closer to finding out who the killer is and growing closer to one another. Near the end of the episode, Adora explains to Camille that her inability to get 'close' to others is a quality she inherited from her absent father and, for this reason, Adora has never loved her. Following this exchange, 'closer' is revealed as an instance of self-harm in the episode's final moments, blurry and overexposed, as Camille and Richard have sex in his motel room. "Closer" is complicated by its revelation in the present moment, allowing new meanings to attach to Camille's body without elucidating why she initially inscribed this particular word, extending and limiting language's signifying ability in the narrative and visual field.

To interrogate the relationship between absence and the symbolic, Copjec's aptly titled essay "Cutting Up" speaks to how signification marks the boundary of its comprehension.[53] Copjec does not read the subject as defined by language in terms of what it *is*, but how language marks what it cannot contain as "the opacity of signifiers means that language does not reveal a reality or truth behind them".[54] Language operates on a process of substitution where symbolic discourse, the signifier, stands in for what it signifies. However, the process of signification bears no representational similarity to the signified, emphasising the fragility in the exchange of signifiers as a discursive mode. This gap between signifier and signified "guarantees that whatever reality or meaning is produced by them will never be able to convince us of its truth or completeness".[55] It is for this reason that Lacan repeatedly describes the unconscious as being "structured like a language", for it is in moments of gaps or stumbles, in slips of the tongue or the pen, that words reveal their failure to generate and relay meaning in a totalised form.

The partiality of the symbolic realm is gestured to in *Sharp Objects* as the analepses toy with a troubled relationship between word and image, with words never finding their correlating images in the flashback sequences. Even when granted some sense of events leading to an act of cutting (as with "Fix"), the words are never direct descriptions or definitions of the events witnessed. The bodily scriptures translate the function of symbolic signification within the narrative schema as stand-ins that cannot fully encompass what they refer to. As such, the series reads signification in the feminine mode, which, as already cited from Ragland, "unveils impasses in the knowledge that bases its claims on certainty".[56]

Translated into the visual and formal parlance of *Sharp Objects*, the linguistic signs displayed upon Camille's body do not reveal the 'truth' of the subject but negate a sense of closure. As Copjec argues, signifiers do not operate on a 'transparent' system of representation:

> [T]hey cannot demonstrate that they are not hiding something behind what they say – they cannot prove that they do not lie. Language can only present itself to the subject as a veil that cuts off from view a reality that is other than what we are allowed to see.[57]

Scrutinising language's process of substitution to create discourse, Copjec speaks to the necessary incompletion of language as a process of signification. Language marks Camille in such a way that it emphasises the structural absence between signifier and signified and informs the series' anachronic temporality, embodying the feminine uncertainty that bears on symbolic law.

For Lacan, "[i]t is in the *name of the father* [*le nom du père*] that we must recognise the support of the symbolic function", as the father traditionally figures the position of authority in kinship networks.[58] Playing on its French homophone 'the no of the father' (*le non du père*), this punning produces a double meaning that situates the subject within the realm of language (the name) and prohibition of 'law' (the 'No!'). The father "functions […] to prop up the symbolic order", "constituted around a sort of void, which is the prohibition of incest".[59] As de Lauretis identifies in her analysis of *Bad Timing*, the masculine claims to knowledge depend upon the linear order of narrative unfolding, articulated by characters who represent judicial law, in Roeg's film and *Sharp Objects* alike. In a literal turn, Camille is 'named' as problematising symbolic law as her own father is palpably absent from the series. Unlike Adora and Amma, who take her stepfather Alan's last name, Crellin, Camille retains Adora's maiden name, Preaker, and thus the name of the father is omitted in the series.

As with the cutting that structures form, narrative and the woman's body, the orderly time that the figures of law enforcement seek to establish recalls the prohibitive law associated with paternal authority as symbolic function. Camille's disrupting of narrative clarity, brought to the surface by enigmatic words written across her body, undermines temporality and the consistency of language in a simultaneous gesture of feminine refusal that problematises the symbolic and judicial law's claim to certainty. As the series develops, this textual lacuna extends beyond Camille's flashbacks and implicates the series' wider geo-political setting and its associated history.

The Return

Noir protagonists are often attempting to flee an uneasy past, suggesting concern with the re-emergence of an American history that threatens the ideals of the films' present day.[60] Scott Loren looks to David Cronenberg's neo-noir film *A History of Violence* (2005) and Jacques Tourneur's classic noir film *Out of the Past* (1947) to exemplify noir's concern with an "inevitable return of an inescapable past", which, he argues, problematises the American myth of self-invention.[61] Building on Loren's analysis, how does Camille trouble national identity as her family legacy is retold in Wind-Gap's public arena?

The opening sequence of *Sharp Objects* situates Wind-Gap in an American past as its public spaces display paintings of traditional consumerist iconography. The crumbling advertisements fill numerous walls, often dominating the town's landscape throughout the series. These images depict the remains of mid-century national idealism that presents white middle-class personhood, suburban living and its associated commodities as essential features of aspirational living.

To borrow from Loren's description of *A History of Violence*, *Sharp Objects* "foreground[s] a split between past and present […] marking the phantasmatic nature of the past as it manifests in the present".[62] The series brings together distinct eras by employing and interrogating visual remembrances of an earlier time, albeit in decline. The surface of Wind-Gap is palimpsestic, replete with deteriorating promises of the 'American dream', detectable in the ghostly traces of faded, yet legible, words like those etched into Camille's body.

According to Loren, the prototypical American dream emerged in the early twentieth century as the increase in the mass production of goods led to a dramatic rise in domestic consumerism. During this period, freedom became associated with one's purchases and purchasing power as "[t]he consumption of (luxury) goods […] was now being made available to the average worker, who was, in turn, often working to produce these goods (directly or indirectly)".[63] Consequently, Loren situates the development of "the idea of consumer empowerment" with the "dream of self-fashioning" that attempts to relinquish history as determining one's social identity.[64] *Sharp Objects* directly references the booming era of American consumerism by including painted advertisements that represent the pinnacle of this period of capitalist reinvention.

It is the trope of a returning past that Loren understands as noir's critique of American capitalism as "film noir tells us that we are not simply free to reinvent ourselves, and in this regard, it goes against the American dream's cultural injunction to believe that you can be free of your past".[65] As 1950s advertisements define the town's contemporary visual environment, Wind-Gap sustains an American fantasy that supposes a subject seemingly without history while re-emphasising an inability to let go of imagery steeped in national nostalgia. The washed-out pastel billboards loom over Wind-Gap, the larger-than-life figures bearing silent witness. Alongside this commercial imagery that exclusively depicts white people, *Sharp Objects* interrogates historical legacies of whiteness that precede the era the billboards hark back to as Wind-Gap stages a celebration of Confederate identity.

Camille's family and their domestic space serve as a conduit for Wind-Gap's – and to some extent America's – past. In episode one, Camille describes Wind-Gap to her editor as being separated into old money and trash (with Camille being "trash from old money"). The family home and the Preaker Farm it sits upon contain her ancestral legacy: Their estate is vast and, along a stretch of road that leads away from the house, is an abattoir that farms and kills pigs. The slaughterhouse employs much of the town's native and immigrant populations, with the blood and guts of the butchered animals kept at a distance from the wealthy domestic space where Camille's family resides. As well as the distinction between gruesome labour and the refined Southern prestige of the house, pigs are a recurring motif that remind town (and viewer) of the Preaker influence over Wind-Gap, appearing as the illustrated pig sign on the door of the local store, while barbecued pigs are served up during the Calhoun Day celebration, and Amma and her friends race pigs after dark as part of their drunken and bored antics. When trying to understand how the killer removed Natalie's and Ann's teeth, Richard buys a pig's head from the butcher to practise this extraction.

The significance of the family history comes into relief during episode five, "Closer". Central to this episode is Calhoun Day, an annual celebration hosted by Adora on the Preaker land and attended by the town's white residents. The event commemorates Confederate identity, organised around the story of Millie Calhoun, an ancestor of the Preaker family who was married to Confederate soldier and founder of Wind-Gap Zeke Calhoun. The Calhoun name, which signifies both family and day of Confederate celebration, calls back to that of the pro-slavery, slave-owning and state's rights-supporting statesman John C. Calhoun, whose political career spanned the first half of the nineteenth century. Wind-Gap's legend describes Millie Calhoun's bravery when Union soldiers came to town and demanded to know her husband's whereabouts. When she refused to say, the Union soldiers tied her to a tree and raped her. In this episode, Millie Calhoun is theatrically embodied by Amma while her friends play the supporting roles. Although there is no visual instantiation of racial difference in this performance, the Union soldiers serve as a conduit for a violence that sustains the vulnerability of the white woman, which has historically functioned to structure fears of blackness, while Millie Calhoun's sacrifice brands her as a heroine who consolidates the town's identity in its origin story.

The story of Millie Calhoun functions as a 'Lost Cause' myth, part of a Southern tradition that recalls the Civil War as "a mawkish and essentially heroic and romantic melodrama, an honorable sectional duel, a time of martial glory on both sides, and triumphant nationalism" that supports a Confederate narrative.[66] Central to the myth, in *Sharp Objects* and as a long-standing piece of misinformation in American history, is the denial that slavery formed the central issue of the Civil War. Alan T. Nolan identifies other key pillars of the Lost Cause myth, including the proposition that enslaved people were well treated and faithful, the idealised home front, and the figure of the brave Confederate soldier.[67]

During "Closer", the iteration of the Lost Cause myth rewrites Wind-Gap's history while connecting more recent rituals of sexual violence to the town's legacy. Prior to the performance of Millie Calhoun's rape, Camille speaks to the teacher who has organised the re-enactment, Kirk Lacey (Jackson Hurte), to ask where Amma is. In previous episodes, Lacey is often seen with a group of men in the local bar and at Natalie's funeral. Intercut into their brief conversation is a flashback that shows Lacey as one of the boys from the football team who sexually coerced Camille in the woods when she was a cheerleader (young Lacey played by Evan Castelloe). Although the flashback is brief, this memory has been witnessed in the previous episode, "Ripe", and the symmetrical framing of the flashback and the present day indicate Lacey as this boy.

As the Calhoun Day performance depicts the arrival of the Union soldiers who attack Millie Calhoun, Lacey's wife, Katie (Reagan Pasternak), looks from the stage to her husband and then back to the stage, emphasising the parallels between the naive re-enactment of rape and the sexual coercion from Camille's past. The similarity of the events is acknowledged by Katie's glance that travels between Lacey and the theatrical scene, indicating her knowledge of what took place between her now-husband and Camille. As the camera cuts to a long shot of the stage, we see that the set resembles the hut in the woods called "the End Zone", where the ritualistic coercion took place.[68] Here, match-cutting creates visual similarities to indicate how violence from the recent past is installed in the interpretation of history, specifically the instance of rape that supports the town's identity and which the public sphere celebrates.

As well as bringing our attention to repetitions of violence in Wind-Gap, the Calhoun Day celebration highlights Camille's ancestral past to articulate tensions of the Civil War, a defining event in American history that continues to inform contemporary identifications along the lines of race and national citizenship. Characters don Confederate flags and shirts, with Chief Vickery and Alan Crellin among the men dressed as Confederate soldiers. When Chief Vickery sees Richard – marked as an 'outsider' and nicknamed "big city" and "Kansas City" – before the celebration, he warns him not to turn up "dress [ed] like a Union soldier". Confederate insignia reference the Civil War, yet slavery, the key conflict of the war, is not incorporated into the diegesis. As such, the Confederate flags and outfits only allude to this silenced dimension of history, while details glimpsed in earlier episodes foreshadow the town's Confederate links.[69] Notably, the makeshift shrine of flowers and toys commemorating the murdered Ann gathers at the foot of a Zeke Calhoun statue. A monument to Wind-Gap's Confederate founder and an exhibition of the public's mourning, this spot becomes a transhistorical memorial site in the town's epicentre. Such a monument to a Confederate 'hero' speaks to a familiar mode of honouring history that has come under scrutiny in recent years as campaigns have sought to remove statues that venerate the violence that Confederate and colonial figures enacted and symbolise.[70]

For Hilary Neroni, attachment to Confederate signifiers such as flags and monuments is "driven by fetishistic disavowal", which describes how an object "takes on a mythical status as it portends to be the object that can finally do away with lack once and for all".[71] Fetishistic disavowal becomes a different way of responding to lack compared with desire. Whereas "desire acknowledges lack and attempts to engage it, [...] fetishistic disavowal sees lack as something that can be permanently erased".[72] Neroni argues that this plays a "key role in the perpetuation of racism" as objects such as Confederate statues are imbued with the fantasy of an American past as "a lost site of plenitude".[73] Such objects become enjoyable for the subjects who display and revere them, as indicated by the way Calhoun Day brings the white community together under the banner of their founding narrative. As if to demonstrate the town's emotional investment in this day, the episode cuts to Amma and her friends taking ecstasy pills minutes before going on stage to re-enact the Calhoun Day myth. Unbeknown to the assembled audience, the drug transforms the amateur play into one performed with immense pleasure as Amma becomes ecstatic while inhabiting the role of the defiant, albeit brutalised, woman who structures the town's identity.

In *Race and Trauma*, George discusses how racial difference gets inferred without being directly acknowledged through discreet references to stereotypes that have been historically attached to persons racialised as black. He uses the example of how Barack Obama was charged with "laziness" and "shuckin and jivin" by some of his white Republican political opponents.[74] Tracing these insults to notions of otherness and "un-Americaness", George highlights how "within language itself is buried the history that unravels to reproduce ready-made structures of *jouissance* that ground racism emerging from the past to shape the present".[75] The Calhoun day re-enactment of history that is brought to life by Amma's *ecstatic* performance (that is, one activated by ecstasy) consolidates the ways the omittance of direct racialised language nonetheless maintains historical and present-day articulations of otherness and nation to support the formation of white identity.

This sequence also incorporates a broader argument made by George that race is articulated as a distribution of *jouissance*, which becomes "embedded in the very signifiers of race themselves", which in turn are bound to the history of slavery in the United States.[76] George reads the master–slave relationship with Karl Marx's theory of surplus value, which in turn led to what Lacan terms "surplus *jouissance*".[77] While surplus value describes a "monetary excess [...] which the labourer returns to the capitalist over and above the quantity of labour he receives for his wages",[78] surplus *jouissance* describes the "unearned excess pleasure the master receives through the slave's work".[79] While this extraction allows the master to mask his lack, it simultaneously denies the slave access to the fantasies which may allow him or her to imagine subjective wholeness. As with *Sharp Objects'* engagement with techniques and images that enact associations across word and image (such as editorial and corporeal *cutting*, or the 'gap' that marks the town's name and history), Amma's recounting of the Confederate myth makes palpable the veritable ecstasy afforded the white Confederate subject in the sustaining of historical narratives of racialised dominance, even as a direct naming of racial difference is repressed in the diegesis. According to Neroni, Confederate insignia "allow[s] people to disavow that the symbols represent slavery, white nationalism, and contemporary racism, while at the same time being steeped in and invested in those traditions".[80] In "Closer", Wind-Gap's myth establishes a balance of celebration and disavowal that silences slavery in the revision of the past as the town's curation of history makes a critical enquiry into the (unspoken) signifier of whiteness which investment in Confederacy upholds.

In *Desiring Whiteness*, Seshadri-Crooks interrogates how whiteness organises racial difference by denying its historical origins. By rendering the invention of whiteness opaque, race is designated as immutably biological *and* constructed, making it particularly challenging to undermine as a system of relationality. Seshadri-Crooks defines whiteness as a "master signifier (without a signified)" that "establishes [...] a signifying chain" which "organises human difference".[81] In other words, race offers a system of categorisation in relation to whiteness, which presents itself as 'natural' as it presupposes a regime of visibility yet eludes a stable category of meaning.

Seshadri-Crooks problematises the assumption of race as a naturalised system by examining Lacan's theory of sexual difference. As already discussed, the feminine pertains to an uncertainty that undermines the masculine quest for knowledge. *Desiring Whiteness* situates the masculine and feminine positions as naming an irrecuperable difference that designates the gap in signification that whiteness then proposes to fill by "promis[ing] a totality, an overcoming of difference itself".[82] Repressing the historical construction of whiteness sustains its position of wholeness and reproduces its power. In *Sharp Objects*, the narrativisation of the town's identity renunciates this historicity to fervently re-establish its dominance in the social realm. The reconstruction of the Lost Cause myth during Calhoun Day becomes an object of fetishistic disavowal as it appears to eliminate the construction of racial difference to affirm the whiteness that contributes towards the town's Confederate identity and imbues it with enjoyment.

Central to Seshadri-Crooks's argument is the idea that confronting the historical construction of racial difference is anxiety-producing because it traverses the fantasy of totality whiteness promises to deliver, a totality that, George argues, is cut off from the enslaved subject and continues to structure African American identity.[83] The anxiety of history permeates the world of Wind-Gap. Despite withholding the violent legacy of slavery in the diegesis, *Sharp Objects* complicates the fantasy of national identity through the contemporary eruptions of murderous violence and the haunting of the past that takes on numerous forms. By examining how slavery becomes a dimension of violence in the series' subtext, the contemporary murders in Wind-Gap are read not as exceptions to the America initially presented in the series but as a result of its history and social order.

During "Closer", several present-day and flashback sequences draw attention to the ivory floor in Adora's bedroom. Intercut across the episode are Camille's memories that speak to her desire and inability to cross the precious tiles, her foot lingering over the doorway's threshold. In one sequence, a photographer shoots Adora for a magazine feature concentrating on the flooring as an important architectural feature of the home. We see a framed cover of *Southern Home* with a spread inside picturing Adora and Marian titled "Legacy & Ivory", which refers to the "Civil War-era ivory floor". During the memory of this photo shoot, Camille walks into the room to pick up the camera the photographer has laid down, accidentally muddying the floor to Adora's dismay. When Camille looks upon the photo shoot, her sense of exclusion from the mother–daughter relationship is palpable as she is rendered absent from the family scene.

As with the abattoir kept at a distance from the family home, refigured in the illustrative pig on the local shop's door, the ivory floor rematerialises a Civil War legacy as a vital feature of the wealthy domestic environment. It is polished and preserved with great care, attested to by its immaculate whiteness, spoiled only by Camille's accidental traipsing. As George details, the owning of enslaved persons served as an "index of [the master's] superiority over both the slave and his white compatriots".[84] The ivory floor, which is haunted by a Confederate past of indentured labour and reasserted as a calcification of social and monetary capital, imagines George's thesis whereby slavery functions as a "foundation of an economics in which the abstract value of both a white man's capital and his superior being were not only signified but also reified by the subjugated body of the enslaved blacks".[85] This legacy of capital that is made available through slavery and secures whiteness haunts episode two, "Dirt", where the family's maid Gayla (Emily Yancy) attends to the tiles, cleaning them in small, circular motions.

Gayla is one of the few black characters seen in the series, along with Frank's wife, Eileen, and Becca (Hilary Ward), Camille's childhood friend from the cheerleading team, who does not conform to the mother and wife roles that her white counterparts have assumed. As the family's maid, Gayla maintains the domestic sphere and supplements (and often eclipses) Adora's maternal role when extending affection towards Camille. Her presence serves as a reminder of the racial difference otherwise absent from Wind-Gap's self-aggrandising narrative, the domestic legacy of the family home, and America's capitalist nostalgia that features across Wind-Gap's public walls. These spaces structure a visual elimination of blackness, which Gayla returns to the frame as she continues to operate in the Preaker–Crellin home. Particularly as the series investigates Southern identity, Gayla becomes reminiscent of the 'mammy' trope, a recurring feature in American iconography. As described by Kimberly Wallace-Sanders, the mammy is "part of the lexicon of antebellum mythology that continues to have a provocative and tenacious hold on the American psyche".[86] Gayla's presence draws on Southern nostalgia and the black domestic servant central to Lost Cause mythology.[87] In her introduction to *Mammy: A Century of Race, Gender, and Southern Memory*, Wallace-Sanders situates the "mammy's body [...] as a tendon between the races, connecting the muscle of African American slave labour with the Skeletal power structure of white southern aristocracy" that Adora is suggestive of.[88] The most famous embodiment of this trope is that of the house servant called Mammy, played by Hattie McDaniel in *Gone with the Wind* (1939), a cinematic rehearsal of the Lost Cause myth that plays out through the film's narrativisation of the American Civil War and Reconstruction period. *Sharp Objects*, as a critical intervention into the pathos of Southern nostalgia, frames Gayla as a living trace of the national and cinematic history of the Confederacy.

During the Calhoun Day celebration, Adora gives Richard a tour of her grand house. She invites him into her bedroom, recounting the history of the ivory floor, which was "a wedding present for [Adora's] great-great-grandmother. Before anybody knew what was 'endangered' was". Because of the emphasis on the floor as a Civil War-era feature and Adora's Confederate ancestry, the family's wealth and 'legacy' become intimately tied to enslavement in America despite this connection remaining unacknowledged. This complex negotiation of the past carries over the series' noir sensibilities, as noirs often employ and question American nostalgia. Loren argues that this tendency situates the past "not only [...] as a historical condition, the 'actuality' of the past upon which a present is contingent" but also as "fantasies and phantoms of the past as they [...] relate[...] to American mythologies".[89] Slavery is a structuring absence that invites us to understand Wind-Gap in terms of its national history and the ways history persists in the social order of the present day.

Unable to be part of Wind-Gap's narrative, the town's repressed history re-emerges in a subverted form in the final scene of the series when Camille realises that Amma murdered Natalie and Ann with the help of Kelsey and Jodes. Throughout the episodes, Amma plays with a doll's house that is a meticulous replica of the family home. In the eighth and final episode, "Milk", Adora is arrested for the town's murders. Richard uncovers that she poisoned Marian and has also been poisoning Amma and Camille as part of her Munchausen syndrome by proxy and, therefore, suspects her of killing the other girls.[90] However, in the concluding moments of "Milk", Camille peers closely at the doll's house in the apartment where she and Amma now live in St. Louis following Adora's imprisonment. Previously, the removal of Ann's and Natalie's teeth has marked the brutality of the Wind-Gap murders. In this closing scene, Camille notices a tooth under a miniature bed before realising that the murdered girls' teeth have been used to construct a facsimile of the ivory floor, whose pristine surface masks the dark underside of the town and implicates the Preaker–Crellin women within their family's violent Confederate legacy.[91]

Camille's revelation frames Amma as a *'fille fatale'*, the 'fatale child' neo-noir trope that came to prominence in the 1990s.[92] Amma is an obedient and sweet daughter in the presence of Adora and rebellious after nightfall, sneaking out of the house to drink, take drugs and party with other local teens. As the murderer, Amma further encourages a reading of woman as a point of narrative difficulty. From the beginning, the police investigators,

Camille's editor and the townspeople all believe the murderer *must* be a man. The young woman cannot be recognised as occupying the place of violence in the social sphere, structuring the investigative narrative action around the point that she is unreadable.

The connection between contemporary and historical violence and whiteness is foreshadowed in episode two, "Dirt", when Camille speaks to a young boy named James Capisi (Dylan Schombing) who claims to have seen Natalie being lured from a playground shortly before she went missing. James tells Camille that it was a "woman in white" who took her, presumed to be referring to local folklore about a woman who kills children, as described by Camille during a conversation with Chief Vickery later in the episode. Following the finale's brief post-credit sequence that reveals Amma murdering Ann, Natalie and a recently introduced young black woman, Mae (Iyana Halley), a short clip of Amma in a white dress shows her moving into the forest by the playground, as described by James. With this myth, 'white' emerges as a signifier that ties contemporary violence to a local legend passed down through generations, supplementing the founding Lost Cause narrative that cannot directly speak of 'whiteness'.

George continues his analysis of African American identity by arguing that slavery imbues bodies with racialised meaning by reducing them to a monetary value and, in doing so, disavows agency and extracts *jouissance* from the enslaved subject. In the move to bar the slave from the fantasy of subjective wholeness to which the master is granted access, George concentrates on the horrific violence inflicted upon slaves and the ways this was rendered permissible. Whereas the social contract maintained by law goes some way to taming violent urges, slavery involves "a suspension or loosening of moral restrictions", as enslaved persons are not recognised as part of the social fabric, and, therefore, their witnessing of violence does not evoke shame for the master who metes out pain to other slaves.[93] When the master "fails to acknowledge" the subjectivity of the other, the slave's capacity as "a source of the shaming gaze that tames one's transgressive desires" is not registered.[94] As the slave is continually reduced to a commodity, the master becomes unmoored from symbolic meaning that dissuades from destructive and evil acts of violence. With this reading of power and the racializing processes in American history, Amma's murderous acts can be framed through their proximity to both her family's and the town's Confederate legacy that is forged through slavery, to exhibit how *jouissance* "begins with a tickle and ends in a blaze of petrol".[95] As slavery functions as the unspoken and unseen 'lost cause' of violence passed down through the generations of women, it rises to the surface through the acts of Amma's and Adora's crimes and Camille's self-harm.[96] By setting Camille's self-harm, Adora's Munchausen syndrome by proxy and Amma's murders against a backdrop of the American Civil War, that which is repressed returns as a symptom that disturbs the face of the town and facilitates a diminishment of symbolic order that would contain the murderous *jouissance* whose reappearance structures the series.

In this sense, slavery becomes not a narrative moment or device but an instance of 'historical trauma' that rewrites town and nation. Coined by Silverman, this term denotes a period that alters the social fabric by bridging the "public social sphere" history gets written into with trauma – a "noun conventionally associated with the psychic or psychosocial shock suffered by an individual person".[97] To articulate this concept, Silverman looks at three films from 1940s Hollywood (*The Best Years of Our Lives* [1946], *It's A Wonderful Life* [1946] and *The Guilt of Janet Ames* [1947]) that focus on masculine subjects and centre narratives that directly or indirectly respond to World War II. In these instances, the traumatic historical event shatters the lives of their male protagonists, who are presented as lacking rather than embodying the masterful phallic subject that Hollywood traditionally codifies. Akin to de Lauretis's discussion of *Bad Timing*, Silverman connects conventional narrative construction with the masculine position, arguing that traumatic dimensions of history erupt as temporal schisms that threaten to puncture the mirage of the coherent egoic subject men have come to be associated with.

In the films that render male figures precarious, Silverman demonstrates how the masculine authority and the social order they preserve are in decline. The protagonists do not merely represent individuals who go through a personal transformation. Rather, formal devices such as deep focus strategy and long takes "differentiate that work from most Hollywood films of the period".[98] In doing so, these texts visually translate how history can "undo our imaginary relation to the symbolic order, as well as to the other elements within the social formation with which that order is imbricated".[99] Ultimately, Silverman recognises how these films repeatedly depict male protagonists as lacking, a condition usually reserved for female characters to "shore up the dominant fiction" of masculine phallocentrism.[100] While her analysis does not feature texts where female characters or questions of whiteness directly disrupt authority, Silverman develops a theory of narrative to analyse how the past returns to the present in a subverted form. As *Sharp Objects* shares this sensibility of complicating certainty and coherence, the series enters a lineage of works that reflect upon historical trauma by destabilising the architecture of whiteness and masculinity as it gets written into the visual and temporal arrangements of the cinematic (and, in this case, serial television) text.

Conclusion (the Black of Noir)

Returning to genre, and as a corrective to the overlooking of race (and, implicitly, whiteness as a racialised position) in the study of noir, E. Ann Kaplan, Manthia Diawara and Eric Lott have each dissected how the visual and narrative economy of this genre suggests racial difference. A common thread in their analyses is the understanding of how race is repressed and re-emerges in their chosen cinematic texts. Kaplan situates race as "film noir's repressed unconscious Signifier", citing the untranslated French 'noir' as indicating an avoidance of directly naming blackness in film analysis.[101] Across their interventions, which bring race to the forefront of noir scholarship, is the rereading of the iconic visual darkness that often dominates noir's mise-en-scène. All three writers read noir's graphic shadows as translating the moral and psychic degeneration of the white male protagonists. Whereas Manon's discussion of chiaroscuro recognises the play of shadow as traversing the distinction between innocent appearances and criminal activity, Lott argues that this lighting schema and "moral focus on the rotten souls of white folks [...] invoked the racial dimension of this figural play of light against dark".[102] The black of 'noir' suggests the erosion of a dominant white culture that alludes to racial otherness without bringing this difference into the consciousness of the cinematic text.

Racialised others featured in a film noir are predominantly marginal characters who overlap or stand in for a white protagonist's criminal actions. Lott identifies examples of this relationality in *Double Indemnity* (1944), *Gilda* and *Kiss Me Deadly* (1955), among others. Following Lott, we can similarly observe how *Sharp Objects* writes Gayla, Eileen, Becca and Mae into the sidelines of the central narrative conceits. Yet, instead of sequestering difference as a benign issue in noir, Lott encourages us to rethink how these instances of otherness "confirm the central symbolic significance of colour to the black-and-white world of many noirs, which revolve upon a racial axis that exerts great force at more key moments in more films than can easily be written off as exceptions".[103] Also suggested by Kaplan and Diawara, racial difference emerges as a central concern in the "dramas of interiority" that depict the turn to 'darkness' enacted by the white protagonists.[104]

In *Sharp Objects*, the haunting of racial difference that supports whiteness is suggested, in part, by Camille, who designates the repressed past. As a figure haunted by her past and someone from Wind-Gap's past who returns to town, Camille comes to signify a spectrum of difference as her presence troubles the otherwise unquestioned myth of the town's Confederate founding. In this way, *Sharp Objects* follows a tradition of noir whereby the central woman contains a multitude of differences, including that of race, as they problematise femininity and, subsequently, the typical gender inscriptions that uphold masculine authority. As Diawara writes, "[w]omen, bad guys, and detectives in film noir are 'Black' by virtue of occupying indeterminate and monstrous spaces that Whiteness traditionally reserves for Black-ness in our culture".[105] Kaplan agrees with Diawara when she argues that "Hollywood discourse" collapses differences so that "the Imaginary white centre can contain its mythic uniqueness. Whiteness is not just one category among many: it is the category through which all other differences are produced as Other".[106] Camille's flashbacks undermine the virtue of violence represented in the re-enactment of Confederate bravery by reintroducing a past repressed in the idealisation of whiteness.

As Seshadri-Crooks proposes, bringing historicity into view produces anxiety in the social fabric that maintains whiteness as a master signifier. *Sharp*

Objects draws out Seshadri-Crooks's thesis when anxiety is connected to the signifier, when written into Camille's flesh, which further complicates skin as a site of gendered and racial meaning. Lott's claim that "the troping of white darkness in noir has a racial source that is all the more insistent for seeming off to the side" seems pertinent when examining the interplay of history, whiteness and trauma in *Sharp Objects*, especially as the series imbues Confederacy with pronounced symbolic importance.[107]

The repression of recent and historical trauma sustains Wind-Gap's America. As the series progresses, the town's projection of nation and community disintegrates. This faltering of the social fabric is not achieved by narrativising the castration of male protagonists. Instead, Camille disturbs textual mastery through the interjection of analepses. As her characterisation links her ancestral line to Wind-Gap's Confederate myth, the understanding of history and its reliance on whiteness becomes problematised by Camille's jarring memories that draw parallels between the town's founding, recent ritualised violence, architectural features in the family home and its doll's house replica, and Gayla's visual persistence. Regarding works that theorise interconnections of history, racialised difference and noir, one can see how *Sharp Objects* follows the cinematic traditions that employ anachronic temporality to interrogate the ways that interpersonal relations and national identities are troubled by the return of the repressed, a return constructed through the feminine side of sexual difference.

Importantly for this series, it is the body that functions as a site of visibility that bears marks of the past. Copjec writes that "[t]he noir hero is embarrassed by a visibility that he carries around like an excess body for which he can find no proper place", a visibility Loren interprets as "the body of the past, or the hero's very historicity".[108] The return of the past, for which Camille is a conduit, is a guiding noir motif in *Sharp Objects*. Her presence brings the personal into the public, the historic into the present, and the singular into the systemic. These complicated strands of the past connect to other noir tropes, such as the flashbacks that create a world of uncertainty and bridge the small American town with its repressed past. On the one hand, Wind-Gap displays picturesque images of post-war capitalism. On the other, the ghosts of transatlantic slavery haunt the text in the form of the eruptive violence perpetrated by Amma, the public embodiment of Confederate heroine Millie Calhoun.

In establishing noir conventions within the geographical and historical contexts of the series, *Sharp Objects* challenges the construction of social and national identities. Examination of the series' analeptic strategy illustrates how the curation of narrative confusion and visual intelligibility performs a version of noir's chiaroscuro lighting as understood by Manon. Because the jarring analepses allude to a time from Camille's past that cannot be otherwise observed in the present-day setting, these instances make a critical intervention into what might otherwise resemble an unremarkable surface of the American town. However, this similarity between flashbacks and chiaroscuro is complicated as

Sharp Objects draws out Wind-Gap's troubled history of routinised violence through Camille's particular perspective. To further complicate this re-articulation of chiaroscuro's effects, her body is an unreliable archive that refuses to provide a cogent understanding of her adolescence. Because the scarred body becomes a privileged point that links the recent past to the present day, *Sharp Objects* rethinks Manon's metaphor that likens normal appearances to the surface of the skin that bears no marks of distress.

Camille is out of sync with linear time. Her allusive memories disrupt the conventional narrative associated with law enforcement, whose representatives drive the plot to uncover the murderer in Wind-Gap and return the town to its previous order. It is a Lacanian understanding of the theory of sexual difference that contextualises the temporality which the series generates and is crucial to reading the staging of language, the body and history. Beyond resurrecting living memories of Wind-Gap's past, the representation of the past's interruption into the present day extends to the nation's history, scrutinised through the rehearsal of myth.

Drawing on the work of Loren, George, Seshadri-Crooks and Silverman, we can see how film noir's concern with the past troubles capitalism's call to self-reinvention, the sustaining of whiteness and textual authority organised through masculinity. Loren argues that the development of American capitalism redefined subjects' relationship with history and encouraged a self-reinvention that attempts to forget the past. Consequently, the noir theme of a returning past that *Sharp Objects* employs problematises this disavowal of history American capitalism has adopted. The threat of history's resurrection is made pertinent by the explicit references to the 1950s era of booming American consumerism in the form of painted advertisements featured throughout the series.

Underpinning the image of suburban contentment that the painted advertisements speak to, the Calhoun Day celebration sustains and complicates Wind-Gap's Southern Confederate identity. Drawing on the Lost Cause myth, the series' re-enactment of Civil War violence and chivalry eliminates racial difference as a readable component in the town's founding legend. In doing so, Wind-Gap's community asserts a legacy of whiteness by denying its historicity, enabled by a Southern nostalgia and Confederate insignia. At the same time, however, whiteness reappears as a signifier in a different Wind-Gap legend, known as "the woman in white", who is said to kill children in the town and who is, like Millie Calhoun, embodied by Amma as she murders Natalie, Ann and, later, Mae.

The town's founding myth and instantiation of whiteness extend to the architecture of the family house. Inside the Preaker–Crellin residence, the floor in Adora's bedroom preserves a "Civil War legacy". As the teeth of the murdered girls later replicate the tiles, this domestic element places the historical past in proximity to the contemporary crimes, revealing a link between the two without staging a causal relationship in the diegesis. Gayla also becomes a site of visual importance as she marks an instance of racialised difference in the domestic sphere. Her presence is a reminder of the black labour otherwise omitted from Wind-Gap's construction of history, both in the Calhoun Day myth and the billboards depicting white suburban consumerism. At the same time, Gayla is also reminiscent of an American literary and cinematic history that positions the black female body as a 'mammy', an invented figure of cheerful domestic servitude during and after the legal enslavement of people in the southern states of America. Only in the closing moments of the final episode, "Milk" – in what serves as another allusion to motherhood and whiteness – do the various threads of violence woven through the series come together. By performing the role of Millie Calhoun, incarnating the legend of the woman in white recalled by James and committing the contemporary murders, Amma collates historical and folkloric violence with her present-day crimes. The enjoyment or *jouissance* that is shown to burst forth in such murderous acts emphasises the affective significance that is generated by modes of violence that have historically been directed across racialised lines, which George analyses as central to understanding the construction of the master–slave arrangement of extracted labour that rewrites the very way in which the subject comes into being.

Seshadri-Crooks's work continues to inform this analysis, as she proposes that racial difference and sexual difference cannot map on to one another. Rather, she provides a refreshed way of reading race by suggesting that sexual difference marks a failure in signification that whiteness attempts to fill by disavowing lack and designating itself as the site of totality. Without confirming or dramatizing the interrelation between sexual and racial difference that Seshadri-Crooks offers, *Sharp Objects* stages an intervention in the myth of American history and its pillars of whiteness and masculinity, which support the dream of capitalism that adorns the surfaces of Wind-Gap. It is through the feminine side of sexual difference, as expressed by Camille, that the series critically interrupts this myth sustained by the disavowal of historical trauma.

Notes

1 *Sharp Objects* is a miniseries that originally aired on HBO in 2018, created by Marti Noxon and directed by Jean-Marc Vallée. It is based on the novel by Gillian Flynn; Gillian Flynn, *Sharp Objects* (London: Pheonix, 2007).
2 James Naremore, *More Than Night: Film Noir in Its Contexts* (Berkeley: University of California Press, 1998), 90–115. 'Queer Noir' in Richard Dyer, *The Culture of Queers* (London: Routledge, 2002), 90–115.
3 James Naremore, *More Than Night: Film Noir in Its Contexts* (Berkeley: University of California Press, 1998), 90–115. 'Queer Noir' in Richard Dyer, *The Culture of Queers* (London: Routledge, 2002), 9.
4 Ben Tyrer, *Out of the Past: Lacan and Film Noir* (Cham: Springer International, 2016), 32, https://doi.org/10.1007/978-3-319-30942-2; Raymond Durgnat, 'Paint It Black: The Family Tree of the Film Noir', in *Notions of Genre*, ed. Barry

Keith Grant and Malisa Kurtz (Austin: University of Texas Press, 2016), 252, https://doi.org/10.7560/303757.

5 Raymond Chandler and Etienne Chaumeton, *A Panorama of American Film Noir (1941–1953)* (San Francisco: City Lights, 2002), 15.

6 Dashiell Hammett, *The Maltese Falcon* (London: Orion, 2005); Raymond Chandler, *The Big Sleep and Other Novels* (London: Penguin Books, 2000). Their respective film adaptations were *The Maltese Falcon* (1941), directed by John Huston, and *The Big Sleep* (1946), directed by Howard Hawks.

7 For a discussion of the difficulty in noir's categorisation, see Joan Copjec, 'Introduction', in Joan Copjec, *Shades of Noir: A Reader* (London: Verso, 1993), vii–xii.

8 Raymond Chandler and Etienne Chaumeton, *A Panorama of American Film Noir (1941–1953)* (San Francisco: City Lights, 2002), 5.

9 Raymond Chandler and Etienne Chaumeton, *A Panorama of American Film Noir (1941–1953)* (San Francisco: City Lights, 2002), 7.

10 Paul Kerr, 'Out of What Past? Notes on the B *film noir*', in Alain Silver and James. Ursini, *Film Noir Reader. 1* (New York: Limelight Editions, 1996), 111; Tyrer includes numerous examples of films that cohere to this claim such as the "flashback narratives of *Double Indemnity* [1944], *The Killers* (Robert Siodmak, 1946), *D.O.A.* (Rudolph Maté, 1950), and *Sunset Blvd.* (Billy Wilder, 1950) [which] present an opening scene – in each case a dead or dying man – whose meaning is determined only at the end of the film; the climactic revelations of *The Maltese Falcon, The Woman in the Window* (Fritz Lang, 1944), *The Postman Always Rings Twice* and *The Lady from Shanghai* (Orson Welles, 1948) effect a transformation of the entire proceedings, retroactively framing them and providing a previously unknown context; and a film such as *Out of the Past* (Jacques Tourneur, 1947) [which] is characterised by overtly retrospective themes". Ben Tyrer, 'Film Noir as Point de Capiton: Double Indemnity, Structure and Temporality', *Film-Philosophy* 17, no. 1 (December 2013): 96–97, https://doi.org/10.3366/film.2013.0006.

11 For example, *Out of the Past, Sunset Boulevard* and *Double Indemnity.*

12 Raymond Chandler and Etienne Chaumeton, *A Panorama of American Film Noir (1941–1953)* (San Francisco: City Lights, 2002), 11–12.

13 For examples of noir films featuring protagonists with amnesia, see *Hangover Square* (1945), *Spellbound* (1945), *The Blue Dahlia* (1946) and neo-noir *Memento* (2000).

14 Georges Sadoul, quoted in Raymond Chandler and Etienne Chaumeton, *A Panorama of American Film Noir (1941–1953)* (San Francisco: City Lights, 2002), 11.

15 Joan Copjec, *Shades of Noir: A Reader* (London: Verso, 1993), x–xi.

16 Joan Copjec, *Shades of Noir: A Reader* (London: Verso, 1993), xii.

17 Joan Copjec, *Shades of Noir: A Reader* (London: Verso, 1993), xii.

18 Richard Dyer, *The Culture of Queers* (London: Routledge, 2002), 90.

19 Hugh S. Manon, 'X-Ray Visions: Radiography, "Chiaroscuro", and the Fantasy of Unsuspicion in "Film Noir"', *Film Criticism* 32, no. 2 (2007): 2–27.

20 Jacques Lacan, *The Seminar of Jacques Lacan/Book XX, On Feminine Sexuality: The Limits of Love and Knowledge: Encore 1972–1972*, ed. Jacques-Alain Miller, trans. Bruce Fink (New York: Norton, 1999).

21 Suzanne Barnard, 'Introduction', in *Reading Seminar XX: Lacan's Major Work on Love, Knowledge, and Feminine Sexuality*, ed. Bruce Fink and Suzanne Barnard (Albany: State University of New York Press, 2002), 1–20. While Lacan uses the terms 'man' and 'woman' in his work, this chapter uses 'masculine' and

'feminine' to designate the Lacanian frame of sexual difference, as distinct from the conventional usage of these positions.

22 Suzanne Barnard, 'Introduction', in *Reading Seminar XX: Lacan's Major Work on Love, Knowledge, and Feminine Sexuality*, ed. Bruce Fink and Suzanne Barnard (Albany: State University of New York Press, 2002), 4.

23 Suzanne Barnard, 'Introduction', in *Reading Seminar XX: Lacan's Major Work on Love, Knowledge, and Feminine Sexuality*, ed. Bruce Fink and Suzanne Barnard (Albany: State University of New York Press, 2002), 4.

24 Jacques Lacan, *The Seminar of Jacques Lacan/Book XX, On Feminine Sexuality: The Limits of Love and Knowledge: Encore 1972–1972*, ed. Jacques-Alain Miller, trans. Bruce Fink (New York: Norton, 1999), 32.

25 With reference to the bestselling book of this title, John Gray, *Men Are from Mars, Women Are from Venus* (New York: HarperCollins, 1992).

26 Jacques Lacan, *The Seminar of Jacques Lacan/Book XX, On Feminine Sexuality: The Limits of Love and Knowledge: Encore 1972–1972*, ed. Jacques-Alain Miller, trans. Bruce Fink (New York: Norton, 1999), 33.

27 Teresa De Lauretis, 'Now and Nowhere: Roeg's *Bad Timing*', in *Alice Doesn't: Feminism, Semiotics, Cinema* (London: Macmillan, 1984), 84–102.

28 Hugh S. Manon, 'X-Ray Visions: Radiography, "Chiaroscuro", and the Fantasy of Unsuspicion in "Film Noir"', *Film Criticism* 32, no. 2 (2007): 2, 3.

29 Hugh S. Manon, 'X-Ray Visions: Radiography, "Chiaroscuro", and the Fantasy of Unsuspicion in "Film Noir"', *Film Criticism* 32, no. 2 (2007): 3.

30 Hugh S. Manon, 'X-Ray Visions: Radiography, "Chiaroscuro", and the Fantasy of Unsuspicion in "Film Noir"', *Film Criticism* 32, no. 2 (2007): 5.

31 Hugh S. Manon, 'X-Ray Visions: Radiography, "Chiaroscuro", and the Fantasy of Unsuspicion in "Film Noir"', *Film Criticism* 32, no. 2 (2007): 10.

32 Hugh S. Manon, 'X-Ray Visions: Radiography, "Chiaroscuro", and the Fantasy of Unsuspicion in "Film Noir"', *Film Criticism* 32, no. 2 (2007): 11.

33 Hugh S. Manon, 'X-Ray Visions: Radiography, "Chiaroscuro", and the Fantasy of Unsuspicion in "Film Noir"', *Film Criticism* 32, no. 2 (2007): 6.

34 Hugh S. Manon, 'X-Ray Visions: Radiography, "Chiaroscuro", and the Fantasy of Unsuspicion in "Film Noir"', *Film Criticism* 32, no. 2 (2007): 3.

35 Hugh S. Manon, 'X-Ray Visions: Radiography, "Chiaroscuro", and the Fantasy of Unsuspicion in "Film Noir"', *Film Criticism* 32, no. 2 (2007): 4.

36 Hugh S. Manon, 'X-Ray Visions: Radiography, "Chiaroscuro", and the Fantasy of Unsuspicion in "Film Noir"', *Film Criticism* 32, no. 2 (2007): 3.

37 Hugh S. Manon, 'X-Ray Visions: Radiography, "Chiaroscuro", and the Fantasy of Unsuspicion in "Film Noir"', *Film Criticism* 32, no. 2 (2007): 5.

38 Hugh S. Manon, 'X-Ray Visions: Radiography, "Chiaroscuro", and the Fantasy of Unsuspicion in "Film Noir"', *Film Criticism* 32, no. 2 (2007): 5.

39 Hugh S. Manon, 'X-Ray Visions: Radiography, "Chiaroscuro", and the Fantasy of Unsuspicion in "Film Noir"', *Film Criticism* 32, no. 2 (2007): 14.

40 Hugh S. Manon, 'X-Ray Visions: Radiography, "Chiaroscuro", and the Fantasy of Unsuspicion in "Film Noir"', *Film Criticism* 32, no. 2 (2007): 14.

41 Teresa De Lauretis, 'Now and Nowhere: Roeg's *Bad Timing*', in *Alice Doesn't: Feminism, Semiotics, Cinema* (London: Macmillan, 1984), 84–102.

42 Teresa De Lauretis, 'Now and Nowhere: Roeg's *Bad Timing*', in *Alice Doesn't: Feminism, Semiotics, Cinema* (London: Macmillan, 1984), 98.

43 Teresa De Lauretis, 'Now and Nowhere: Roeg's *Bad Timing*', in *Alice Doesn't: Feminism, Semiotics, Cinema* (London: Macmillan, 1984), 98.

44 Teresa De Lauretis, 'Now and Nowhere: Roeg's *Bad Timing*', in *Alice Doesn't: Feminism, Semiotics, Cinema* (London: Macmillan, 1984), 97

45   Ellie Ragland-Sullivan, *Essays on the Pleasures of Death: From Freud to Lacan* (New York: Routledge, 1995), 184–185.

46   Elizabeth Freeman, 'Introduction: Queer and Not Now', in *Time Binds: Queer Temporalities, Queer Histories* (Durham: Duke University Press, 2010), 1–19; Lee Edelman, *No Future: Queer Theory and the Death Drive* (Durham: Duke University Press, 2004).

47   Teresa De Lauretis, 'Now and Nowhere: Roeg's *Bad Timing*', in *Alice Doesn't: Feminism, Semiotics, Cinema* (London: Macmillan, 1984), 95

48   Mary Ann Doane, *Femmes Fatales* (London: Taylor & Francis, 1991), 1.

49   Mary Ann Doane, *Femmes Fatales* (London: Taylor & Francis, 1991), 99.

50   Mary Ann Doane, *Femmes Fatales* (London: Taylor & Francis, 1991), 99.

51   Mary Ann Doane, *Femmes Fatales* (London: Taylor & Francis, 1991), 100.

52   Mary Ann Doane, *Femmes Fatales* (London: Taylor & Francis, 1991), 101.

53   Joan Copjec, *Read My Desire: Lacan against the Historicists* (Cambridge: MIT Press, 1994), 39–63.

54   Joan Copjec, *Read My Desire: Lacan against the Historicists* (Cambridge: MIT Press, 1994), 54.

55   Joan Copjec, *Read My Desire: Lacan against the Historicists* (Cambridge: MIT Press, 1994), 54.

56   Ragland, *Essays on the Pleasure of Death*, 185.

57   Joan Copjec, *Read My Desire: Lacan against the Historicists* (Cambridge: MIT Press, 1994), 54, emphasis in original.

58   Jacques Lacan, *Écrits: A Selection*, trans. Alan Sheridan (London: Routledge, 1989), 67, emphasis in original.

59   François Regnault, 'The Name-of-the-Father', in *Reading Seminar XI: Lacan's Four Fundamental Concepts of Psychoanalysis* (New York: State University of New York Press, 1995), 66.

60   For an analysis of how film noir thematises concerns around American citizenship, particularly during the Cold War era, see Jonathan Auerbach, *Dark Borders: Film Noir and American Citizenship* (Durham: Duke University Press, 2011).

61   Scott Loren, 'Self-Fashioning, Freedom, and the Problem of His-Story: The Return of Noir', *European Journal of American Studies* 3, no. 1 (21 January 2008): 2, https://doi.org/10.4000/ejas.1842.

62   Scott Loren, 'Self-Fashioning, Freedom, and the Problem of His-Story: The Return of Noir', *European Journal of American Studies* 3, no. 1 (21 January 2008): 1.

63   Scott Loren, 'Self-Fashioning, Freedom, and the Problem of His-Story: The Return of Noir', *European Journal of American Studies* 3, no. 1 (21 January 2008): 6.

64   Scott Loren, 'Self-Fashioning, Freedom, and the Problem of His-Story: The Return of Noir', *European Journal of American Studies* 3, no. 1 (21 January 2008): 7.

65   Scott Loren, 'Self-Fashioning, Freedom, and the Problem of His-Story: The Return of Noir', *European Journal of American Studies* 3, no. 1 (21 January 2008): 7.

66   Alan T. Nolan, 'The Anatomy of the Myth', in *The Myth of the Lost Cause and Civil War History*, ed. Alan T. Nolan and Gary W. Gallagher (Bloomington: Indiana University Press, 2000), 12.

67   Alan T. Nolan, 'The Anatomy of the Myth', in *The Myth of the Lost Cause and Civil War History*, ed. Alan T. Nolan and Gary W. Gallagher (Bloomington: Indiana University Press, 2000), 16–18.

68 The "End Zone" is shown to Richard in the previous episode, "Ripe". In the scene, Camille takes Richard into the woods during their exchange of knowledge. She describes the clearing as "The End Zone. Double entendre intended. This is where the football team would have their way with that week's lucky cheerleader", indicating a pattern of sexual violence. It should be noted that, while I am referring to the implied events as sexual coercion, this is not the language Camille uses. When Richard comments that "some would call that rape, you know?", Camille responds with "some would call that consensual, you know?".

69 This collective gesture of the fictional town follows a long history of repressing slavery from narratives of freedom, for which Millie Calhoun serves as a figure. In 'Hegel and Haiti', Susan Buck-Morss meticulously demonstrates how the practice and subjects of enslavement remain unspoken while the rhetoric of freedom and slavery is widely taken up as a central metaphor across philosophical works of eighteenth-century European Enlightenment and subsequent historical accounts of this period. See Susan Buck-Morss, 'Hegel and Haiti', *Critical Inquiry* 26, no. 4 (2000): 821–865.

70 See Audra D. S. Burch, 'How a National Movement Topples Hundreds of Confederate Symbols', *The New York Times* [online], 28 February 2022. Available at: https://www.nytimes.com/interactive/2022/02/28/us/confederate-statue-removal.html [Accessed 10/10/2014].

71 Hilary Neroni, 'Confederate Signifiers in Vermont: Fetish Objects and Racist Enjoyment', in *Lacan and Race: Racism, Identity, and Psychoanalytic Theory*, ed. Derek Hook and Sheldon George (London: Routledge, 2021), 54, https://doi.org/10.4324/9780429326790.

72 Hilary Neroni, 'Confederate Signifiers in Vermont: Fetish Objects and Racist Enjoyment', in *Lacan and Race: Racism, Identity, and Psychoanalytic Theory*, ed. Derek Hook and Sheldon George (London: Routledge, 2021), 54, https://doi.org/10.4324/9780429326790, 54.

73 Hilary Neroni, 'Confederate Signifiers in Vermont: Fetish Objects and Racist Enjoyment', in *Lacan and Race: Racism, Identity, and Psychoanalytic Theory*, ed. Derek Hook and Sheldon George (London: Routledge, 2021), 54, https://doi.org/10.4324/9780429326790, 55.

74 Sheldon George, *Race and Trauma: A Lacanian Study of African American Racial Identity* (Texas: Baylor University Press, 2016), 11.

75 Sheldon George, *Race and Trauma: A Lacanian Study of African American Racial Identity* (Texas: Baylor University Press, 2016), 11.

76 Sheldon George, *Race and Trauma: A Lacanian Study of African American Racial Identity* (Texas: Baylor University Press, 2016), 13.

77 Cited in Sheldon George, *Race and Trauma: A Lacanian Study of African American Racial Identity* (Texas: Baylor University Press, 2016), 22.

78 Karl Marx, *Theories of Surplus Value: Part 1* (New York: Prometheus Books, 2000), 46, cited in Sheldon George, *Race and Trauma: A Lacanian Study of African American Racial Identity* (Texas: Baylor University Press, 2016), 22.

79 Sheldon George, *Race and Trauma: A Lacanian Study of African American Racial Identity* (Texas: Baylor University Press, 2016), 23.

80 Hilary Neroni, 'Confederate Signifiers in Vermont: Fetish Objects and Racist Enjoyment', in *Lacan and Race: Racism, Identity, and Psychoanalytic Theory*, ed. Derek Hook and Sheldon George (London: Routledge, 2021), 54, https://doi.org/10.4324/9780429326790, 55.

81 Kalpana Seshadri-Crooks, *Desiring Whiteness: A Lacanian Analysis of Race* (London: Routledge, 2000), 3–4.

82 Kalpana Seshadri-Crooks, *Desiring Whiteness: A Lacanian Analysis of Race* (London: Routledge, 2000), 7.

83   Kalpana Seshadri-Crooks, *Desiring Whiteness: A Lacanian Analysis of Race* (London: Routledge, 2000), 45.

84   Sheldon George, *Race and Trauma: A Lacanian Study of African American Racial Identity* (Texas: Baylor University Press, 2016), 26.

85   Sheldon George, *Race and Trauma: A Lacanian Study of African American Racial Identity* (Texas: Baylor University Press, 2016), 26.

86   Kimberly Wallace-Sanders, *Mammy: A Century of Race, Gender, and Southern Memory* (Ann Arbor: University of Michigan Press, 2008), 2.

87   Kimberly Wallace-Sanders, *Mammy: A Century of Race, Gender, and Southern Memory* (Ann Arbor: University of Michigan Press, 2008), 4.

88   Kimberly Wallace-Sanders, *Mammy: A Century of Race, Gender, and Southern Memory* (Ann Arbor: University of Michigan Press, 2008), 3.

89   Scott Loren, 'Self-Fashioning, Freedom, and the Problem of His-Story: The Return of Noir', *European Journal of American Studies* 3, no. 1 (21 January 2008): 1.

90   In episode seven, "Falling", Richard's investigation into Camille leads him to Marian's medical records. He seeks out the nurse (Cristine Rose) who tended to Marian in the hospital. After attempting to alert the authorities to Adora's Munchausen syndrome by proxy and poisoning, the nurse was fired and forced to work in a different clinic as part of a cover-up that Chief Vickery was involved in. It is also implied on several occasions throughout the series that Chief Vickery and Adora have had an affair.

91   Kalpana Seshadri-Crooks, *Desiring Whiteness: A Lacanian Analysis of Race* (London: Routledge, 2000), 94.

92   See Samantha Lindop, 'What Are (Fatal) Little Girls Made of?', in Samantha Lindop, *Postfeminism and the Fatale Figure in Neo-Noir Cinema* (Basingstoke: Palgrave Macmillan, 2018), 93–103.

93   Sheldon George, *Race and Trauma: A Lacanian Study of African American Racial Identity* (Texas: Baylor University Press, 2016), 28.

94   Sheldon George, *Race and Trauma: A Lacanian Study of African American Racial Identity* (Texas: Baylor University Press, 2016), 29.

95   Jacques Lacan, *The Seminar of Jacques Lacan Book XVII: The Other Side of Psychoanalysis*, trans. Russell Grigg (New York: Norton, 2007), 72, cited in Sheldon George, *Race and Trauma: A Lacanian Study of African American Racial Identity* (Texas: Baylor University Press, 2016), 29.

96   In episode six, "Cherry", Alan also talks to Camille about how Adora's mother, Joya, would pinch her in the middle of the night and treat Adora with cruelty.

97   Kaja Silverman, 'Historical Trauma and Male Subjectivity', in *Male Subjectivity at the Margins* (New York: Routledge, 1992), 55.

98   Kaja Silverman, 'Historical Trauma and Male Subjectivity', in *Male Subjectivity at the Margins* (New York: Routledge, 1992), 66.

99   Kaja Silverman, 'Historical Trauma and Male Subjectivity', in *Male Subjectivity at the Margins* (New York: Routledge, 1992), 55.

100   Kaja Silverman, 'Historical Trauma and Male Subjectivity', in *Male Subjectivity at the Margins* (New York: Routledge, 1992), 89.

101   E. Ann Kaplan, ed., '"The Dark Continent of Film Noir": Race, Displacement and Metaphor in Tourneur's Cat People (1942) and Welles' The Lady from Shanghai (1948)', in *Women in Film Noir* (London: Bloomsbury Publishing, 1978), 183, https://doi.org/10.5040/9781838710163.

102   Eric Lott, 'The Whiteness of Film Noir', *American Literary History* 9, no. 3 (1997): 543.

103   Eric Lott, 'The Whiteness of Film Noir', *American Literary History* 9, no. 3 (1997): 545.

104 Eric Lott, 'The Whiteness of Film Noir', *American Literary History* 9, no. 3 (1997): 545.
105 Manthia Diawara, 'Noir by Noirs: Towards a New Realism in Black Cinema', *African American Review* 27, no. 4 (1993): 525, https://doi.org/10.2307/3041886.
106 E. Ann Kaplan, ed., '"The Dark Continent of Film Noir": Race, Displacement and Metaphor in Tourneur's Cat People (1942) and Welles' The Lady from Shanghai (1948)', in *Women in Film Noir* (London: Bloomsbury Publishing, 1978), 191–92.
107 Eric Lott, 'The Whiteness of Film Noir', *American Literary History* 9, no. 3 (1997): 545.
108 Joan Copjec, *Shades of Noir: A Reader* (London: Verso, 1993), ix; Scott Loren, 'Self-Fashioning, Freedom, and the Problem of His-Story: The Return of Noir', *European Journal of American Studies* 3, no. 1 (21 January 2008): 2.

References

Auerbach, Jonathan. *Dark Borders: Film Noir and American Citizenship* (Durham: Duke University Press, 2011).
Barnard, Suzanne. 'Introduction.' In *Reading Seminar XX: Lacan's Major Work on Love, Knowledge, and Feminine Sexuality*, edited by Bruce Fink and Suzanne Barnard, 1–20. Albany: State University of New York Press, 2002.
Buck-Morss, Susan. 'Hegel and Haiti.' *Critical Inquiry* 26, no. 4 (2000): 821–865.
Burch, Audra D.S. 'How a National Movement Topples Hundreds of Confederate Symbols.' *The New York Times* [online]. 28 February 2022. Available at: https://www.nytimes.com/interactive/2022/02/28/us/confederate-statue-removal.html [Accessed 10/10/2014].
Chandler, Raymond. *The Big Sleep and Other Novels*. London: Penguin Books, 2000.
Chandler, Raymond, and Etienne Chaumeton. *A Panorama of American Film Noir (1941–1953)*. San Francisco: City Lights, 2002.
Copjec, Joan. *Read My Desire: Lacan against the Historicists*. Cambridge: MIT Press, 1994.
Copjec, Joan, ed. *Shades of Noir: A Reader*. London: Verso, 1993.
De Lauretis, Teresa. *Alice Doesn't: Feminism, Semiotics, Cinema*. London: Macmillan, 1984.
Diawara, Manthia. 'Noir by Noirs: Towards a New Realism in Black Cinema.' *African American Review* 27, no. 4 (1993): 525. doi:10.2307/3041886.
Doane, Mary Ann. *Femmes Fatales*. London: Taylor & Francis, 1991.
Durgnat, Raymond. 'Paint It Black: The Family Tree of the Film Noir.' In *Notions of Genre*, edited by Barry Keith Grant and Malisa Kurtz. Austin: University of Texas Press, 2016. doi:10.7560/303757.
Dyer, Richard. *The Culture of Queers*. London: Routledge, 2002.
Edelman, Lee. *No Future: Queer Theory and the Death Drive*. Durham: Duke University Press, 2004.
Flynn, Gillian. *Sharp Objects*. London: Pheonix, 2007.
Freeman, Elizabeth. 'Introduction: Queer and Not Now.' In *Time Binds: Queer Temporalities, Queer Histories*, 1–19. Durham: Duke University Press, 2010.
George, Sheldon. *Race and Trauma: A Lacanian Study of African American Racial Identity*. Texas: Baylor University Press, 2016.
Gray, John. *Men Are from Mars, Women Are from Venus*. New York: HarperCollins, 1992.

Hammett, Dashiell. *The Maltese Falcon*. London: Orion, 2005.

Kaplan, E. Ann. *Women in Film Noir*. London: Bloomsbury, 1978.

Kerr, Paul. 'Out of What Past? Notes on the B film noir.' In Alain Silver and James Ursini, *Film Noir Reader*, 1. New York: Limelight, 1996.

Lacan, Jacques. *Écrits: A Selection*. Translated by Alan Sheridan. London: Routledge, 1989.

Lacan, Jacques. *The Seminar of Jacques Lacan: Book XX, On Feminine Sexuality: The Limits of Love and Knowledge: Encore 1972–1972*. Edited by Jacques-Alain Miller. Translated by Bruce Fink. New York: Norton, 1999.

Lacan, Jacques. *The Seminar of Jacques Lacan: Book XVII: The Other Side of Psychoanalysis*. Translated by Russell Grigg. New York: Norton, 2007.

Lindop, Samantha. *Postfeminism and the Fatale Figure in Neo-Noir Cinema*. Basingstoke: Palgrave Macmillan, 2018.

Loren, Scott. 'Self-Fashioning, Freedom, and the Problem of His-Story: The Return of Noir.' *European Journal of American Studies* 3, no. 1 (2008): 1–7. doi:10.4000/ejas.1842.

Lott, Eric. 'The Whiteness of Film Noir.' *American Literary History* 9, no. 3 (1997): 543–545.

Manon, Hugh S. 'X-Ray Visions: Radiography, "Chiaroscuro", and the Fantasy of Unsuspicion in "Film Noir".' *Film Criticism* 32, no. 2 (2007): 2–27.

Marx, Karl. *Theories of Surplus Value*. New York: Prometheus Books, 2000.

Naremore, James. *More Than Night; Film Noir in Its Contexts*. Berkeley: University of California Press, 1998.

Neroni, Hilary. 'Confederate Signifiers in Vermont: Fetish Objects and Racist Enjoyment.' In *Lacan and Race: Racism, Identity, and Psychoanalytic Theory*. Edited by Derek Hook and Sheldon George, 54. London: Routledge, 2021. doi:10.4324/9780429326790.

Nolan, Alan T. 'The Anatomy of the Myth.' In *The Myth of the Lost Cause and Civil War History*. Edited by Alan T. Nolan and Gary W. Gallagher. Bloomington: Indiana University Press, 2000.

Ragland-Sullivan, Ellie. *Essays on the Pleasures of Death: From Freud to Lacan*. New York: Routledge, 1995.

Regnault, François. 'The Name-of-the-Father.' In *Reading Seminar XI: Lacan's Four Fundamental Concepts of Psychoanalysis*, 66. New York: State University of New York Press, 1995.

Seshadri-Crooks, Kalpana. *Desiring Whiteness: A Lacanian Analysis of Race*. London: Routledge, 2000.

Silverman, Kaja. *Male Subjectivity at the Margins*. New York: Routledge, 1992.

Tyrer, Ben. 'Film Noir as Point de Capiton: Double Indemnity, Structure and Temporality.' *Film-Philosophy* 17, no. 1 (2013): 96–97. doi:10.3366/film.2013.0006.

Tyrer, Ben. *Out of the Past: Lacan and Film Noir*. Cham: Springer International, 2016. doi:10.1007/978-3-319-30942-2.

Wallace-Sanders, Kimberly. *Mammy: A Century of Race, Gender, and Southern Memory*. Ann Arbor: University of Michigan Press, 2008.

Chapter 3

Welcome 2 Reality

Ryan Trecartin's *Priority Innfield*

Two sorority girls giggling and petting a horse, their blonde synthetic wigs shinier than any natural locks could hope to be, the camera darting around while also moving in and out. Two different girls for a moment, their faces shimmering and contoured, one in a red sleeveless top with her arms painted blue. Someone shot from below, large lights above them, a couple of toilets in the room? They sway off-beat to the camera's swerving movement, their auto-tuned singing made from a string of incoherent words, painted-on beard and moustache smudged, lopsided pigtails sprouting out of their baseball cap, waistcoat with camouflage on the front and the American flag on the back. They wander 'off-stage', a stage that shares its edges with the camera. Artist Ryan Trecartin calls his works "movies", a tongue-in-cheek descriptor since the works are decidedly not cinematic: They are not shown in cinemas and tend towards 'video art' as they employ various digital techniques, including a pronounced layering of images, image filtering and swerving mobility made possible by light-weight camcorders.

In its first iteration, *Center Jenny* was part of Trecartin's video and sculptural installation *Priority Innfield* created in collaboration with artist Lizzie Fitch, which premiered at the fifty-fifth Venice Biennale in 2013.[1] Alongside *Center Jenny*, three other new video works were also exhibited: *Junior War*, *Comma Boat* and *Item Falls*, projected across multiple screens. Viewers were encouraged to enter and move between the screens as they were filled with the frantic activity filmed with multiple handheld cameras. Living beyond the gallery exhibition environment, Trecartin's work is also available for online streaming on the video-sharing platforms YouTube and Vimeo, where one can pause and resume or jump through time on command.

Conventional narrative films prioritise diegetic realism by hiding crew members, equipment and set boundaries while employing editing techniques and shot conventions designed to be unnoticeable. Together, these devices minimise the interruption of action within the *fabula* construction. In contrast, *Center Jenny*'s experimental staging incorporates features of its assembly, which post-production continues to accentuate. The synthetic quality of objects is ready to be seen as the videos do not present any body, environment

DOI: 10.4324/9781003527244-4

or prop in a naturalised way. Sound and lighting equipment remains in full view, and green screens, typically used to superimpose content, remain unfilled. Words and phrases carried over from previous or upcoming moments compile a concert of speech, forced to compete with samples of upbeat pop music, ballads and sirens. Sound builds in a manner reminiscent of Girl Talk's pop music mash-ups, or when a car radio gets set to run through stations, playing mere seconds from each detectable frequency. People film people filming, and spectators are made aware of the cutting between the numerous camera positions. Editing ignores conventions such as shot-reverse shot, and cameras avoid established 'rule of three' framing, the use of long shots to establish location and close-ups to generate pathos.[2] Colours change from highly saturated to night-vision to black and white without any discernible reason.

One can trace Trecartin's techniques to avant-garde and experimental film traditions. For instance, filmmaker Jean Luc Godard often breached cinematic conventions while referencing classical Hollywood tropes. In his film *Le Mépris* (1963), Godard opens with a long shot of Gorgia Moll walking from a distant point towards the camera while being tracked by a small film crew. As she approaches the camera, the crew and camera in shot turn to face the spectatorial viewpoint, encouraging us to confront the construction of the cinematic image. Godard's later eight-part film essay *Histoire(s) du Cinema* (1988–1998) creates an encyclopaedic tapestry of cinematic moments and images, which are repeated, stilled and overlaid with other clips, images and written and spoken words. Across this vast project, Godard produces a complex and evolving palimpsestic screen that Trecartin's work resembles as simultaneous images morph and collapse into one another in an eruption of visual information, albeit newly created rather than mined from cinema's archive. Trecartin's DIY aesthetics also extend to his pervasive use of handheld cameras. As well as being associated with candid footage shot on personal camcorders and phones, Trecartin's filming style mimics that seen in the 1999 independent picture *The Blair Witch Project* and the 2008 feature *Cloverfield*, which appeared to be compiled of 'found footage' to render naturalistic (and, therefore, more unnerving) their supernatural themes and action.

Trecartin has been dubbed the "most radical representative of a generation of artists for whom the Internet is always in the corner of their eye" and, famously, "the most consequential artist to have emerged since the nineteen-eighties".[3] Such responses are presumably due in part to the intensely disorientating effect of the videos. Viewing *Center Jenny* on a loop, as is the case during gallery exhibitions of Trecartin's work, one would be hard-pressed to discern what point in the 'movie' one was viewing.[4] There is an opening title card and a closing credit sequence but little else to indicate a beginning, middle or end. As numerous critics have commented, Trecartin's saturated environments are characteristic of the contemporary Western world's reliance on internet technologies for communication, socialising, dating, work, economic transactions, the production and consumption of media, education, art, gaming and sex.[5]

Bright beams of light pound the many talking faces, their voices high-pitched squeals or, occasionally, slowed down, deep and melting. The incessant cutting, in combination with streams of non sequitur speech, gives an appearance of improvisation, but Trecartin notably storyboards and scripts everything with precision.[6] It is for this reason that Ricardo E. Zulueta's monograph *Queer Art Camp Superstar*, to date the only one dedicated solely to Trecartin's work, examines the artist's oeuvre to establish its narrative content even though the works themselves resist such an approach. Examinations of Trecartin's work tend to focus on its aesthetic character and intense rate of action and editing, "forgo[ing] close readings of his dense narratives".[7] In an alternative approach, Zulueta subjects the pieces to a scrutiny that attempts to tame them into linear, sensible plotlines. The five chapters comprising this monograph take a chronological look at the artist's output over a thirteen-year period, from 2001 to 2014, detailing individual videos and tracking themes and techniques developed across the artist's career.

Zulueta cites a wealth of influences he discerns in Trecartin's body of work. These include Raoul Hausmann, whose collages "transmit [...] a sense of chaos and disorder that Trecartin's cinematic montages successfully convey"; experimental filmmakers Stan Brakhage, Jonas Mekas, Kenneth Anger and Jack Smith; video installation artist Nam June Paik; and the pop art of Andy Warhol, among others.[8] One of the most overlooked influences – not only on Trecartin's work but on the reality genre and the internet's surveillance and broadcasting capacities – is Josh Harris, whom Zulueta does not mention.

As a corrective to the oversight of this figure, Ondi Timoner offers a detailed portrait of the lesser-known Harris in her 2009 documentary *We Live in Public*, which provides a singular investigation into the internet mogul and his wildest offerings, including his 1999 social experiment *Quiet: We Live in Public*. After becoming a millionaire during the dot-com boom of the 1990s, Harris constructed a large-scale underground bunker in Manhattan where he invited 100 people to live. During their stay, participants agreed to be constantly filmed by over 100 cameras and, in each of their pods, had access to a TV monitor where they could tune into the cameras' live footage. To capture as much as possible, participants had no private space. Much like in *Center Jenny*, toilets and showers were open plan. Such moments are witnessed in Timoner's film, which shares footage captured from the bunker, including instances of cameras coming into intimate proximity with participants whose behaviour becomes increasingly erratic as the experiment continues.

As well as experimental and independent film and artworks, Trecartin's departure from narrative also bears similarities to mainstream and independent music videos. Such media will regularly move through a series of locations, brought into a continuum by the music track and the artist's performance, which often unites distinct spaces. Michel Chion argues that music videos resist cinematic rules as their "only constraint [is] to synch up audio and video at certain points to solder the image to the music: this way the image can move around at will in time and space".[9] Chion finds music videos appealing as the image is "fully liberated from the linearity normally imposed by sound".[10] Trecartin's work similarly stages audio-visual disconnect as speech from one moment may be sampled and inserted into previous or following scenes. Because of these devices, we can trace other resonances between Trecartin's work and Chion's reflection on the music video format, which he describes as "a joyous rhetoric of images" that "liberates the eye".[11] At the same time, Chion acknowledges that some people find music videos "eye-assaulting", expressing a "dislike of the stroboscopic effect of rapid editing" and the "succession of shots [that] creates a sense of visual polyphony".[12] As discussed later in this chapter, the dynamic flitting whereby "no scene [is] anchored in a coherent spatiotemporal continuum" has been increasingly enabled with the rise of the internet and is cited as a feature of postmodernity by David Harvey.[13] Trecartin's works similarly straddle the divisive affective environment Chion identifies in music videos, as they often tip from jubilant to overbearing.

For Zulueta, *Priority Innfield*'s four videos map a similar visual, spatial and rhythmic environment as that encountered in gaming systems, narratively rehearsing "game levels [that] must be surpassed in order to gain experience".[14] *Center Jenny* opens with handheld shots of a green corridor and overlaid images of feet walking, alluding to the first-person shooter perspective of early video games such as *Doom*.[15] The sorority girl characters, almost all called a variation of 'Jenny', are understood by Zulueta as personifications of gaming levels. 'Basic Jenny' represents "the simplest, most rudimentary incarnation possible in the gaming system", and her non-sorority outfit, white contact lenses and the treatment she receives from the other Jennies confirm this status.[16] Zulueta assigns a linear order to the *Priority Innfield* videos as he excavates an overarching narrative whereby the protagonists "gain experience points by advancing to higher levels. In doing so, they acquire more skills and attributes, including individual names".[17] Basic Jenny's "main goal is not to win, but rather [...] to attain the highest level of herself", which she supposedly achieves in *Item Falls*.[18] Even assisted by Zulueta's dedication to detail, *Priority Innfield*'s narrative remains opaque, as bodies stand in for 'systems' as much as distinguishable characters. When displayed as an installation, a sense of linearity across the four videos is further upended as viewers can roam between the various screens in no particular order.

Close narrative reading is not an unusual mode of analysis in film studies, but scrutinising Trecartin's work in this way is no easy feat. *Queer Art Camp Superstar*'s approach seems counter-intuitive given the videos exhibit purposeful visual and aural distortion. Although he convincingly clarifies Trecartin's 'movie' narratives, Zulueta ignores the purposeful disorganisation of their structure. In contrast to Zulueta's project, I move away from narrative rationale to examine how temporality, exhibitions of enjoyment, and the presentation of bodies bring visions of capitalism and queerness into contact and contradiction. With these themes and devices in mind, how is the late capitalist environment emulated, and how does queerness configure a critical upheaval of this contemporary era? To answer these questions, this chapter examines how *Center Jenny, Comma Boat* and *Item Falls* (and, to a lesser extent, *Junior War*) emulate reality television.

Trecartin pastiches reality television by imitating it in an excessive fashion that goes beyond what we may reasonably expect from it. Richard Dyer defines pastiche as a mode of artistic imitation "of other art, not of life or reality itself"; always an "imitation of an imitation" for which we may never find an 'original'.[19] Tracing the term and practice through literary, musical and visual works of art, Dyer presents numerous definitions for pastiche that coalesce in a comprehensive examination of the practice. Central to his study is the likeness of pastiche to its referent, guided in part by a knowledge of this formal proximity by audience members who can recognise the textual resemblance: "[T]he text itself, while being enough like that which it pastiches to be recognisable as such, must also be unlike it to be recognisable as pastiche."[20] It is not, therefore, a straight imitation or part of a generic category. Rather, "[p]astiche deforms the style of its referent: it selects, accentuates, exaggerates, concentrates".[21] Because of the similarity between referent and imitation, one's textual knowledge becomes crucial when assessing the role of pastiche in an artwork, as pastiche only works "if you know what is being imitated".[22] Owing to this relationship between artefact and viewer, it is important to give an overview of reality television conventions to support an analysis of *Priority Innfield* that hinges on familiarity with this genre.

Mark Andrejevic's book *Reality TV: The Work of Being Watched* provides a comprehensive study of the reality genre.[23] Throughout this chapter, I return to Andrejevic as he studies elements of surveillance, labour practices and notions of authenticity, which feature across Trecartin's work. In tandem with an analysis of the visual strategies of reality television, Harvey's and Jonathan Crary's investigations into emerging forms of postmodernism and late capitalism contextualise the temporal and spatial collapse Trecartin creates with erratic editing,[24] while Hito Steyerl's category of the "poor image" situates the kind of heterogeneous aesthetic combinations that Trecartin employs as products of the increasingly digitised world.[25]

Alongside discussions of *Priority Innfield*'s inclusion of generic tropes, this chapter investigates Trecartin's strategies of on-screen enticement that draw attention to the rendition of enjoyment favoured by reality programming. Central to my argument is an understanding of enjoyment as an authorial position that intensifies in late capitalism, contextualised by psychoanalytic works from Todd McGowan and Juliet Flower MacCannell.[26] McGowan, along with other Lacanian thinkers, uses 'enjoyment' and *jouissance* interchangeably. Although the French *jouissance* translates into English as 'enjoyment', it is often left untranslated in the work of Jacques Lacan to denote a sensation "beyond pleasure" that borders on pain.[27] This chapter retains 'enjoyment' instead of jouissance, which Chapter Four of this book examines in greater detail. Here, 'enjoyment' is connected to fantasy, which Yannis Stavrakakis summarises as "the imaginary promise of recapturing our lost/impossible enjoyment that provides, above all, the fantasy support for many of our political projects and choices".[28] In comparison, jouissance – as used in the following chapter – designates an enjoyment in the *failure* to attain the object of desire that the topology of the drive inscribes. In summary, this book differentiates the English and French translations by their relation to desire and drive, respectively.[29]

Like Harvey and Crary, McGowan is concerned with the specifics of contemporary capitalism, situating the "superego commanding enjoyment and the epoch of global capitalism [as] exist[ing] in a symbiotic relationship".[30] McGowan cites the "ultimate expression of this idea of enjoyment as a social duty [coming] from the first George Bush in 1992" with his explicit encouragement to Americans to shop to help their country's economy.[31] The term 'late capitalism' is favoured by Crary and is similar to 'neoliberalism', which defines a market-centric economic regime that supports an ideological mandate on individuality.

The imbricated relationship between late capitalism and neoliberalism is elaborated by Toby Carroll, who suggests that neoliberal governments, institutions and policies produce a "globalised" capitalism that informs the "late capitalist" environment.[32] For Carroll, late capitalism "is composed of [...] the ideological and institutional elements of neoliberalism", including a "particular set of social relations [...]; advanced means of production [...]; the transnational disaggregation of production rendering non-neoliberal development extremely challenging; heightened dynamics of competition [...]; regular crises; increased inequality; and environmental exploitation and damage on a vast scale".[33] Without conflating late capitalism and neoliberalism, their proximity allows the former to cover many of the defining features of the latter.

While drawing from reality television motifs, how does Trecartin then distort this popular genre? Bung-Chul Han's critical enquiry into how technology regenerates the authority of surveillance and control helps to unpack the intricate affective landscape of late capitalism that Trecartin evokes, further supported by Andrejevic's analysis of reality television and the internet's transformation of labour.[34] Fredric Jameson's account of postmodernism and the function of pastiche contextualises *Priority Innfield*'s formal properties and mode of critique, which Dyer's reading of pastiche in cinema somewhat departs from.

Finally, the closing section of this chapter asks how queerness, as a category of (non-)meaning, disturbs and un-anchors the traditional prescriptions of desire and enjoyment found in spectacles of the reality genre. Two central features of Trecartin's work – capitalist enjoyment and queerness – collide in such ways that the latter refuses to be the guarantee of the former as the particular identities needed to secure the 'normative' order of late capitalist society dissolve. Aesthetic and sonic extremity and looping time develop a sense of queerness across the *Priority Innfield* video set, contextualised by contemporary artworks from Bod Mellor, Flo Brooks and Jenkin van Zyl. Whereas Zulueta's analysis deciphers order in Trecartin's work, this chapter proposes that Trecartin's purposeful *dis*order troubles late capitalism with chaotic invocations of queerness that resist coherent characterisation and narrative elucidation.

Coding Reality

The reality television format can be traced back to the American television show *Candid Camera* (1948–2014), developed by Allen Funt. The premise involved hidden cameras filming people responding to scenarios staged without their knowledge, thus forgoing television's then-typical scripting.[35] In addition to its entertainment content, the show's documentation sparked interest in the social sciences, which viewed Funt's work as "capable of providing a critical analysis of modern society within mass culture", suggesting potential educational merits of early reality programming.[36] Over the decades, reality television has developed and adopted a wide array of formats. It has seen a pronounced rise over the last twenty-five years following the success of the *Big Brother* franchise (1999–), first broadcast in the Netherlands in 1999 before being turned into the successful USA and UK versions in 2000. As Helen Piper points out, the popularity of *Big Brother* brought with it a deluge of "histrionic commentaries in magazines, tabloids and websites with which 'reality' forms are now inter-dependent", as well as a wealth of academic essays and monographs.[37]

Trecartin's work reproduces a plethora of reality television conventions. These include first-person confessionals replete with associated verbal inflexions, handheld cameras, the presence of recording equipment in the mise-en-scène, seemingly improvised activity and fast-paced editing, all of which contribute to a 'candid' appearance. By staging these familiar tropes, the artist also draws from the socio-political environment the genre engages. Andrejevic argues that the development of the internet and digital recording technology is crucial for understanding reality television's appeal. By combining spectacle, surveillance and consumerism, reality television resituates the typical viewer as a consumer, contributor, voyeur and potential celebrity.

Center Jenny, Comma Boat and *Item Falls* frequently show people holding recording equipment rather than hiding production crew off-screen, as is typical for mainstream fiction and documentary film and television media. Although reality television tends to omit footage of the camera and production staff, surveillance provides much of the entertainment content in shows such as *Big Brother*, indicated by its transition shots and opening credit sequences that use close-ups of CCTV cameras tracking movements. As Laurie Ouellette and Susan Murray summarise, the reality genre "acknowledge[s] [...] the manufactured artifice that coexists with truth claims", such as when non-actor participants respond to devised challenges within a constructed set.[38]

Trecartin's worlds seem to be under constant surveillance. Rapid editing presents viewers with a flurry of perspectives from the on-screen camera operators, foregoing the authority of a master shot that would conventionally serve to organise the images. Figures adorn sorority sweatshirts printed with the words "WITNESS 360" to emphasise the panoptic circularity of total surveillance, including the process of surveillance itself, packaged as an exclusive collegial membership. As well as "WITNESS 360", Basic Jenny wears a sweatshirt printed with "STORY TELLING" in *Item Falls*, while *Center Jenny* features people wearing "WASTE" sweatshirts, and sweatshirts printed with "AUDITION XXX&XXX Straight <3" are worn across *Center Jenny, Comma Boat* and *Item Falls*. The self-referential sartorial statements of watching ("witness"), being watched ("audition", "story telling") or being detritus and disposable ("waste") all share similar varsity-style lettering associated with American sports teams and their jocular exhibitions (see Figure 3.1).

Figure 3.1 Item Falls, 2013. Courtesy of the artist, Sprüth Magers, and Morán Morán.

The mix of overcrowding, unpredictable movements and multiple screens relaying a single moment creates a visual claustrophobia. At times, *Priority Innfield* bears similarities to the erratic editing practices used in *The Real Housewives* franchise (2006–) and *America's Next Top Model* (2003–), where numerous cameras film a scenario. Cutting between supposedly concurrent events in different locations is also part of the familiar rhythm of the genre, often interspersed with talking-head commentary filmed after the fact but spoken about in the present tense. Studios, production companies and enthusiastic fans regularly recut shows to create montages for YouTube, collecting clips of the 'most explosive fights' or the 'funniest moments' and intensifying the rate of action and editing while disintegrating the already precarious narrative cohesion.

'Scripted reality' or 'docu-soaps' often absorb character 'types' from coming-of-age Hollywood films and narrative television. The incorporation of mainstream tropes speaks to reality television's popular appeal that Ouellette and Murray distinguish from "the twin expectations of unpopularity and unprofitability that have historically differentiated 'serious' factual formats from popular entertainment".[39] *Priority Innfield* rehashes exaggerated American clichés as figures don synthetic wigs and heavily contoured faces, consistently address cameras in a manner indicative of talking-head narration, and reference 'new-age' energy, spiritualism and magic. They speak in affected 'valley girl' accents, a dialect associated with rich Californian women such as socialites Nicole Richie and Paris Hilton, who starred in the reality show *The Simple Life* (2003–2007), and the dynastic reality television family the Kardashian–Jenners of *Keeping Up with the Kardashians* (2007–2021, henceforth referred to as *KUWTK*) and its recent reboot, *The Kardashians* (2022–). Often peppering their speech with "like" and an 'upspeak' inflexion, Trecartin's figures also suggest sorority girl and cheerleader stereotypes: Elle Woods (Reese Witherspoon) from *Legally Blonde* (2001) or Torrance Shipman (Kirsten Dunst) from *Bring It On* (2000). In *Center Jenny*, a group gathers over Basic Jenny. Their faces display hints of sneers as they resemble the 'popular group' archetype, their uniformity of dress and expression reminiscent of the 'plastics' in *Mean Girls* (2004, played by Rachel McAdams, Lacey Chabert and Amanda Seyfried), the satirical teen film *Heathers'* (1988) titular group (Shannen Doherty, Lisanne Falk and Kim Walker) and the aforementioned Kardashians.

The incessant speech, action and editing of *Center Jenny, Comma Boat* and *Item Falls* unravel time as an undefined 'now' within unspecified technology-saturated locations. Trecartin's curation of non-stop action has become a familiar rhythm in reality television, which often compresses twenty-four hours into thirty-to-sixty-minute episodes, either televised or streamed, with the latter allowing audiences to 'binge-watch'. Early seasons of the US *Big Brother* broadcast 24/7 live streams of the contestant house, supplemented by the official website's chatroom feature, which enabled viewers to discuss the series and provide ongoing commentary.

These forms of production and engagement chime with Crary's character-isation of 'late capitalism' as a 24/7 temporal environment that demands subjects be constantly alert.[40] Regional time zones are of reduced importance as people tune into endless streams of online activity that exist in excess of the traditional working day or week, seasonal patterns and geographic locations. Akin to the shift away from conventional arrangements of labour and leisure, *Priority Innfield* imagines environments that do not comply with standardised time or a series of definable places. Instead, figures arrive in the throes of movement with no explanation given as to where they have come from or where they are going.

The displacement and reduction of sleep are central to Crary's enquiry into the emerging 24/7 society. Unlike other bodily needs such as "hunger, thirst, sexual desire, and recently the need for friendship", which "have been remade into commodified or financialized forms", sleep has yet to be successfully mined for marketable information and labour.[41] Slumber is a necessity that maintains an "interval of time that cannot be colonized and harnessed to a massive engine of profitability".[42] However, the average decline of sleep over the decades and the scientific research dedicated to maintaining human func-tioning without sleep demonstrates that its reduction is of increasing concern for capitalist society.[43]

Big Brother and recent dating shows such as *Love Island* (2015–) and *Too Hot to Handle* (2020–) film contestants using cameras strategically placed throughout the staged quasi-domestic spaces. After the extensive footage has been edited, clips of contestants eating and sleeping are minimal, if included at all, while dramatic conflict and energetic tasks take priority. As if to demonstrate Crary's argument that capitalism cannot mine sleep for value, the rendition of reality created for entertainment reduces it to a mere indica-tion that one day has ended and another is beginning. Like this restless life presented in reality television, nobody sleeps in *Priority Innfield*.

Trecartin's abrupt transitions follow the erratic patterns of globalised online networks that reduce temporal and spatial barriers as they transport infor-mation across huge distances with increasing speed, intensifying what Harvey has termed "time–space compression". In *The Condition of Postmodernity*, Harvey studies the reconfiguration of time and space from the Enlightenment up to the post-1970s period of postmodernity.[44] First published in 1990, Harvey's thesis on time–space compression and its "disorientating and dis-ruptive impact" across "political-economic practices, the balance of class power [...] [and] cultural and social life" has become increasingly evident since the advent of high-speed internet that underpins much of Crary's and Andrejevic's analyses.[45]

Drawing on cartography, technological advancements, labour practices, and art and literature, Harvey traces how labour and capital accumulation sped up with capitalist economic expansion from the 1970s to the late 1980s. Technological advancements such as "[i]mproved systems of communication and information flow", computerised trading, "[e]lectronic banking and plastic money" and the subcontracting and outsourcing of manufacturing facilitated this acceleration.[46] Changes in the labour infrastructure created "a shift from the consumption of goods [...] into the consumption of services – not only personal, business, educational, and health services, but also into entertainments, spectacles, happenings, and distractions".[47] For Harvey, it is the acceleration of "the turnover times of capital" observed in the growing emphasis on instantaneous gratification and disposability that comes to define postmodernity.[48]

Harvey's analysis is largely historical as he connects political, artistic and geographic fluctuations to emerging cultural changes and the development of norms. While Crary's project is more polemical and tends to draw from philosophical works, he also traces historical instances that paved the way for the contemporary moment under examination. A lineage of technological advancement predating the relatively recent invention and widespread uptake of personal computers, the internet and 'smart' technologies helps situate the 24/7 epoch. Introducing the Industrial Revolution's impact on labour practices, Crary refers to Joseph Wright's 1782 painting *Arkwright's Cotton Mills by Night*, which depicts the cotton mill's windows as small rectangles of light beneath a bright moon. Drawing attention to these simultaneous forms of illumination, Crary shows how the image depicts a turning point where "[t]he artificial lighting of the factories announces the rationalized deployment of an abstract relation between time and work, severed from the cyclical temporalities of lunar and solar movements".[49] The painting indicates a shift in labour practices made possible by technological innovation, a tradition that has mutated into the intensified collapse of designated working patterns today.

Trecartin's concentrated stacking of audio-visual material is indicative of Crary's late capitalist temporality and Harvey's shrinking world that condenses the rate of production, exchange and accumulation. In *Item Falls*, there is no 'outside' to the interiors where action occurs, no sense of day or night. Artificial lighting brightens the spaces, enhancing the characters' alienation from organic environmental factors. There is no weather here. The windows are not glass but flat metallic cards, not windows but images of windows. Action and speech create a saturation of activity, with post-production animations advancing the intensity of the visual field. *Center Jenny, Comma Boat* and *Item Falls* feature live-action and virtual elements that combine into dense palimpsests. *Item Falls* utilises cartoon filters, 3D-rendered bodies, heads warped into spheres and digital tennis balls, with red party cups and mailboxes superimposed over faces.

Such layering displaces high-definition images in favour of glitches and distortion as Trecartin incorporates features of what Steyerl has termed the "poor image". This aesthetic regime emerged from cyberspace where files can be easily shared and manipulated, "squeezed through slow digital connections, compressed, reproduced, ripped, remixed, as well as copied and pasted into other channels of distribution".[50] Although Trecartin's work does not recycle existing data, *Item Falls'* visual tendencies embrace the reduction of image quality that files experience as they disperse across the web.

Steyerl considers the poor image's once subordinate status to the sharp picture of widely distributed cinema, with "high-end economies of film production [...] firmly anchored in systems of national culture, capitalist studio production, the cult of mostly male genius, and the original version", which are "often conservative in their very structure".[51] Mainstream film is deemed "conservative" because it dominates the media industry with specific ideas represented in the efficiency of narrative execution and aesthetic quality predominantly reproduced by the Euro-American, profit-driven and male subject positions Steyerl suggests. However, "[p]oor images are [...] popular images – images that can be made and seen by the many", as the internet has allowed once obscure or niche interests to find a wider reception.[52] The rhizomatic patterns of distribution that proliferate across the internet allow poor images to generate a combination of contrasting aesthetics that rub up against each other online.

As well as these temporal and spatial schemas that articulate the acceleration of capitalism, *Priority Innfield* suggests an emerging psychic imperative to enjoy.[53] In particular, McGowan argues that we are experiencing "a new epoch of social relations" marked by a transformation of authority that commands enjoyment rather than ruling through prohibition.[54] According to McGowan, the contemporary authority of enjoyment became more pronounced in the late 1980s and early 1990s. As referenced in the introduction to this chapter, McGowan cites the encouragement to shop as indicative of this turn, much like Harvey's characterisation of postmodernism, which sees the speeding up of production and consumption of services, experiences and material objects.

> Whereas formerly society has required subjects to renounce their private enjoyment in the name of social duty, today the only duty seems to consist in enjoying oneself as much as possible. The fundamental social duty in contemporary American society lies in committing oneself to enjoyment. Advertisements, friends, movies, parents, television shows, internet sites, and even authority figures all call on us to maximize our enjoyment.[55]

The year 2004, the same year McGowan published *The End of Dissatisfaction?*, saw the release of *Laguna Beach* (2004–2006), a pioneer of the 'scripted reality' subgenre that followed a group of wealthy teenagers in Orange County, California. Journalists and podcasters Pandora Sykes and Sirin Kale chart how *Laguna Beach* and its follow-up, *The Hills* (2006–2010), were early examples of "lifestyle consumerism that is now a founding tenet of reality TV".[56] In this sense, these examples illustrate McGowan's connection between accumulation and enjoyment as the cast's obscene accrual of possessions contributes to the shows' entertainment content. More recent shows such as *The Real Housewives* and *KUWTK* continue this trend that prioritises the consumption of luxury items. However, programs such as *The Real World* (1992–2019), *Big Brother* and *Survivor* (2000–) strip contestants of their ability to exercise their 'free choice' in the marketplace of goods. Despite this, they utilise the increasingly synonymous status of commodity and subject as contestants' image, charisma and narratives of 'self-improvement' replace the traditional commodity, which shows such as *The Real Housewives* and *KUWTK* also achieve with great success.

In their book *Better Living through Reality TV*, Ouellette and James Hay argue that reality programming has "become the quintessential technology of advanced or 'neo' liberal citizenship" as it develops the individual as an "entrepreneur of the self" through a range of strategies that are now hallmarks of the genre.[57] For instance, the extensive 'makeover' reality subgenre situates physical reinvention as an investment in contestants by turning them into "managers of their 'greatest assets' – themselves".[58] By engaging the rhetoric of finance, makeover shows present flexibility as necessary for adapting to life's challenges and making oneself a desirable hire, partner and citizen. However, the need for reinvention obfuscates an acknowledgement of the structural difficulties that may hinder someone's access to services such as healthcare, dental care, childcare and healthy food, without which acquiring standardised beauty becomes extremely challenging. Nor do such shows recognise the racialised, gendered and class positions implicitly supported or disavowed in the regimes being advanced.[59] Because of these features, neoliberal individuality finds a concentrated expression in reality television that informs much of *Priority Innfield*'s formal and affective qualities. In this media formulation, the capitalist enjoyment distilled in accumulation extends to self-betterment, framed as a commodity in the social, political and economic marketplace.

Defining the psychic logic of the turn to enjoyment, McGowan suggests that there has been a cultural shift from the symbolic order, broadly designated by language, to the imaginary. Part of Lacan's triad, along with the symbolic and the real, the imaginary is designated by the regime of the image that structurally disavows the lack installed by the signifier. McGowan identifies the cultural inclination to the image in examples of art and literature, and the increasing "ubiquity of television and video".[60] He outlines how the imaginary order offers an "illusion of wholeness", which contributes to the ego as it "serves to obscure both the lack in the subject and the lack in the big Other", an organising authority that bears a structural similarity to the Freudian 'superego'.[61]

In what is likely Lacan's best-known essay, "The Mirror Stage", the mirror "manufactures for the subject, caught up in the lure of spatial identification, the succession of phantasies that extends from a fragmented body-image to a form of its totality".[62] The body's coherent appearance on an external plane of reflection "generates the inexhaustible quadrature of the ego's verifications".[63] Whereas the symbolic signals the lack between signifier and signified as there is no direct correlation between them, McGowan explains how the imaginary allows the subject to "visualize an image of enjoyment, an image that seems to overcome all lack" as the ideals we hold of ourselves do not contain the lack we experience.[64] However, we become alienated from others as they appear to embody the image of a wholeness that contrasts with our felt lack. In "The Function and Field of Speech and Language in Psychoanalysis", Lacan probes the tension in the subject's relation to their ego, associated with the imaginary order.[65] He asks:

> Does the subject not become engaged in an ever-growing dispossession of that being of his, concerning which – by dint of sincere portraits which leave its idea no less incoherent, of rectifications that do not succeed in freeing its essence, of stays and defences that do not prevent his statue from tottering, of narcissistic embraces that become like a puff of air in animating it – he ends up by recognizing that this being has never been anything more than his construct in the imaginary and that this construct disappoints all his certainties?[66]

Rather than shoring up the self, attempts to distil the subject into consistency cannot arrest the meaning (including the absence of and in meaning) that exceeds the imaginary. Lacan's question, interjected with examples of the failure to reconcile certainty of oneself, speaks to the partiality of the ego and imaginary order that nonetheless appear total. Following McGowan's thesis that characterises the command to enjoy as distilled by the imaginary, the place of the image in society has only intensified with the rise of social media.

Two of the most popular online platforms, Instagram and TikTok, proliferate images while the written word typically appears as a small supplementary caption to the main picture or video. Miya Tokumitsu suggests a similar link between alienation and the saturation of images as that made by McGowan. In her essay "Tell Me It's Going to be OK", Tokumitsu defines online platforms as encompassing a "paradox of neoliberal social retreat" whereby "people gravitate to social media in order to *feel* connected".[67] However, "Instagram in particular[,] has a tendency to make people feel worse about themselves".[68] This reaction does not occur because of a proliferation of 'negative' content. Instead,

> even the feel-good content featured on Instagram breeds a perverse sort of invidious malaise, with each new post about an excellent meal leaving a powerful residual sense that the onlookers' own lives are acutely lacking in the material to generate similarly celebratory posts.[69]

Though she does not employ psychoanalytic terminology, Tokumitsu touches on how the appearance of enjoyment transmitted in the image contrasts with subjects' experience of lack in ways that produce alienation rather than affinity.

McGowan's analysis also echoes MacCannell's concerns in her book *The Regime of the Brother*. Here, MacCannell refers to Sigmund Freud's origin myth of society from *Totem and Taboo* to argue that modernity replaces the traditional father who rules from above with the brother, whose seemingly equal fraternal position shrouds his authority.[70] MacCannell's investigation into the shift in authority's expression points to the danger of the brother's non-threatening appearance. Rather than a figure distinct from the patriarchal order, the fraternal order is a "mutant" of patriarchy which "exploit[s] [...] images of equality and ecological balance to the real detriment of genders (feminine), classes (those whose desires and energies are fully engaged in labor), and races (generally non-white)".[71] Because of the apparent proximity of the brother – he is 'one of us' – he maintains power not from a distance but through a closeness in a society where we believe that *"[a]ny one can grow up to be president"*.[72] But this guise of equality enhances power, instead of detracting from it, "for what is licensed by the mechanism of identification and exchange as the exclusive collective form in democracy also fosters the greatest of inequalities".[73] Under the 'regime of the brother', authority is permitted by a belief that the ordinary citizen could obtain power. The watchful eye of reality television's *Big Brother* enacts this shift as it constitutes a symbol of entertainment and opportunity rather than punishment. McGowan engages a different familial position, designating the figure of enjoyment as an "anal father", borrowed from Slavoj Žižek, compared with the "father of prohibition".[74] Like MacCannell, McGowan argues that the command to enjoy is more persuasive than a prohibitive master because it eludes our expectations of authority's appearance: We are more likely to embrace the kind figure of authority than the one who punishes.

Trecartin's work resonates with McGowan's analysis of a structural transfer from symbolic to imaginary as the videos enact a dual dismissal of spoken and visual clarity with a staging of a palpable *over*abundance in the image. Although there appears to be no conclusive resolution to the action, the screen's excess also omits any 'gaps' in spectatorial knowledge that would usually permit a comprehendible narrative organisation by structuring viewers' desire around a missing object, which is either retrieved or remains lost. The looping exhibition of the videos and their unspecified viewing order contribute to this confusion as they hinder audiences from following character trajectories or identifying emerging or ongoing plotlines. While speech rattles through the videos, the spoken word follows the erratic patter of the image as it starts and halts, is interrupted and never seems to finish a line of enquiry. Sound and vision promote confusion by refusing apparent causal action, making Zulueta's analysis of the videos' dormant narratives counter-intuitive.

As if taking the command to enjoy at its word, *Junior War* is a compilation of nocturnal video footage Trecartin recorded as a teenager and shows his adolescent peers partying, drinking, smoking, driving around and vandalising suburban America. The riotous activities are viewed through a green-tinted night-vision filter or flooded by car headlights. Like Crary's late capitalist temporality, night is refused as a time of turning in or off, rest or recuperation. *Center Jenny* and *Comma Boat* also include sequences set outside, yet floodlights brighten the wild action and vanquish the dark sky.

Inside, *Center Jenny*, *Comma Boat* and *Item Falls* often stage action in interiors akin to those used in reality shows. John Corner describes *Big Brother*'s social architecture as one of display, as "living space is also performance space".[75] In rooms that are open-plan yet enclosed, *Big Brother*'s physical and social environments are "tightly spatial and urgently temporal".[76] Trecartin reproduces the contrived gatherings seen in *Big Brother*, *America's Next Top Model*, *The Bachelor* (2002–) and *RuPaul's Drag Race* (2009–, henceforth *Drag Race*) that contribute to an overcrowding of the mise-en-scène and take enjoyment to its teetering edge (see Figure 3.2).

Discussing *Priority Innfield*, Lisa Åkervall describes how "the tentacles of neoliberalism have gradually encircled the globe, undermining the outsider perspective long prized by the artist and the cultural critic alike". Neoliberalism's ability to assimilate previously 'outsider' positions complicates the idea that a critique of capitalism can "stand [...] outside a given phenomenon and comment [...] on it from afar".[77] Trecartin's uncanny embrace of contemporary entertainment tropes indicates how neoliberalism incorporates criticism of consumerist culture by creating another market. Like MacCannell's and McGowan's new forms of authority, the jubilant and energetic manifestations of Trecartin's audio-visual world do not present viewers with a figure who asserts control from 'above'. Instead, the actors are awash in a confusing stream of environments. Filming and editing practices draw from contemporary

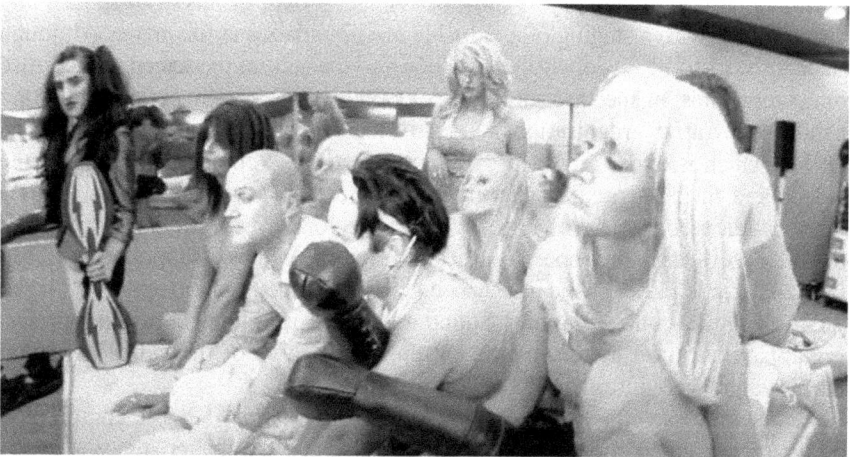

Figure 3.2 Center Jenny, 2013. Courtesy of the artist, Sprüth Magers, and Morán Morán.

enactments of capitalist enjoyment, including consumerism and celebrity, while distorting reality television's webs of value and expression.

The Regime of the (Big) Brother

Andrejevic suggests that "the emergence of relatively inexpensive highly sophisticated technologies for comprehensive consumer monitoring coincides with a trend in popular culture towards the portrayal of surveillance as a means of self-expression and a shortcut to fame and fortune".[78] Andrejevic develops this claim by detailing how reality television often includes interactive elements, such as audience voting on the singing competition *American Idol* (2002–) and *Big Brother*'s early online community. Unlike scripted narrative television, which closes the possibility of direct audience influence, the opportunity to affect reality television's on-screen content lends viewers a sense of participation by integrating technology with the televised format.

The 'regular people' cast in many reality shows willingly submit to surveillance, which promises potential prize money, celebrity or, in the makeover subgenre, a full roster of cosmetic surgeries that will make them look like a celebrity.[79] Rather than being viewed as an infringement on our private lives, monitoring is now the norm when advertising and entertainment content is created. The collapse of private and public space repeatedly staged in reality television becomes "a compact metaphor for the productivity of the online economy" where "self-disclosure of even the most mundane variety is increasingly economically valuable in a mass-customized economy".[80] The streams of speech spoken as direct address in *Item Falls* suggest the ubiquity of the confessional mode that populates the internet in the form of vlogs and online journals and that is an essential dimension of reality programming. The framing of the self as the product for consumption reflects the shift towards customised advertising, where internet users provide information that algorithms collate into profiles based on specific demographics. Gender, age, race and sexuality are approximated and identified by algorithms tracing online activity and storing, exchanging and selling personal data to companies. Andrejevic describes this online system of data production and consumption as functioning in a "digital enclosure" that "established an ongoing relationship of surveillance via interactivity".[81] Reality programming that relies on surveillance to generate entertainment helps render online tracking benign or even desirable. This mutual reliance between subjects and technologies pervades the general milieu of Trecartin's videos as figures appear undeterred by a lack of privacy. Rather than ignoring or recoiling from the cameras, figures lean into them, look to the lens and perform for their multiple viewpoints, actively enticing their attention.

Early reality programming such as *An American Family* (1973) and, later, *The Osbournes* (2002–2005) purported to show "the daily lives of real people", which Andrejevic suggests "corresponds to the *return* of an era of increasing economic inequality".[82] The boom in reality programming in the early 2000s grew with a "public awareness of the return of the robber-baron capitalist/industrialist".[83] This renewed inequality is evidenced by statistics such as "CEO compensation jump[ing] from thirty-nine times the pay of an average worker in the early 1970s to more than a thousand times the pay of an average worker thirty years later".[84] As material discrepancies in the United States became harder to ignore, reality television's spotlighting of 'regular' people supported neoliberalism's assurance that 'anyone' could rise to the echelons of wealth and success despite the increased absorption of assets by a small minority.[85] Instead of tackling structural inequality, reality television maintains that individuals can achieve what is reserved for the few if they enter one of the numerous (but oversubscribed) shows on offer. As with reality programming, Trecartin's work does not draw an explicit line between the fantasy of transformation from ordinary citizen to celebrity and rising inequality. Nevertheless, its emulation of the genre suggests that surveillance transforms 'candid' behaviour into labour, which contestants can monetise as excitable action becomes potentially profitable content.

Reality television has been central in changing the figure of Big Brother from "hostile and forbidding during the Cold War era" to "a nonthreatening – even entertaining and benevolent – pop culture icon".[86] The show *Big Brother* is, of course, the most obvious example of the transformation of an omnipresent and controlling Orwellian authority into a publicly transmitting eye in service of entertainment.[87] In the fourth chapter of his book, "The Kinder, Gentler Gaze of Big Brother", Andrejevic examines *Big Brother* and *The Real World* and describes cast members leaning into a sense of 'authenticity', which supposedly allows them to show audiences who they 'really are'. Chapter One of this thesis problematises 'authenticity' when examining the serial melodrama *Pose* (2018–2021). Though generically distinct, the signifier 'authenticity' attempts to stabilise a truth value across these heterogeneous forms of television.

Starring in a reality series invites "self-disclosure as a form of personal growth" and assumes it is difficult, if not impossible, to hide or edit oneself under constant surveillance, despite the production and editing that construct the aired episodes.[88] Corner cites this contradiction in *Big Brother* as "its interest and pleasure" develops around "real characteristics of real people, even if the material and temporal conditions for the behaviour have been entirely constructed by television itself" as well as the "larger contrivance of them being [...] in front of the camera in the first place".[89] The tension between the supposed 'unedited' self within the edited series troubles authenticity as producers mediate subjects' appearances for filming and screening.

Justin Lewis suggests that reality television "remorselessly blends ideas of authenticity and contrivance", collapsing "the conceptual divisions that distinguish fact from fiction".[90] Lewis takes the paradoxes of the genre as indicative of television more generally. As we typically differentiate between our social reality and the world of television shows, Lewis reminds us that viewing television is part of our lived experience, and separating "fiction and reality" is "fraught with contradiction and ambiguity".[91] For instance, while the popular cartoon series *The Simpsons* (1989–) is "loaded with impossibilities", it can also "be seen as closer to real life than a more conventionally realist form of television" as the members of the titular family are "not especially gifted or attractive and spend much of their time in front of the TV set".[92] Consequently, reality television produces contradictions with its claims to present reality within the televised format.

Figures in Trecartin's videos rehearse reality vernacular by talking with exaggerated intonation and heightened emotion. At the same time, their delivery verges on the surreal and indecipherable, abandoning the sense of 'realism' marginally maintained by reality programs while clinging on to a performance of 'authenticity' sustained by the confessional mode. Near the beginning of *Item Falls*, a woman in a pink sorority hoodie talks to the camera, jerking her head to punctuate her speech and speaking a string of disjointed sentences that share sentiments of competition and self-promotion:

> I am super simple. [...] We're trying to get into the system. From now on, I'm managing myself. The sorority I fell in love with – uh – Can we turn the lights off? [...] I've bitten off so many hands I'm back to first level 'cos my goal is to make it to level centre. Who wants to be in first place? Centre me bitch! Don't make that dumb girl become a hippie.

The video then cuts to various people sitting on beds in a communal room spouting similar sentences: "The last time someone threw money at me, I was so upset I was offended." "If you want to talk to me, talk to me via this." "The last time I auditioned for something, I was so offended I was angry. And every time I get letters from my friends, they're interesting." During this sequence, the video moves between medium shots of people lounging on beds and standing with cameras and close-ups of lips, sweatshirts, cameras, hands and faces struck by white light. Cameras swivel and move towards and away from bodies, shaking and tilted, causing the room to blur with motion. Post-production adds zooming, colour saturation and reduced frame rates. Occasionally, a split screen shows two simultaneous camera perspectives. Modulated voices speak with digital reverb, and the non-diegetic sounds include tinny and jarring, dissonant synthesised musical notes. In *Center Jenny*, a group of girls dressed in beige tank tops and shorts run through the sets screaming with hen party- and spring break-style excitement, red party cups in their hands, arms flailing, stumbling through corridors as shaking cameras capture them from all sides before they gather around a pool. Such moments are indicative of *Priority Innfield*'s general affect and action that create, to borrow from Jameson, "a world transformed into sheer images of itself and for pseudo-events and 'spectacles'".[93]

In a similar vein to Andrejevic's 'kinder, gentler' Big Brother, Han defines authority in neoliberalism as a "Friendly Big Brother".[94] In his compact polemical *Psychopolitics*, Han draws direct lines between ideas of freedom with surveillance and social media as a "digital panopticon".[95] Like Andrejevic's reading of reality television's impact on surveillance, Han argues that digital communication encourages users to "willingly expose themselves", creating a society where "data is not surrendered under duress so much as offered out of an inner need".[96] After citing a description of George Orwell's Big Brother from his dystopian novel *Nineteen Eighty-Four*, Han characterises neoliberalism's "Friendly Big Brother" as permitting rather than prohibiting, fostering a world where "[c]onsumption is not held in check, but maximized".[97] Like McGowan's "anal father" of enjoyment and MacCannell's "regime of the brother", Han sees "[t]he principle of negativity" as having "yielded to the principle of positivity".[98] However, the shift in authority articulated by McGowan, MacCannell, Andrejevic and Han is complicated by *Priority Innfield* as the videos are not all that enjoyable to watch.

Narrative incoherence and relentless energetic movement dominate *Priority Innfield*, making the videos overstimulating yet boring as it becomes difficult to concentrate on them for sustained periods. Because of this, Trecartin's work is well suited to the looping playback and immersive gallery environment, which viewers can easily move through, compared with the set viewing times that televised programming invites. Even in the more extreme stylings of reality television that prioritise enjoyment by staging consumption and emotional outpouring, such shows maintain ideological imperatives to accumulate and sustain norms, including family, romantic relationships and identity. In comparison, Trecartin's work largely abandons these sites of narrative and affective investment.

For instance, *KUWTK* and its new iteration *The Kardashians* follow the Kardashian–Jenner women through trivial, interchangeable plotlines concerning work commitments and interpersonal drama before resolving episodes by reinforcing the familial bonds that unite the cast members. Family relationships double as business relationships, with matriarch Kris Jenner managing her children and dubbing herself a "momager", a portmanteau that explicitly conflates business with the maternal role. Enjoyment, both the spectators' and the cast members', is held together by family, narrow beauty ideals and monogamous heterosexual coupledom, which anchor the series' frantic activity. In competition shows, that which determines value is explicitly stated. For instance, the winner of *Big Brother* receives a large sum of money, *America's Next Top Model* winner secures a modelling contract, *The Batchelor* and *The Bachelorette* (2003–) winners leave coupled with the titular man or woman, and *Drag Race* winners are awarded a cash prize and the title of "America's next drag superstar". Such media repeatedly rehearse the spectacle of enjoyment, valorising a fantasy of what capitalism can provide, which is sustained by the hope of those who do not have access to this version of the 'American dream'.

By excluding an obviously organising narrative structure while retaining visual and rhetorical elements from reality television, *Priority Innfield* enacts bureaucracy hollowed of purpose, a display of excess fodder that usually supports a larger plot. It is replete with sequences of enjoyment that retain the fluster and bustle of frantic activity while stripping the diegetic world of an object of desire that such movement would ordinarily orbit. Action is purposely *dis*organised and refuses to offer routes to success and fame despite the proliferation of cues lifted from media that do precisely this. The excess of narrative purpose proliferates without direction, erupting like laughter without the joke that provokes it.

Despite its studied emulation, *Priority Innfield*'s commitment to the semiotics of reality television does not produce a 'passable' version of the genre. For this reason, Trecartin does not comply with Dyer's definition of pastiche in cinema, which he studies by turning to the Western and neo-noir genres. When considering pastiche in Westerns, Dyer cites *The New Frontier* (1939) and *Hearts of the West* (1975), which reveal the contrived staging of the Western landscape and action to produce "retrospective pastiche", and *Westworld* (1973), which depicts the Western spectacle as a simulation that reproduces the environment and fills it with android actors.[99] In these examples, the recognisable Western elements become "displays of generic form qua form, that is, pastiche" as the genre is acknowledged and self-consciously rehearsed.[100]

Dyer then turns to neo-noir, where the "prefix 'neo' suggests [...] a return to an earlier form that has been in abeyance, and at times [...] seems almost a synonym for pastiche".[101] Studying *Body Heat* (1981), Dyer identifies the film's inclusion of numerous noir tropes across its mise-en-scène and narrative.[102] Although there are many recognisable elements of noir, and the film is loosely based on the classic noir *Double Indemnity* (1944), Dyer argues that "[o]ne would not mistake *Body Heat* for a 1940s/1950s noir. It does film noir but not quite like earlier film noir did it and it is especially this that makes it reasonable to describe *Body Heat* as pastiche".[103] Importantly, in Dyer's examples, the films read as pastiche enter the generic canon they emulate. For instance, a film that "plays with being a Western [...] by the end becomes one".[104] Similarly, neo-noirs subvert and engage the conventions that distinguish the noir genre. *Priority Innfield*, however, takes generic cues yet is definitively *not* reality television. Importantly, it *only appears* as such, a distinction confirmed by the extent of Trecartin's meticulous scripting, which indicates the implementation of acting and performance purposefully expunged from the reality genre. The uncanny resemblance to familiar conventions renders Trecartin's work a form of imitation more aligned with Jameson's understanding of pastiche as 'blank parody'.

In "Postmodernism, or, the Cultural Logic of Late Capitalism", Jameson designates postmodernism as a departure from previous forms of capitalism, characterised in part by a speeding-up of production, distribution and disposal, which Harvey, Crary and Andrejevic note in their respective works.[105]

Jameson examines the emerging aesthetic regimes of postmodernism in contrast with earlier works of 'high modernism'. A central feature identified is "a new depthlessness" of images that complicates modes of sincerity and political critique, which Trecartin's work takes up in its uncanny incorporation of familiar reality semiotics.[106]

To demonstrate the postmodern shift in cultural production, Jameson compares a "canonical work of high modernism", Vincent van Gogh's 1886 painting *A Pair of Boots*, with Andy Warhol's 1980 screen print *Diamond Dust Shoes*.[107] The former representation of shoes invites us to read the "world of agricultural misery, of stark rural poverty, and the whole rudimentary human world of backbreaking peasant toil", which contextualises the boots' transformation into a "[u]topian gesture" of pigment and painted texture.[108] The latter, in contrast, is a screen print of high-heeled shoes that appear as "a random collection of dead objects hanging together on a canvas".[109] Their flatness, rendered by the graphic reduction of detail that screen printing invites, gives no hint of a "larger lived context" that van Gogh's boots evoke.[110]

Trecartin's rehearsal of reality television's eccentric codes gives an impression of the 24/7 temporality described by Crary and the labour practices studied by Andrejevic. However, it resists sentimentality and refuses to become an overtly political statement concerning the behaviour it broadcasts. *Priority Innfield* borrows recognisable conventions from popular media and displays them with the "decorative exhilaration" and "gratuitous frivolity" that Jameson detects in Warhol's work.[111] Trecartin's emulation demonstrates a media literacy that produces a version, but not a replica, of the reality genre. Like Warhol's *Campbell's Soup Cans* paintings (1962), Trecartin presents viewers with a familiar commodity of late capitalism – the spectacle of reality television – without becoming or critiquing it with pointed certainty.

Priority Innfield's ambiguity contrasts with reality television parodies such as those performed on the American comedy show *Saturday Night Live* (1975–).[112] In these instances, sketches make fun of well-known reality shows such as *The Real Housewives* or *Love Island* by staging farcical reproductions that emphasise their incessant dramatic action or the supposed stupidity of their contestants. Unlike these forms of mimicry played for laughs, *Center Jenny, Comma Boat* and *Item Falls* are confusing and chaotic rather than humorous. Because of this, Trecartin's work is again better understood as pastiche as defined by Jameson, rather than parody or satire. For Jameson, pastiche is similar to parody in that it is an "imitation of a peculiar or unique, idiosyncratic style" but "without any of parody's ulterior motives, amputated of the satiric impulse, devoid of laughter and of any conviction that alongside the abnormal tongue you have momentarily borrowed, some healthy linguistic normality still exists".[113] Accordingly, parodic imitation makes comedic sleights that contrast with one's presupposed position that performs the mimicry. In doing so, parody restages existing productions by forging a critical distance between what it emulates and what it performs. *Center

Jenny, Comma Boat and *Item Falls* shrink this critical distance by rehearsing the conventions of a popular media genre without mocking it, which Jameson also terms "blank parody", even as the formal praxis is distinct in terms of genre.[114]

Other (though perhaps not similar) examples of works that reproduce conventions without mocking or entering the canon they rehearse include Harmony Korine's film *Spring Breakers* (2012), which cast famous Disney stars Selena Gomez and Vanessa Hudgens in a coming-of-age film that distorts the expectations these actors purposefully invite. Instead of following the upbeat and family-friendly Disney format that Gomez and Hudgens are associated with, the young women become swept up in a criminal gang headed by Alien (James Franco) and spend most of the film in neon bikinis getting drunk, taking drugs and robbing people at gunpoint. David Cronenberg's film *Maps to the Stars* (2014) is another film that renders uncanny generic expectations without becoming parodic. The film follows numerous figures in the Hollywood area, including troubled actor Havana Segrand (Julianne Moore), teenage child star Benjie Weiss (Evan Bird), limo driver Jerome Fontana (Robert Pattinson) and the enigmatic Agatha Weiss (Mia Wasikowska), who has recently arrived in Los Angeles. Like *Spring Breakers, Maps to the Stars* casts well-known figures only to subvert the initial expectations of the conventional Hollywood production. As the narrative unfolds, the film takes a series of dark turns, including murder and suicide, and is filmed and edited in ways that subtly alter framing and rhythmic conventions to give an off-kilter appearance and disturbing affective field.

Although Trecartin does not use narrative and casting to obviously subvert expectations of reality television, his work creates a version of a popular genre that plays on its well-established conventions without mocking them. Instead of making a pointed critique, *Priority Innfield* empties itself of the overarching logic that holds reality television's semiotic field in place and makes it a seductive object of contemporary enjoyment. In the media that Trecartin imitates, the command to enjoy is to do so in a particular way, by satiating particular desires. Trecartin traverses the fantasy of enjoyment by omitting the master-signifier that otherwise secures identification with the people and environments on screen. By including tropes that support late capitalism as enjoyable, without securing the values that provide its shape and consistency, its meaning falls apart.

The Exploded Body

Central to the undoing of reality television in *Priority Innfield* is the way bodies are displayed. Although shows such as *The Real Housewives* frequently descend into screaming matches, transforming the titular women into a series of crying and snarling faces, this contrasts with their quaffed and smoothed composure. In *Priority Innfield*, however, intoxicated stumbles and guttural rants are the primary modes of behaviour performed by the recorded populations. The bodies are messy, with edges of make-up, hairlines and clothing bleeding, voices warbling, steps staggering, everything smudged.

How can one define Trecartin's character who recurs across *Center Jenny, Comma Boat* and *Item Falls*? The hair is a black synthetic bob; the face pasty and white; the stubble a blackened smudge; the voice an often screeching pitch; the words voiced with a whiney American accent; the gestures an effeminate array of limp wrists and flailing arms; fingers moving hair out of the face, along with flicks and jerks of the neck; the mouth forming big, gurning smiles; shouting; commanding; pulling faces of accentuated disgust; cartoonish wide eyes moving between cameras; distorted expressions, sticking out tongues and biting teeth.

This figuration is not the T-1000 (Robert Patrick) from *Terminator 2: Judgement Day* (1991) who, beneath his angular policeman body, is a globule of metallic liquid that can morph with ease in order to capture John Conner (Edward Furlong). Nor is it Agent Smith (Hugo Weaving) in *The Matrix* (1999), whose streamlined efficiency allows him to reactivate and respawn indefinitely and without injury. Trecartin's rendition of online systems also departs from the technologies personified in the episodic television series *Black Mirror* (2011–2023), which repeatedly rehearses a philosophical interest in the consciousness of artificial intelligence, rendered as human figures with emotional capacities to match.[115] Instead, bodies in *Priority Innfield* suggest something other than or beyond the human without employing the smooth-skinned digital animations featured in the artwork of Ed Atkins or Kate Cooper. Visually, they have a quality like that found in the faces of Bod Mellor paintings, where skin is smeared with violent gestures of pigment, disturbing the recognisable faces of celebrities, their usual photogenic shimmer transformed into some clawing darkness that appears as scrawls of text across their painted flesh.

Numerous writers label Trecartin's work as 'queer', but what this term means is not always obvious. Wes Hill names the figures that populate Trecartin's videos "straight, gay, transsexual, bisexual, inter-sexual, racial, post-racial, mainstream, alternative, capitalist or anarchist", and Alexander Gawronski locates the "queered dimension of Trecartin's work" in "the fact that many performing in his videos are either transgender or in drag".[116] Patrick Langley notes queer as one theme in a list of many: "identity as roleplay, the struggle between individual expression and communal belonging, family politics, queer culture, globalisation".[117] For Åkervall, the characters in *Center Jenny* are "[s]exually ambiguous and sometimes transgender", "queered in every possible way", but with the meaning of 'queer' vague as she observes how "queering generates no novelty, innovation or subversion per se".[118] 'Queer' is the first word used in Zulueta's book title, and the author begins by identifying Trecartin's figures as embodying non-normative sexualities and gender presentations, with terms such as "butch queens, vogue femmes, girlfags, guydykes, and other genderqueer characters".[119] These assessments of Trecartin's work position queer as a subversion of the physical attributes and normative desires that contribute to the social distinguishment of woman from man or black from white. Such understandings of queerness in Trecartin's work implicitly use unnamed but intelligible categories as a benchmark from which the figures deviate.

Zulueta reads 'fluidity' in the videos in terms of race as well as sexuality and gender, observing how the artist will "cast Asian, Black, Hispanic, and/or White actors in his work" while "destabiliz[ing] the very concept of racial identity by cross-accessorizing their looks with unexpected non-traditional hair and skin choices manifested for example through blue wigs, ghostly white faces, or stripes of makeup of varying skin tones".[120] Here, Zulueta affirms the mode of racial identification that he argues Trecartin undoes and does not explain how such categories are known if Trecartin deliberately obscures the classification they typically rely upon. *Priority Innfield* disrupts the particularities that guide identification based on supposedly physical attributes by juxtaposing tropes commonly associated with racialised and gendered positions. In this move, the artist complicates racial determinism (and perhaps identity more broadly) that proposes physicality as the basis of meaning.

Make-up and clothing also transform Trecartin's characters so that they "no longer represent human beings, but rather embody our commodifying culture in which time, space, and identity are no longer necessarily straightforward, linear, quantifiable, and/or classifiable", implicitly affiliating the 'human' with the ability to be measured and differentiated by a non-descript outside perspective.[121] Zulueta sees these qualities in Trecartin's work as "align[ing] [...] with the concept of open-endedness articulated in queer theory" rather than the ways neoliberalism transforms a myriad of physical characteristics into commodities, which consumers may access with their purchasing power.[122] Zulueta admits that LGBT categories cannot encompass the presentation of characters in Trecartin's work, yet 'queer' continues to refer to "both nonstraight sexualities, as well as nonheteronormative and nonfixed positions".[123] Although there is an emphasis on opting out from conventions with the prefix 'non', 'queer' remains paired with an ability to profess genders and sexualities as they relate to the bodies under scrutiny.

Even if we forgo Zulueta's simultaneous disavowal of and reliance on intelligible categories, the assumption that Trecartin's figures are straight, gay or transgender encounters difficulty. Although action on screen ignores civility and refinement, any display of nudity, sex or overt defining of characters is largely absent, implicitly proposing queerness as a social identity that breaks with norms rather than referring to identities that describe specific desires or sex acts. As with his reading of race, which depends on a pre-existing system of categorisation to which Trecartin's work does not appear to subscribe, Zulueta's situating of gender and sexuality evokes discrete positions he implicitly presumes have a basis from which the videos depart.

In contrast to Zulueta and the other critics cited above, who regard queer as non-normative identities (that one cannot locate when scrutinising the videos), I regard Trecartin's figures as queer to the extent they defy the idea that identity persists 'beneath' their physical and behavioural markers. As with Jameson's reading of postmodern 'depthlessness', queer emphasises surfaces that relish in the fluctuating play of semiotic uncertainty. *Center Jenny, Comma Boat* and *Item Falls* display irreverence towards the orderly presentation of the body as intelligible identity categories fall apart and signifiers fluctuate in a manner akin to the heterogeneous image types that collide across cyberspace.

In addition to the disorderly presentation of bodies, the videos also include voices, sets, filming techniques and post-production effects that surpass regular visual and audio boundaries. The toilets casually sat upon throughout *Center Jenny* merge the public space of the stage with the private acts of bodily excretion. Detritus clutters the rooms, spilling out from nowhere in particular. The voices run at modulated pitches and speak at high speed, their rambling qualities evoking the idea of 'word vomit' where language seems to overflow from the mouth, building into a cacophony of sound. Handheld cameras fitted with glaring lights create pools of white illumination across faces that bleach out features and obliterate them with short-lived brilliance. As Žižek has commented on David Lynch's use of this technique, the beams of light create "moments of sensual over-intensity" that "threaten to overflow the screen and to grab us into it".[124] Consequently, our attention is drawn to the image's construction as "the fictional, narrative space [...] gets too intense and reaches out towards us spectators so that we lose ourselves".[125] Such visual excess secures Trecartin's work in the category of video art as the streamlined efficiency of mainstream cinema often represses these elements.

Borrowing from Laura Mulvey's description of artist Cindy Sherman's "disgust" photographic series, there are many scenes across *Priority Innfield* that display "sexual detritus, decaying food, vomit, slime, menstrual blood, hair" that "represent the end of the road, the secret stuff of bodily fluids that the cosmetic is designed to conceal".[126] In *Junior War*, teenagers actively engage in producing detritus as mailboxes and lawn furniture are dashed and smashed, playthings for urges of angst, moving from commodities to the waste of suburban living, tables and chairs made into plastic debris under the blanket of nocturnal boredom.

The seemingly impulsive action and chatter of *Priority Innfield* engages a "politics of disgust", as theorised by Anna Breckon in her analysis of John Waters' cult film, *Pink Flamingos* (1972).[127] For Breckon, *Pink Flamingos'* dedication to unruliness and perversion often omits intelligibility pertaining to narrative and characters. In the vein of Lee Edelman's "anti-social" queer, this disorder rejects the liberal politics of social inclusion based on extending empathy to others: "Perverse, aversive, immoral, abject, united only in that [the characters] all defy the conditions necessary for recognition within the category of the human, they exceed empathy's capaciousness."[128] *Priority Innfield* shares

Pink Flamingos' disregard for the sensible, which Breckon details by evaluating how the film impedes the "spectator's ability to form an imaginary alignment with any of the characters".[129] The hindering of a conventional spectatorial relation is partly achieved by the way scenes lack "sufficient narrative scaffolding to assist the spectator to understand, and potentially identify with, the situation".[130] *Priority Innfield* is similarly stuffed with occurrences that exceed the regulatory boundaries of the somatic and filmic body, causing the limits that demarcate particularities to disintegrate. In *Center Jenny* and *Comma Boat*, cinder blocks are chopped and thrown with the weight of bodies behind them, crumbling into dusty fragments by screaming figures in green bikinis, make-up caked and lifting from the skin, wigs barely clinging to their heads, without reason other than the sheer pleasure of their unexamined destructive impulse.

Extension beyond the confines of what is deemed the 'proper' forms of physicality is similarly at play in the paintings of Flo Brooks. In Brooks's work, ambiguous and often unseen bodies come to the fore, along with visual instances of waste and detritus. In their 2018 series *Scrubbers*, paintings spill over from the ordinary construction of the four-sided canvas as illustrative cleaners work in cumbersome tornados of surfaces in need of wiping. In *U Bend but It's Still a Trap*, a public bathroom fractures; hand dryers, cleaning products, toilet paper, shaving gel and a razor float around bodies cleaning, washing their faces and changing their clothes. Brooks paints the inside-outside borders of the body and the wider environment into a liminal swirl. Hints of the 'feminine' float amid the masculine bodies; a green sports bra on one of the figures, a moon cup balancing upon an incongruous black pole. Cleaners are pictured as part of the storm, performing the labour necessary for the functioning of society but usually hidden by nocturnal working hours before or after everyone has entered or exited the office. Like these often-unseen bodies, tubes of shit and sludge normally concealed by architecture spring into the scene, while thick scrawls of colour exceed the sensible limits of the image. Brooks's work – palpably different from Trecartin's, not least because these are static paintings – nonetheless evokes a time–space compression through the collapse of environments as painterly gestures disrupt a coherent image and narrative in the frame.

Jenkin van Zyl is another artist who shares themes and exhibition features with Trecartin, including looping video, obscure narratives and an interest in bodily surfaces. The video component of Zyl's 2019 installation *Looners* takes place in a fortress of crumbling grandeur, populated by large inflatable latex animals – kangaroos, zebras and donkeys with protruding breasts, butts and swollen bellies – along with people in full-head silicon masks that look like old men, buried in wigs, padding and make-up. Folds of silicon flesh visibly flap, not fully fixed to the bodies and faces they cover, which are overflowing with an abundance of skins and guises as bodies bulge with rubbery flesh and leak like busted batteries. The surfaces and structures of the built environments in the videos function like the bodies. From aerial shots, we see walls held up by scaffolding, interiors of peeling wallpapers and makeshift theatre spaces. Characters wear and hold cameras, phones and 360° GoPros, achieving shots filmed from confined spaces such as the interiors of the inflated balloons into which characters have climbed. Post-production effects distort and merge faces, sound cuts in and out, moments of quiet and black screens punctuate the action, and scrawled and typed text appears intermittently, written from the perspective of an unseen narrator.

Åkervall describes how the installation setup of *Priority Innfield* includes furniture and props from the videos. "As a result, the fictional space of the videos extends into the exhibition space and, conversely, the exhibition space is integrated into the videos' fictional space."[131] The installation environment for *Looners* similarly contains many components that appear as excretions of the screened action: One enters up a ramp towards red curtains, a latex tail is pressed between plexiglass, a big red kiss mark smudged in the middle. Inside are rows of cinema seats facing the screen. Ripped wallpapers and theatrical façades of a brick building plaster the walls that flank both sides of the video projection, with two small channels set into theatre-build windows. Rows of props, from axes to crutches, line the top of the room, and an easily missable miniature of a character stands by one of the entrances. For Åkervall, the expansion of the *Priority Innfield* environment "offers a perspectival twist that includes the position of the viewer in the artwork", where the "viewer doubles as performer".[132] One may feel as if one is entering the belly of the work, being digested, becoming part of the debris, blurring the typical differentiation between spectator and artwork. As with Trecartin's work, Zyl communicates something queer but nothing one can 'identify'. For both artists, the uncanniness of bodies on the cusp of multiple liminalities, brought forth by the excess of jumbled signification and somatic leaking, communicates an irreverence towards the normative desires that govern bodily containment.

Patricia Gherovici reads Trecartin's work as "reject[ing] the binarism of real versus virtual, male and female, self and other, gay and straight, rationality and madness, surface and depth, style and content, time and space".[133] Instead of figures being presented as men or women, signifiers stick to bodies in seemingly random clusters, relinquishing their determining power when not arranged in recognisable styles. Gherovici's sense of fluidity resonates with the lack of distinction between work and leisure in reality television. However, in the case of bodily presentation, this collapse of previously distinct forms undermines – rather than reinforces – the seemingly benevolent authority of late capitalism. *Center Jenny, Comma Boat* and *Item Falls* reject the stability of the bodies on screen and the broader textual system. The crux of capitalist desire can find no resting ground in Trecartin's storm of reality television conventions and masculine, feminine and racial signifiers.

Reality television plays on coordinated components that sustain identifications with the ordinariness of participants and their access to money and celebrity through surveillance (*Big Brother, Survivor*) or the work, beauty and romantic worlds of the already wealthy and established (*The Anna Nicole Show* [2002–2004], *The Real Housewives, KUWTK*). Across the genre's various incarnations, the overarching fantasy of fulfilment via attainment (be it of a specific prize or status) invites viewers to invest in cast members' authenticity and growth. Trecartin presents a detailed emulation of reality television throughout *Priority Innfield*. Yet he also subverts the narrative intelligibility that establishes capitalist success by framing figures as all surface and no 'substance' beneath their visual, acoustic and linguistic play. The videos insist that the signifiers used to determine gender and race are fictitious and decorative rather than innate and able to be guaranteed. The work's refusal to present a coherent narrative structure reinforces this negation of identity.

Many reality shows demonstrate the potential plasticity of their cast members, including the physical transformations seen in makeover shows and the personal 'journeys' that feature across the genre. However, these transformative possibilities reaffirm beauty ideals (*The Swan* [2004], *Extreme Make Over* [2008–], *What Not to Wear* [2001–2007]), individual motivation and the virtue of self-care (*Queer Eye* [2018–]), and strength in the rigorous personal pursuit of success in the face of adversity (*American Idol, The X Factor* [2010–2018]). In the looping exhibition format of *Priority Innfield*, the pointed rejection of narrative arcs disinvites a strategic and curated 'lack' to be filled by a fantasy object as bodies fly in the face of beauty regimes and the demand to be a unified and productive 'self'.

Conclusion

Reality television promotes the rhetoric of authenticity amid a general recognition of its contrivance. Handheld cameras, talking heads, confessionals and the extra-diegetic world of social media and tabloids contribute to a confusing blend of non-fiction and staged action. Storylines have quick turnarounds in lifestyle shows such as *KUWTK* or *The Real Housewives*. Like soap operas, there is no definitive end in sight. Dramatic tensions ebb and flow in overlapping directions: As one storyline ends, another takes off. *Big Brother* and *Survivor* refresh their roster of contestants each season, creating an updated microcosm of society that audiences watch as they live under the scrutiny of CCTV or the film crews who follow them. In many ways, the typical trappings of the Hollywood narrative seem to be in remission in reality formats, replaced with 'unpredictability' and 'candid' reactions. Yet, despite the divergent set of formal codes and constraints, reality television often returns to the familiar tropes of narrative causality. People learn and grow, they fall in love, they lose something, they find it again. Rather than meditate on non-directional or vague wandering unlikely to find significant viewership, reality television follows traditional screen media by prioritising the recovery or development of selfhood through the hallmarks of capitalism's social and material systems of accumulation. However, the reality genre frequently casts 'regular' people in competitions and 'social experiments' or expresses a 'relatability' of the famous families now embedded in mainstream television culture to enhance the sense that these opportunities are attainable for the viewing public.

Trecartin complicates the conventions developed in reality television as his direction frees figures from narrative arcs. The videos are often hard to watch but not because they are too graphic, too gruesome or too vapid. A difficulty occurs because there is no way for viewers to occupy a space of desire. The coordinates that situate spectators as desiring subjects in narrative meaning do not exist in Trecartin's work. Instead, audiences encounter figures who revel in the very confusion promoted by their catch-phrase lingo and smatters of sartorial and pigmented garb. In combination with the restlessness of time and space, and the strategic disregard of linear movements from here to there or then to now, *Priority Innfield* displays jumbles of stimulus that viewers further chop up by moving between screens in the exhibited installations or by clicking across the web.

However, refusing narrative sense is not the same as refusing meaning. In the sea of tumbling action and speech, one can glimpse fleeting media or bodily gestures that provide momentary instances of recognition before being swept back into the fray. The familiarity of reality television and the chaotic undoing of temporality, spatiality and somatic registration come together in a curated combination of competing registers of meaning. As a result, *Priority Innfield* becomes a blended textual environment that critiques how the harnessing of desire is essential for investment in late capitalism by refusing to reproduce this very guarantee.

Notes

1   Originally exhibited in *Il Palazzo Enciclopedico* (The Encyclopaedic Palace), the Fifty-Fifth International Art Exhibition, la Biennale di Venezia, curated by Massimiliano Gioni, 1 June–24 November 2013.
2   For details on convention see David Bordwell, *Narration in the Fiction Film* (London: Methuen, 1985).
3   Gesine Borcherdt, 'Ryan Trecartin', *ArtReview*, 20 August 2014. Available at: https://artreview.com/summer-2014-feature-ryan-trecartin/;   Peter   Schjeldahl, 'Party On: Ryan Trecartin at P.S. 1.', *The New Yorker*, 20 June 2011. Available at: https://www.newyorker.com/magazine/2011/06/27/party-on-peter-schjeldahl.
4   I have seen Trecartin's work first-hand at *Information Superhighway (2016–1966)*, Whitechapel Gallery, London, 29 January 2016–15 May 2016, and *Strange Days: Memories of the Future*, 180, The Strand, London, 02 October 2018–09 December 2018.
5   For a sample of articles and essays that comment on Trecartin's work in relation to the internet, see Lisa Åkervall, 'Networked Selves: Ryan Trecartin and Lizzie Fitch's Postcinematic Aesthetics', *Screen* 57, no. 1 (1 March 2016): 35–51, https://doi.org/10.1093/screen/hjw004; Wes Hill, 'The Automedial Zaniness of Ryan Trecartin', *M/C Journal* 21, no. 2 (25 April 2018), https://doi.org/10.5204/mcj.

1382; Katie Kitamura, 'Ryan Trecartin: Any Ever', *Art Monthly*, no. 349 (September 2011): 28–29; Michael Waugh, '"My Laptop Is an Extension of My Memory and Self": Post-Internet Identity, Virtual Intimacy and Digital Queering in Online Popular Music', *Popular Music* 36, no. 2 (2017): 233–251, https://doi.org/10.1017/S0261143017000083.

6 Ricardo E. Zulueta, *Queer Art Camp Superstar: Decoding the Cinematic Cyberworld of Ryan Trecartin* (New York: SUNY Press, 2018), xix.

7 Ricardo E. Zulueta, *Queer Art Camp Superstar: Decoding the Cinematic Cyberworld of Ryan Trecartin* (New York: SUNY Press, 2018), xiv.

8 Ricardo E. Zulueta, *Queer Art Camp Superstar: Decoding the Cinematic Cyberworld of Ryan Trecartin* (New York: SUNY Press, 2018), xix, xx–xxiii.

9 Michel Chion, *Audio-Vision: Sound on Screen*, trans. Claudia Gorbman, Second edition (New York City: Columbia University Press, 2019), 80, https://doi.org/10.7312/chio18588.

10 Michel Chion, *Audio-Vision: Sound on Screen*, trans. Claudia Gorbman, First edition (New York City: Columbia University Press, 1994), 167.

11 Michel Chion, *Audio-Vision: Sound on Screen*, trans. Claudia Gorbman, First edition (New York City: Columbia University Press, 1994), 166.

12 Michel Chion, *Audio-Vision: Sound on Screen*, trans. Claudia Gorbman, First edition (New York City: Columbia University Press, 1994)`, 166.

13 Michel Chion, *Audio-Vision: Sound on Screen*, trans. Claudia Gorbman, Second edition (New York City: Columbia University Press, 2019), 80; David Harvey, 'Time–Space Compression and the Postmodern Condition', in *The Condition of Postmodernity: An Enquiry into the Origins of Cultural Change* (Cambridge: Basil Blackwell, 1990), 284–307.

14 Ricardo E. Zulueta, *Queer Art Camp Superstar: Decoding the Cinematic Cyberworld of Ryan Trecartin* (New York: SUNY Press, 2018), 99.

15 Ricardo E. Zulueta, *Queer Art Camp Superstar: Decoding the Cinematic Cyberworld of Ryan Trecartin* (New York: SUNY Press, 2018), 101.

16 Ricardo E. Zulueta, *Queer Art Camp Superstar: Decoding the Cinematic Cyberworld of Ryan Trecartin* (New York: SUNY Press, 2018), 103.

17 Ricardo E. Zulueta, *Queer Art Camp Superstar: Decoding the Cinematic Cyberworld of Ryan Trecartin* (New York: SUNY Press, 2018), 104.

18 Ricardo E. Zulueta, *Queer Art Camp Superstar: Decoding the Cinematic Cyberworld of Ryan Trecartin* (New York: SUNY Press, 2018), 104.

19 Richard Dyer, *Pastiche* (London: Routledge, 2007), 2.

20 Richard Dyer, *Pastiche* (London: Routledge, 2007), 56.

21 Richard Dyer, *Pastiche* (London: Routledge, 2007), 56.

22 Richard Dyer, *Pastiche* (London: Routledge, 2007), 60.

23 Mark Andrejevic, *Reality TV: The Work of Being Watched* (Lanham: Rowman & Littlefield, 2004).

24 David Harvey, 'Time–Space Compression and the Postmodern Condition', in *The Condition of Postmodernity: An Enquiry into the Origins of Cultural Change* (Cambridge: Basil Blackwell, 1990), 284–307; Jonathan Crary, *24/7: Late Capitalism and the Ends of Sleep* (London: Verso, 2014).

25 Hito Steyerl, 'In Defense of the Poor Image', *E-Flux Journal*, no. 10 (November 2009): 1–9; Lisa Åkervall, 'Networked Selves: Ryan Trecartin and Lizzie Fitch's Postcinematic Aesthetics', *Screen* 57, no. 1 (1 March 2016): 35–51.

26 Todd McGowan, *The End of Dissatisfaction?: Jacques Lacan and the Emerging Society of Enjoyment* (Albany: State University of New York Press, 2004); Juliet Flower MaccCannell, *The Regime of the Brother: After the Patriarchy* (London: Routledge, 1991).

27 Néstor Braunstein, 'Desire and Jouissance in the Teachings of Lacan', in *The Cambridge Companion to Lacan*, ed. Jean-Michel Rabaté (Cambridge: Cambridge University Press, 2003), 104.

28 Yannis Stavrakakis, *The Lacanian Left: Psychoanalysis, Theory, Politics* (Albany: State University of New York Press, 2007), 196.

29 In the previous chapter, my account of 'sexual difference' focuses on the subject's relationship to the signifier. However, Lacan designates 'jouissance' as a component of sexual difference, with phallic jouissance and feminine jouissance corresponding with the sides of sexuation. Briefly, the enjoyment referred to in this chapter could be associated with phallic jouissance, whereas the jouissance referred to in the following chapter more closely resembles feminine jouissance.

30 Todd McGowan, *The End of Dissatisfaction?: Jacques Lacan and the Emerging Society of Enjoyment* (Albany: State University of New York Press, 2004), 34.

31 Todd McGowan, *The End of Dissatisfaction?: Jacques Lacan and the Emerging Society of Enjoyment* (Albany: State University of New York Press, 2004), 36.

32 Toby Carroll, 'Neoliberalism, Globalization, and Late Capitalism: Capital, Ideology, and Making the World Market', in *The Oxford Handbook of Economic Imperialism*, ed. Zak Cope and Immanuel Ness (Oxford: Oxford University Press, 2022), 135–152, https://doi.org/10.1093/oxfordhb/9780197527085.013.11.

33 Toby Carroll, 'Neoliberalism, Globalization, and Late Capitalism: Capital, Ideology, and Making the World Market', in *The Oxford Handbook of Economic Imperialism*, ed. Zak Cope and Immanuel Ness (Oxford: Oxford University Press, 2022), 137.

34 Byung-Chul Han, *Psychopolitics: Neoliberalism and New Technologies of Power*, trans. Erik Butler (London: Verso, 2017); Juliet Flower MacCannell, *The Regime of the Brother: After the Patriarchy* (London: Routledge, 1991); Todd McGowan, *The End of Dissatisfaction?: Jacques Lacan and the Emerging Society of Enjoyment* (Albany: State University of New York Press, 2004).

35 Susan Murray and Laurie Ouellette, *Reality TV: Remaking Television Culture* (New York: New York University Press, 2004), 3. For a history of reality television, see the podcast by Pandora Sykes and Sirin Kale, 'Unreal: A Critical History of Reality TV', 17 May 2022. Available at: https://www.bbc.co.uk/programmes/p0c5w0zm.

36 Anna McCarthy, '"Stanley Milgram, Allen Funt, and Me": Postwar Social Science and the "First Wave" of Reality TV', in Susan Murray and Laurie Ouellette, *Reality TV: Remaking Television Culture* (New York: New York University Press, 2004), 21.

37 Helen Piper, 'Understanding Reality Television, Reality TV – Audiences and Popular Factual Television, Reality TV – Realism and Revelation', *Screen* 47, no. 1 (1 January 2006): 133, https://doi.org/10.1093/screen/hjl012.

38 Susan Murray and Laurie Ouellette, 'Introduction', in *Reality TV: Remaking Television Culture* (New York: New York University Press, 2004), 3.

39 Susan Murray and Laurie Ouellette, 'Introduction', in *Reality TV: Remaking Television Culture* (New York: New York University Press, 2004), 3.

40 Jonathan Crary, *24/7: Late Capitalism and the Ends of Sleep* (London: Verso, 2014).

41 Jonathan Crary, *24/7: Late Capitalism and the Ends of Sleep* (London: Verso, 2014), 10.

42 Jonathan Crary, *24/7: Late Capitalism and the Ends of Sleep* (London: Verso, 2014), 10–11.

43 Crary opens *24/7* by discussing military and government projects dedicated to finding ways to keep human beings functional without sleep for long durations

and cites a general reduction in sleep time in North America where "the average [...] adult now sleeps approximately six and a half hours a night, an erosion from eight hours a generation ago, and (hard as it is to believe) down from ten hours in the early twentieth century". Jonathan Crary, *24/7: Late Capitalism and the Ends of Sleep* (London: Verso, 2014), 11.

44   David Harvey, 'Time–Space Compression and the Postmodern Condition', in *The Condition of Postmodernity: An Enquiry into the Origins of Cultural Change* (Cambridge: Basil Blackwell, 1990), 284–307.

45   David Harvey, 'Time–Space Compression and the Postmodern Condition', in *The Condition of Postmodernity: An Enquiry into the Origins of Cultural Change* (Cambridge: Basil Blackwell, 1990), 284.

46   David Harvey, 'Time–Space Compression and the Postmodern Condition', in *The Condition of Postmodernity: An Enquiry into the Origins of Cultural Change* (Cambridge: Basil Blackwell, 1990), 285.

47   David Harvey, 'Time–Space Compression and the Postmodern Condition', in *The Condition of Postmodernity: An Enquiry into the Origins of Cultural Change* (Cambridge: Basil Blackwell, 1990), 285.

48   David Harvey, 'Time–Space Compression and the Postmodern Condition', in *The Condition of Postmodernity: An Enquiry into the Origins of Cultural Change* (Cambridge: Basil Blackwell, 1990), 285.

49   Jonathan Crary, *24/7: Late Capitalism and the Ends of Sleep* (London: Verso, 2014), 61–62.

50   Hito Steyerl, 'In Defense of the Poor Image', *E-Flux Journal*, no. 10 (November 2009): 1.

51   Hito Steyerl, 'In Defense of the Poor Image', *E-Flux Journal*, no. 10 (November 2009): 3.

52   Hito Steyerl, 'In Defense of the Poor Image', *E-Flux Journal*, no. 10 (November 2009): 6.

53   For other works on enjoyment and authority not specifically discussed in this chapter, see Mari Ruti, *The Ethics of Opting Out: Queer Theory's Defiant Subjects* (New York: Columbia University Press, 2017); Yannis Stavrakakis, *The Lacanian Left: Psychoanalysis, Theory, Politics* (Albany: State University of New York Press, 2007); Slavoj Žižek, *For They Know Not What They Do: Enjoyment as a Political Factor* (London: Verso, 2008).

54   Todd McGowan, *The End of Dissatisfaction?: Jacques Lacan and the Emerging Society of Enjoyment* (Albany: State University of New York Press, 2004), 1.

55   Todd McGowan, *The End of Dissatisfaction?: Jacques Lacan and the Emerging Society of Enjoyment* (Albany: State University of New York Press, 2004), 2.

56   Pandora Sykes and Sirin Kale, episode five, 'The Birth of Scripted Reality: Laguna Beach & The Hills', in 'Unreal: A Critical History of Reality TV' (podcast), 17 May 2022. Available at: https://www.bbc.co.uk/programmes/p0c5w0zm.

57   Laurie Ouellette and James Hay, *Better Living Through Reality TV: Television and Post-Welfare Citizenship* (Malden: Blackwell, 2008), 4.

58   Laurie Ouellette and James Hay, *Better Living Through Reality TV: Television and Post-Welfare Citizenship* (Malden: Blackwell, 2008), 103.

59   Laurie Ouellette and James Hay, 'Makeover TV: Labors of Reinvention', in *Better Living Through Reality TV: Television and Post-Welfare Citizenship* (Malden: Blackwell, 2008), 99–133.

60   Todd McGowan, *The End of Dissatisfaction?: Jacques Lacan and the Emerging Society of Enjoyment* (Albany: State University of New York Press, 2004), 60. McGowan is unable to extend this analysis to the rise in social media as *The End of Dissatisfaction?* was published in 2004, the same year Facebook was founded.

61 Todd McGowan, *The End of Dissatisfaction?: Jacques Lacan and the Emerging Society of Enjoyment* (Albany: State University of New York Press, 2004), 66.

62 Jacques Lacan, *Écrits: A Selection*, trans. Alan Sheridan (London: Routledge, 1989), 4.

63 Jacques Lacan, *Écrits: A Selection*, trans. Alan Sheridan (London: Routledge, 1989), 4.

64 Todd McGowan, *The End of Dissatisfaction?: Jacques Lacan and the Emerging Society of Enjoyment* (Albany: State University of New York Press, 2004), 66.

65 Jacques Lacan, *Écrits: A Selection*, trans. Alan Sheridan (London: Routledge, 1989), 30–113.

66 Jacques Lacan, *Écrits: A Selection*, trans. Alan Sheridan (London: Routledge, 1989), 42.

67 Miya Tokumitsu, 'Tell Me It's Going to Be OK', *The Baffler*, no. 41 (2018): 11, emphasis in original.

68 Miya Tokumitsu, 'Tell Me It's Going to Be OK', *The Baffler*, no. 41 (2018): 11.

69 Miya Tokumitsu, 'Tell Me It's Going to Be OK', *The Baffler*, no. 41 (2018): 11.

70 Sigmund Freud, *Totem and Taboo: Resemblances Between the Psychic Lives of Savages and Neurotics* (Harmondsworth: Penguin, 1938).

71 Juliet Flower MacCannell, *The Regime of the Brother: After the Patriarchy* (London: Routledge, 1991), 23.

72 Juliet Flower MacCannell, *The Regime of the Brother: After the Patriarchy* (London: Routledge, 1991), 176, emphasis in original.

73 Juliet Flower MacCannell, *The Regime of the Brother: After the Patriarchy* (London: Routledge, 1991), 176.

74 Slavoj Žižek, *The Metastases of Enjoyment: Six Essays on Women and Causality* (London: Verso, 2005), 206.

75 John Corner, 'Performing the Real: Documentary Diversions', *Television & New Media* 3, no. 3 (2002): 257, https://doi.org/10.1177/152747640200300302.

76 John Corner, 'Performing the Real: Documentary Diversions', *Television & New Media* 3, no. 3 (2002): 257, https://doi.org/10.1177/152747640200300302..

77 Lisa Åkervall, 'Networked Selves: Ryan Trecartin and Lizzie Fitch's Postcinematic Aesthetics', *Screen* 57, no. 1 (1 March 2016): 39.

78 Mark Andrejevic, *Reality TV: The Work of Being Watched* (Lanham: Rowman & Littlefield, 2004), 8.

79 Examples of make-over shows that use cosmetic surgery to transform contestants include *The Swan* (2004–2005), *Extreme Makeover* (2002–2007) and *Ten Years Younger* (2004–2009).

80 Mark Andrejevic, *Reality TV: The Work of Being Watched* (Lanham: Rowman & Littlefield, 2004), 35.

81 Mark Andrejevic, *Reality TV: The Work of Being Watched* (Lanham: Rowman & Littlefield, 2004), 37.

82 Mark Andrejevic, *Reality TV: The Work of Being Watched* (Lanham: Rowman & Littlefield, 2004), 67, emphasis in original.

83 Mark Andrejevic, *Reality TV: The Work of Being Watched* (Lanham: Rowman & Littlefield, 2004), 68.

84 Mark Andrejevic, *Reality TV: The Work of Being Watched* (Lanham: Rowman & Littlefield, 2004), 68.

85 Mark Andrejevic, *Reality TV: The Work of Being Watched* (Lanham: Rowman & Littlefield, 2004), 68.

86 Mark Andrejevic, *Reality TV: The Work of Being Watched* (Lanham: Rowman & Littlefield, 2004), 95.

87 George Orwell, *Nineteen Eighty-Four* (London: Secker & Warburg, 1984).

88 Mark Andrejevic, *Reality TV: The Work of Being Watched* (Lanham: Rowman & Littlefield, 2004), 109.

89 John Corner, 'Performing the Real: Documentary Diversions', *Television & New Media* 3, no. 3 (2002): 256.

90 Justin Lewis, 'The Meaning of Real Life', in *Reality TV : Remaking Television Culture*, ed. Susan Murray and Laurie Ouellette (New York: New York University Press, 2004), 288.

91 Justin Lewis, 'The Meaning of Real Life', in *Reality TV : Remaking Television Culture*, ed. Susan Murray and Laurie Ouellette (New York: New York University Press, 2004), 290.

92 Justin Lewis, 'The Meaning of Real Life', in *Reality TV : Remaking Television Culture*, ed. Susan Murray and Laurie Ouellette (New York: New York University Press, 2004), 291.

93 Fredric Jameson, *Postmodernism, or, The Cultural Logic of Late Capitalism* (London: Verso, 1991), 18.

94 Byung-Chul Han, *Psychopolitics: Neoliberalism and New Technologies of Power*, trans. Erik Butler (London: Verso, 2017), 37.

95 Byung-Chul Han, *Psychopolitics: Neoliberalism and New Technologies of Power*, trans. Erik Butler (London: Verso, 2017), 8.

96 Byung-Chul Han, *Psychopolitics: Neoliberalism and New Technologies of Power*, trans. Erik Butler (London: Verso, 2017), 8, 9.

97 Byung-Chul Han, *Psychopolitics: Neoliberalism and New Technologies of Power*, trans. Erik Butler (London: Verso, 2017), 34.

98 Byung-Chul Han, *Psychopolitics: Neoliberalism and New Technologies of Power*, trans. Erik Butler (London: Verso, 2017), 38.

99 Richard Dyer, *Pastiche* (London: Routledge, 2007), 98.

100 Richard Dyer, *Pastiche* (London: Routledge, 2007), 102.

101 Richard Dyer, *Pastiche* (London: Routledge, 2007), 119.

102 Richard Dyer, *Pastiche* (London: Routledge, 2007), 120–122.

103 Richard Dyer, *Pastiche* (London: Routledge, 2007), 123.

104 Richard Dyer, *Pastiche* (London: Routledge, 2007), 100.

105 Fredric Jameson, 'The Cultural Logic of Late Capitalism', in *Postmodernism, or, The Cultural Logic of Late Capitalism* (New York: Duke University Press, 1992), 1–54.

106 Fredric Jameson, *Postmodernism, or, The Cultural Logic of Late Capitalism* (London: Verso, 1991), 6.

107 Fredric Jameson, *Postmodernism, or, The Cultural Logic of Late Capitalism* (London: Verso, 1991), 6.

108 Fredric Jameson, *Postmodernism, or, The Cultural Logic of Late Capitalism* (London: Verso, 1991), 7.

109 Fredric Jameson, *Postmodernism, or, The Cultural Logic of Late Capitalism* (London: Verso, 1991), 8.

110 Fredric Jameson, *Postmodernism, or, The Cultural Logic of Late Capitalism* (London: Verso, 1991), 8.

111 Fredric Jameson, *Postmodernism, or, The Cultural Logic of Late Capitalism* (London: Verso, 1991), 10.

112 See *SNL Presents Reality TV Sketches*, YouTube video, 5 February 2020. Available at: https://www.youtube.com/watch?v=Fe6cBZJnf3w.

113 Fredric Jameson, *Postmodernism, or, The Cultural Logic of Late Capitalism* (London: Verso, 1991), 17.

114 Fredric Jameson, *Postmodernism, or, The Cultural Logic of Late Capitalism* (London: Verso, 1991), 17.

115 See *Black Mirror* episodes S2E1 "Be Right Back" (2013), S2E4 "White Christmas" (2014), S4E1 "USS Callister" (2017), S4E4 "Hang the DJ" (2017) and S5E3 "Rachel, Jack and Ashley Too" (2019).
116 Wes Hill, 'The Automedial Zaniness of Ryan Trecartin', *M/C Journal* 21, no. 2 (25 April 2018); Alexander Gawronski, 'Art as Critique under Neoliberalism: Negativity Undoing Economic Naturalism', *Arts* 10, no. 1 (2021): 11, https://doi.org/10.3390/arts10010011.
117 Patrick Langley, 'Ryan Trecartin: The Real Internet Is Inside You', *The White Review*, April 2022. Available at: https://www.thewhitereview.org/feature/ryan-trecartin-the-real-internet-is-inside-you/.
118 Lisa Åkervall, 'Networked Selves: Ryan Trecartin and Lizzie Fitch's Postcinematic Aesthetics', *Screen* 57, no. 1 (1 March 2016): 43.
119 Ricardo E. Zulueta, *Queer Art Camp Superstar: Decoding the Cinematic Cyberworld of Ryan Trecartin* (New York: SUNY Press, 2018), xxi.
120 Ricardo E. Zulueta, *Queer Art Camp Superstar: Decoding the Cinematic Cyberworld of Ryan Trecartin* (New York: SUNY Press, 2018), xxxi.
121 Ricardo E. Zulueta, *Queer Art Camp Superstar: Decoding the Cinematic Cyberworld of Ryan Trecartin* (New York: SUNY Press, 2018), xxxi.
122 Ricardo E. Zulueta, *Queer Art Camp Superstar: Decoding the Cinematic Cyberworld of Ryan Trecartin* (New York: SUNY Press, 2018), xxxi.
123 Ricardo E. Zulueta, *Queer Art Camp Superstar: Decoding the Cinematic Cyberworld of Ryan Trecartin* (New York: SUNY Press, 2018), xxxvi.
124 *The Pervert's Guide to Cinema* (P Guide, ICA Projects, 2006).
125 *The Pervert's Guide to Cinema* (P Guide, ICA Projects, 2006).
126 Laura Mulvey, 'A Phantasmagoria of the Female Body: The Work of Cindy Sherman', *New Left Review* 188, no. 188 (1991): 144.
127 Anna Breckon, 'The Erotic Politics of Disgust: Pink Flamingos as Queer Political Cinema', *Screen* 54, no. 4 (1 December 2013), https://doi.org/10.1093/screen/hjt041.
128 Anna Breckon, 'The Erotic Politics of Disgust: Pink Flamingos as Queer Political Cinema', *Screen* 54, no. 4 (1 December 2013): 517. See also Lee Edelman, *No Future: Queer Theory and the Death Drive* (Durham: Duke University Press, 2004).
129 Anna Breckon, 'The Erotic Politics of Disgust: Pink Flamingos as Queer Political Cinema', *Screen* 54, no. 4 (1 December 2013): 522.
130 Anna Breckon, 'The Erotic Politics of Disgust: Pink Flamingos as Queer Political Cinema', *Screen* 54, no. 4 (1 December 2013): 522.
131 Lisa Åkervall, 'Networked Selves: Ryan Trecartin and Lizzie Fitch's Postcinematic Aesthetics', *Screen* 57, no. 1 (1 March 2016): 48.
132 Lisa Åkervall, 'Networked Selves: Ryan Trecartin and Lizzie Fitch's Postcinematic Aesthetics', *Screen* 57, no. 1 (1 March 2016): 48.
133 Patricia Gherovici, *Transgender Psychoanalysis: A Lacanian Perspective on Sexual Difference* (London: Routledge, 2017), 114.

References

Åkervall, Lisa. 'Networked Selves: Ryan Trecartin and Lizzie Fitch's Postcinematic Aesthetics.' *Screen* 57, no. 1 (1 March 2016): 35–51. doi:10.1093/screen/hjw004.
Andrejevic, Mark. *Reality TV: The Work of Being Watched.* Lanham: Rowman & Littlefield, 2004.

Borcherdt, Gesine. 'Ryan Trecartin.' *ArtReview*, 20 August 2014. Available at: https://artreview.com/summer-2014-feature-ryan-trecartin/.

Bordwell, David. *Narration in the Fiction Film*. London: Methuen, 1985.

Braunstein, Néstor. 'Desire and Jouissance in the Teachings of Lacan', in *The Cambridge Companion to Lacan*, edited by Jean-Michel Rabaté. Cambridge: Cambridge University Press, 2003.

Breckon, Anna. 'The Erotic Politics of Disgust: Pink Flamingos as Queer Political Cinema.' *Screen* 54, no. 4 (1 December 2013): 517. doi:10.1093/screen/hjt041.

Carroll, Toby. 'Neoliberalism, Globalization, and Late Capitalism: Capital, Ideology, and Making the World Market', in *The Oxford Handbook of Economic Imperialism*, edited by Zak Cope and Immanuel Ness, 135–152. Oxford: Oxford University Press, 2022, doi:10.1093/oxfordhb/9780197527085.013.11.

Chion, Michel. *Audio-Vision: Sound on Screen*. Translated by Claudia Gorbman. First edition. New York City: Columbia University Press, 1994.

Chion, Michel. *Audio-Vision: Sound on Screen*. Translated by Claudia Gorbman. Second edition. New York City: Columbia University Press, 2019. doi:10.7312/chio18588.

Corner, John. 'Performing the Real: Documentary Diversions', *Television & New Media* 3, no. 3 (2002): 257. doi:10.1177/152747640200300302.

Crary, Jonathan. *24/7: Late Capitalism and the Ends of Sleep*. London: Verso, 2014.

Dyer, Richard. *Pastiche*. London: Routledge, 2007.

Edelman, Lee. *No Future: Queer Theory and the Death Drive*. Durham: Duke University Press, 2004.

Freud, Sigmund. *Totem and Taboo: Resemblances Between the Psychic Lives of Savages and Neurotics*. Harmondsworth: Penguin, 1938.

Gawronski, Alexander. 'Art as Critique under Neoliberalism: Negativity Undoing Economic Naturalism.' *Arts* 10, no. 1 (2021): 11. doi:10.3390/arts10010011.

Gherovici, Patricia. *Transgender Psychoanalysis: A Lacanian Perspective on Sexual Difference*. London: Routledge, 2017.

Han, Byung-Chul. *Psychopolitics: Neoliberalism and New Technologies of Power*. Translated by Erik Butler. London: Verso, 2017.

Harvey, David. 'Time-Space Compression and the Postmodern Condition', in *The Condition of Postmodernity: An Enquiry into the Origins of Cultural Change*, 284–307. Cambridge: Basil Blackwell, 1990.

Hill, Wes. 'The Automedial Zaniness of Ryan Trecartin.' *M/C Journal* 21, no. 2 (25 April 2018). doi:10.5204/mcj.1382.

Jameson, Fredric. *Postmodernism, or, The Cultural Logic of Late Capitalism*. London: Verso, 1991.

Kitamura, Katie. 'Ryan Trecartin: Any Ever.' *Art Monthly*, no. 349 (September 2011): 28–29.

Lacan, Jacques. *Écrits: A Selection*. Translated by Alan Sheridan. London: Routledge, 1989.

Langley, Patrick. 'Ryan Trecartin: The Real Internet Is Inside You.' *The White Review*, April 2022. Available at: https://www.thewhitereview.org/feature/ryan-trecartin-the-real-internet-is-inside-you/.

Lewis, Justin. 'The Meaning of Real Life', in *Reality TV : Remaking Television Culture*, edited by Susan Murray and Laurie Ouellette, 288–302. New York: New York University Press, 2004.

MacCannell, Juliet Flower. *The Regime of the Brother: After the Patriarchy.* London: Routledge, 1991.

McCarthy, Anna. '"Stanley Milgram, Allen Funt, and Me": Postwar Social Science and the "First Wave" of Reality TV', in *Reality TV: Remaking Television Culture,* edited by Susan Murray and Laurie Ouellette, 21. New York: New York University Press, 2004.

McGowan, Todd. *The End of Dissatisfaction?: Jacques Lacan and the Emerging Society of Enjoyment.* Albany: State University of New York Press, 2004.

Mulvey, Laura. 'A Phantasmagoria of the Female Body: The Work of Cindy Sherman.' *New Left Review* 188, no. 188 (1991): 144.

Murray, Susan, and Laurie Ouellette. *Reality TV: Remaking Television Culture.* New York: New York University Press, 2004.

Orwell, George. *Nineteen Eighty-Four.* London: Secker & Warburg, 1984.

Ouellette, Laurie, and James Hay. *Better Living Through Reality TV: Television and Post-Welfare Citizenship.* Malden: Blackwell, 2008.

Piper, Helen. 'Understanding Reality Television, Reality TV – Audiences and Popular Factual Television, Reality TV – Realism and Revelation.' *Screen* 47, no. 1 (1 January 2006): 133. doi:10.1093/screen/hjl012.

Ruti, Mari. *The Ethics of Opting Out: Queer Theory's Defiant Subjects.* New York: Columbia University Press, 2017.

Schjeldahl, Peter. 'Party On: Ryan Trecartin at P.S. 1.' *The New Yorker,* 20 June 2011. Available at: https://www.newyorker.com/magazine/2011/06/27/party-on-peter-schjeldahl.

Stavrakakis, Yannis. *The Lacanian Left: Psychoanalysis, Theory, Politics.* Albany: State University of New York Press, 2007.

Steyerl, Hito. 'In Defense of the Poor Image.' *E-Flux Journal,* no. 10 (November 2009): 1–9.

Sykes, Pandora, and Sirin Kale. 'Unreal: A Critical History of Reality TV.' BBC, 17 May 2022. Available at: https://www.bbc.co.uk/programmes/p0c5w0zm.

Tokumitsu, Miya. 'Tell Me It's Going to Be OK', *The Baffler,* no. 41 (2018).

Waugh, Michael. '"My Laptop Is an Extension of My Memory and Self": Post-Internet Identity, Virtual Intimacy and Digital Queering in Online Popular Music.' *Popular Music* 36, no. 2 (2017): 233–251. doi:10.1017/S0261143017000083.

Žižek, Slavoj. *For They Know Not What They Do: Enjoyment as a Political Factor.* London: Verso, 2008.

Žižek, Slavoj. *The Metastases of Enjoyment: Six Essays on Women and Causality.* London: Verso, 2005.

Zulueta, Ricardo E. *Queer Art Camp Superstar: Decoding the Cinematic Cyberworld of Ryan Trecartin.* New York: SUNY Press, 2018.

Chapter 4

Bodies That Shatter

The Negative Content of *120 BPM*

A man speaks on a stage, seen through a gap in the curtains. He is unaware of the cluster of bodies standing in agitated hush on the other side of the drapes. The handheld camera is among the bodies, peering, with anticipation, through the curtain to the illuminated side of the fabric wall. It moves around the claustrophobic and low-lit space as the man on stage shifts his weight, causing his body to interfere with the light's beam, making its brilliance quiver. The hidden group surges on to the stage following the announcement – "Let's go!" – which the following scene contextualises as the eruption of protest.

This opening sequence of *120 BPM* (2017) emphasises light and shadow to frame the political activity, which functions as one of the film's central narrative concerns. The articulation of form and action takes place in the diegetic conversion of stasis into animation that occurs via the literal staging of a political body, whereby a dark and still crowd moves forth into light to initiate its political demonstration. During the sequence, audiences are introduced to a sense of revolution – 'revolution' not only as political "change, upheaval" but also as a circulation of illumination.[1] The latter definition, traced from French (*revolution*), describes celestial circuits that manifest as points of discernible light which move "about a centre of mass" and, later, designates movement around "an axis or centre; rotation", the act of the turn, a cyclical course.[2] The scene's play of light and movement resonates with later sequences from the film that again stage scenes under brief, bright flashing and flickering lights. In particular, it is the technique known as 'strobe' that this chapter examines in detail to argue that *120 BPM* brings a queer politics to the screen through its notable distortion of light and movement.

'Strobe' is shortened from 'stroboscopic', taken from the Ancient Greek *strobos*, meaning "a twisting or whirling round", and *skopein*, meaning "to view or examine", sharing the etymological theme of 'revolution' as it pertains to movement and light.[3] Strobe lighting was initially named after the stroboscopic disc, an optical toy invented in 1832 by Simon von Stampfer. This early device featured a series of still sequential images around the edge of a disc. When spun or *twisted* and *whirled*, the disc was *looked at* and *examined* in a mirror via small slits at the circle's edge, producing the

DOI: 10.4324/9781003527244-5

appearance of movement. Along with other pre-cinematic devices, such as the zoetrope or the flip book, the stroboscopic disc creates an illusion of movement from still images. Such rudimentary mechanisms remind us that cinema relies upon our *mis*recognition. For optical toys and advanced cinematic technologies alike, the compelling impression of movement hinges on the human eye's *inability* to read the rapid display of sequential images as static. In a reversal of film projection's creation of animation, strobe's pulsating light appears to reduce and fragment action, making movement (re)appear as a series of photographic instances. As such, *120 BPM*'s strobe sequences develop a mise-en-scène that refers to cinema's history, which is lodged in the photographic index.

It is perhaps impossible to simultaneously comprehend still images *and* the movement they collectively produce. Contemplating this juncture is like imagining a temporal equivalent of the classic optical illusion where one tries to see both duck and hare at the same time but can only restlessly jump between them. With this challenge in mind, this chapter argues that *120 BPM*'s strobe sequences curate negative 'content' that informs the temporal visual field and invites spectators to see what is *not* there. Strobe does not create instances dominated by shadow but is a schema that includes a rhythmic exclusion of light and movement. In doing so, this lighting design inflects the perception of the specific historical and political context of the film's diegesis. By closely examining *120 BPM*'s invocation of negativity, this chapter continues this book's critical enquiry into queerness and capitalism, understood as conflictual positions that alternately map subjectivity's extinguished dimension of meaning.

In a rigorous close reading of the film *Open Water* (2003), Eugenia Brinkema sets herself the task of assessing absence in the visual field while resisting the desire to transform it into a metaphor for displaced content, to "read for the form of the nothing without obliterating it, to read with loss instead of reading to fill loss".[4] Brinkema's challenge underscores the following critical assessment of *120 BPM*, which turns to the film's use of light and shadow and asks how this mode contributes to a mapping of social and political subjectivity on screen. To examine the complex negotiations that reveal and conceal the absent meaning that psychoanalysis terms the 'real', this chapter introduces the Freudian and Lacanian theory of the 'drive', a repetitive psychic structure that circulates 'nothing'. It also further contextualises strobe on screen by attending to other notable lighting sequences, including those from the experimental film *Exploding Plastic Inevitable* (1967), the action film *Blade* (1998), the photographic installation work of Mat Collishaw, and Gaspar Noé's 'extreme cinema' feature *Irréversible* (2002), to deepen an understanding of how strobe can affect perceptions of time, movement and space and chart how the visual inscription of negativity expresses the topology of the drive.

The following three sections draw from texts by Laura Mulvey, Leo Bersani, Lee Edelman and Todd McGowan to address the function of the drive, which structures my analysis of *120 BPM*'s mise-en-scène and temporality. Regarding these related but divergent interpretations, how does negative space help us see precisely that which is not there? And how does this situate queerness as a political mode on screen? The stroboscopic field offers a diegetic context (such as a party or a protest) that masks the lack nonetheless displayed in the frame while drawing attention to cinema's mechanical history.

To begin, I introduce the Freudian death drive and its relationship to stasis in cinema. The 'death drive' was first theorised by Sabina Spielrein in her 1912 paper "Destruction as the Cause of Coming into Being" before being taken up by Sigmund Freud in his 1920 essay "Beyond the Pleasure Principle".[5] After witnessing soldiers returning from World War I suffering from 'war neurosis', Freud advanced the death drive as a theory of psychical action that displaced pleasure as the fundamental unconscious motivation experienced by subjects. Freud rethinks the psychic importance of the pleasure principle as "the purposes of wish-fulfilment are certainly not being served by the dreams of patients with accident-induced neurosis when they thrust them back – as they regularly do – into the original trauma situation".[6] Attempting to make sense of this phenomenon, Freud distinguishes between life drives ('Eros') and death drives ('Thanatos'), with the latter designating a repetition of trauma, understood as the living organism's compulsion to return to the 'inorganic' state it originated from:

> If we may reasonably suppose, on the basis of all our experience without exception, that every living thing dies – reverts to the inorganic – for *intrinsic* reasons, then we can only say that *the goal of all life is death*, or to express it retrospectively: *the inanimate existed before the animate.*[7]

Freud conceptualises the death drive as a return to stasis by examining the interrelation of biological and psychic activity. In *Death 24× a Second*, Mulvey employs Freud's theory to reflect on cinema's oscillation between stillness and movement, from early photography to home-viewing technologies such as DVDs that allow spectators to pause movement at will.[8] Mulvey does not look at strobe as part of her investigation, but her analysis contextualises its distortive effect on movement and time. Regarding Mulvey's interpretation of the death drive and the cinematic medium, the opening section of this chapter addresses how stasis informs *120 BPM*'s manifestation of loss in the historical context of the AIDS epidemic in France during the 1990s. Taking absence as a visual instance, how does loss (dis)appear as the limit of the representational frame and introduce an understanding of queerness as a refusal to be filled with content?

This chapter then turns to the Lacanian queer theory of Bersani and Edelman and Jacques Lacan's interpretation of the drive. Rather than distinguishing between life drives and the death drive, Lacan collapses the drives into a topology that splits 'aim' and 'goal' to indicate how the drive continuously circulates and misses the 'object' of desire (the *objet petit a*) and, in this missing, passes through the 'rim' of the erogenous zone (see Figure 4.1). Importantly, the drive is

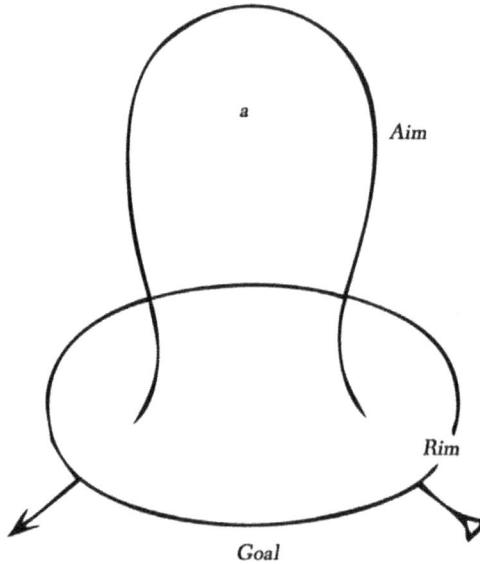

Figure 4.1 Lacan's diagram of the drive, *Seminar XI*, 1979.[9]

not a biological instinct. Rather, it is the difficulty that emerges at the meeting of biology and the signifier, with the latter reframing the former through the symbolic order of language, which inaugurates the subject into a structure of negativity.

Lacan expresses the web of language as symbols that "envelop the life of man in a network so total that they join together, before he comes into the world, those who are going to engender him 'by flesh and blood'".[10] The universe of signifiers precedes the subject's being, yet this sense of being is articulated by participating in chains of signification. As Edelman summarises, "the order of a social and linguistic reality [is] articulated from somewhere else" that cannot coalesce with a coherent sense of interiority.[11] The signifier "only bestows a sort of *promissory* identity, one with which we can never succeed in fully coinciding".[12] Although we may consciously and unconsciously attempt to "clos[e] the gap that divides us", we become subjects *"through that act of division alone"*, introduced by the signifier.[13] Language does not only install lack in the subject; from this position, we also construct a time of fulfilment that preceded lack. Lacan emphasises the drive as always partial and acquiring satisfaction not from attaining a realisable object but from continually missing the *object a*: "Even when you stuff your mouth – the mouth that opens in the register of the drive – it is not the food that satisfies it, it is, as one says, the pleasure of the mouth."[14] The process of signification disjoins the subject from the world and introduces a separation that was never sutured but that one nevertheless retroactively imagines as a mythic totality to which the pre-discursive being had access. Language creates a desire to return to an original, unsplit self, but this longing only exists with the advent of the signifier.

Joan Copjec suggests that a paradox is introduced between the signifier and nature by drawing our attention to Freud's exclamation "oh, inch of nature!" from his later work *Civilisation and Its Discontents*, first published in 1930.[15] This expression uses a measurement ('inch'), which "is itself unnatural, found not in nature but in the rods and rules by which culture calculates", to designate nature.[16] Copjec's erudite reading of this relationship demonstrates that the natural can be articulated only through the cultural prism, and the biological cannot be understood outside of or beyond our imbrication with language. It is with this difficulty that the drive emerges.

Lacan implies a rift between the logic of the drive and the logic of desire by contrasting the perceived object of satisfaction with the aim of the drive, "which is in fact simply the presence of a hollow, a void, which can be occupied [...] by any object, and whose agency we know only in the form of the lost object, the petit a".[17] The object is a momentary placeholder for the lack that causes desire rather than a material thing. Food and the oral function again mark how the *objet a* is "not introduced as the original food, it is introduced from the fact that no food will ever satisfy the oral drive, except by circumventing the eternally lacking object".[18] Satisfaction cannot be achieved by attaining the perceived object of desire but emerges as one perpetually misses the object: "[T]he object of desire, in the usual sense, is either a phantasy that is in reality the support of desire, or a lure."[19] In other words, the objects we encounter that seem to offer satiation always fail to deliver.

With this in mind, the second section of this chapter reads *120 BPM*'s strobe sequences and their repetition of absence alongside Lacan's topology of the drive and Bersani's essay "Is the Rectum a Grave?". In this seminal essay, Bersani traces how conservative media outlets perpetuated connections between the figure of the homosexual, death and sex during the eruption of AIDS by introducing *jouissance*. This Lacanian term speaks to a 'self-shattering' enjoyment that evokes pleasure and pain, or pleasure *as* painful.[20] Bersani's Lacanian resituating of homosexuality frames *120 BPM*'s displays of enjoyment and loss in its historical and political setting. Edelman continues Bersani's connections between sex, death and jouissance while examining the drive to introduce queerness as resistant to political sensibility.[21] With regard to the Freudian and Lacanian influence in Bersani's and Edelman's work, how does *120 BPM* communicate jouissance in the visual field, and how does this interpretation of the film's mise-en-scène continue to develop the understanding of queerness as that which resists signification?

In the third section of this chapter, McGowan's analysis of cinematic time introduces the drive as articulating a politics of form, which I extend to *120 BPM*'s scenes depicting demonstrations and the ways these overlap with strobing sequences. For McGowan, the drive informs capitalism's seductive regime that promises, but never delivers, satiation through accumulation.

Although language predates capitalism, the signifier structures the subject in a way that makes capitalism particularly appealing: If "[t]he essence of capitalism is accumulation", then "the key to capitalism's staying power lies in the fact that this ultimately satisfying object doesn't exist".[22] If it did, we would not continue to accumulate. Psychoanalysis teaches us that satiation is mythic even as it is structured by and perpetuates desire. McGowan argues that capitalism skilfully exploits subjects by suggesting a path to satiation that is never delivered. For this reason, McGowan proposes that "[c]apitalism's emergence and its psychic appeal are related to the nature of human subjectivity, though this subjectivity is itself unnatural, a function not of natural processes but of a disjunction from the natural world".[23] Compared with capitalism's insistence on extinguishing lack through accumulation, the topology of the drive presents a relationship to lack that disabuses us of the fantasy that the subject can recoup the lost object, which this chapter connects to queerness and negative space on screen.

Across McGowan's work, an embrace of lack develops an ethical stance that questions capitalism's promise. In his book *Out of Time*, the drive guides a conceptualisation of the politics of anachronic temporality in cinema.[24] McGowan focuses on a selection of films whose narrative structures depart from conventional linearity and, in doing so, demonstrates how the drive resituates desire.[25] Regarding this theoretical intervention, can lighting in *120 BPM* enact a queer temporality that resists capitalist commands to desire? Building on cinematic materiality established in the first section, the notion of jouissance in the second and atemporality in the third, the exclusion of visual content in *120 BPM* offers a refreshed imagining of how queerness infiltrates the cinematic text to undo the capitalist demands on identity.

Stasis = Loss

The opening sequence of *120 BPM* sees the eruption of protest that emerges from behind curtains and moves on to a lit stage. This scene materialises the negative content of darkness-stillness and its transformation into its positive counterpart, movement-light, with the former depleted of what the latter makes visible. Here, negative and positive are distinguished sites that are nonetheless able to transform into one another. However, the same cannot be said for the film's discussion of HIV, where someone's 'negative' status is distinct from, but can become, a 'positive' and yet, crucially, cannot turn back. The film's enigmatic introduction depicts its central ACT UP activist group progressing into animated movement to suggest its collective fight as a vehicle for political change – braiding political action with narrative action – before the following scene establishes the film's present day in the early 1990s.

In a bright lecture hall, a man greets a small group: "Hello and welcome to ACT UP." New members of the activist group and film viewers alike receive an introduction to ACT UP Paris: What they do ("defend the rights of people with AIDS") and what to expect ("whatever your HIV status, you must accept to be viewed [...] as HIV positive"). Implicit in preparing for participation in ACT UP, those who are negative must be willing to *be viewed as* positive during the acts of protest that target government and corporate bodies who have neglected the overwhelmingly marginalised people who have contracted HIV. The "whatever" that refers to one's status during the introductory message presumably includes negative, positive and the quasi-status of not knowing – unknown, unsure and perhaps, implicitly, untested. In being the recipient of another's view, negative is read as positive, extinguished of its missing content and filled with a positive one. This meeting is the first of its kind for the film's protagonist, Nathan (Arnaud Valois), who is HIV-negative. Nathan's negative status positions him 'outside' the immediate corporeal consequences of AIDS, in contrast with Sean (Nahuel Pérez Biscayart), a long-term member of ACT UP who is HIV-positive, with whom Nathan develops a sexual and romantic relationship over the course of the film. This distinction between the positive and negative body, collapsed into positive in the view from the 'outside', is reopened within the group during an early scene of political action.

Sick of waiting for results following a new drug trial that could help those suffering with HIV, the ACT UP group storms the Melton Pharm pharmaceutical company offices. As members swarm the building, entering the lift and jumping over its foyer barriers after getting awkwardly tangled in the revolving doors, they proceed to make their way up to the appropriate floor. Nathan hurries to join those in the lift, only to opt for the stairs after Sean jokingly declares that the lift is for "HIV-positive only". This spoken line establishes the often uncertain boundary between positive and negative, affirmed by the horizontal track of the closing door as the lift raises one group to the upper levels of the building while Nathan presumably runs the zigzag of the staircase. Within the group of activists, there is no forgone absorbing of the negative into the positive. The collapse in the optical arena of the media (where one is *viewed*) suggests that appearances alone cannot differentiate HIV statuses. Instead, knowledge of T-cell numbers and their likelihood of diminishing, which indicates HIV infection, is often necessary to distinguish positive from negative. It is, as it were, what is on the inside that 'counts', where being named 'positive' relates to a decrease and diminishment of what the 'negative' status retains. In these early scenes, positive and negative are established as uncertain sites that can convert, not only in terms of HIV contraction (where one may turn from negative to positive) but also in how one is viewed by the public, which transforms the presumed status in the same direction. The film's concern with positive and negative not only relates to people's bodily status but also becomes absorbed into the film's mise-en-scène as it repeatedly stages stark graphic fluctuations of light's positive and negative inscription.

There are two nightclub scenes in the film's first half, two in the second half, and a final protest scene, which all feature strobing or flickering light while dispensing with dialogue. In the first instance, blue, red and orange lights wash over bodies with a texture reminiscent of sunlight through water. Time dips into slow motion as a wave of hands reaches upwards through the rippling illumination, recalling and foreshadowing the gestures of elongated arms that hold placards at protests or signal consensus during the ACT UP general meetings. From above, we witness a sea of limbs before the focus shifts from the crowd to floating particles, reducing figures to blurred shapes as specks of dust surf on air and images of white blood cells form against the dark background. These particles conjure the materiality of the human and cinematic body, reminding us of the desiccated consistency of flesh's inevitable reduction and the dance of grain when meeting light in the celluloid film process.

Chronicling the expanded cinema events of the mid 1960s, critic and film-maker Jonas Mekas and artist Steve Durkee summon a similar combination of imagery when describing the experience of dancing under strobe lighting:

JM: On the dance floor, under the strobes, very often you lose the sense of the musical rhythm, you pick up the strobe rhythm, instead – you can't even hear the sound, you lose the sense of sound […].

SD: Or who you are – because all you see are fragments of yourself. It's really like being in a movie.

JM: You become a particle, a grain of the movie. Maybe that's what it is. We are cut by strobe light into single frames, to eight frames per second or whatever the strobe frequency is […].

SD: Like movies becoming real.[26]

Mekas and Durkee evoke strobe's cinematic quality by referring to grain and frames to convey the time that such lighting seems to set one's body to. In drawing out these elements, *120 BPM* visually ponders the fragility of bodies by arousing the texture of the pre-digital cinematic medium. For Mulvey, there is a "fundamental and irreconcilable opposition between still-ness and movement that reverberates across the aesthetics of cinema", between the static frames and the "entrancing images moving on screen in a darkened space".[27] *120 BPM* charts this contradiction as the strobe redoubles the illusion of movement into an illusion of stillness, drawing attention to the "'before' for the moving image as a film-strip, as a reference back to photo-graphy or its own original moment of registration".[28] By breaking with the naturalistic relay of motion, strobe is reminiscent of the breaks between frames on a spool of celluloid, the editorial cuts that organise shot and scene sequences (the syuzhet) and the unstable beams of light that shone from pro-jectors, which gave early cinema its informal name, 'the flicks'. By emphasis-ing the gap in the flow of movement and drawing our attention to celluloid's photographic index in a curious reversal of stasis and action, strobe reminds viewers of cinema's construction. In such instances, the staging of light com-plicates viewers' perceptual failure to read motion pictures as still.

In *120 BPM*, the starkest use of strobe comes during the film's final moments, when ACT UP stages a political funeral for Sean at an insurer's gathering, following his death from HIV. Unlike the obscured commotion detected during the film's opening, viewers have a clear perspective of the room and the ensuing action. Intercut with this closing scene, the recently bereaved Nathan and fellow activist Thibault (Antoine Reinartz) have sex, presumably the evening before the protest we now witness. Their bodies are made visible by a hint of light, and their rhythmic movement halts as Nathan sits up to cry, unable to make sex forestall another wave of grief following Sean's death. During the protest, the group of now-familiar faces disperse Sean's ashes across the banquet room, causing grey plumes to rise and settle over the elaborate canopies, flower arrangements, towers of champagne and bewildered patrons. Inexplicably, and in a departure from the nightclub sequences that use strobe as part of the diegesis, the room becomes flooded with strobing lights, and time shifts into slow motion. The chants of political action fade as the group begins dancing, and strobe introduces a space that extends as a supplement to the diegesis. A faint thudding sound reminiscent of a heartbeat leads into melancholic dance music, escalating as strobing comes to dominate the frame. Building into a crescendo of rhythmic light and sound, *120 BPM* moves to an intensified point for its close. Throughout the film, strobe marks scenes of dancing and protest before dramatically punctuating the final moments. As such, there is a visual circularity that *120 BPM* plays on through the motif of light, ending with the activists forged into poses by strobe's rapid flash. Their faces momentarily appear frozen in the orange tinge and blue-white glare of light; their hair seems suspended in mid-air as they sling their heads back in dancing abandon.

When examining film endings, Mulvey reads cinema's negotiation of stasis and action as enacting Freud's theory of the death drive, an unconscious compulsion to return to an original inert state. Mulvey suggests this connection by observing how cinema gives an impression of stillness with its mechanical revving of photographic images into movement, and by studying narrative designs that open and close with a reduction of motion. To exemplify the narrative formulas that generate such circularity, Mulvey cites cinema's "two grand conventions of narrative closure, devices that allow the drive of a story to return to stasis: death or marriage", as well as versions of these tropes, including the final screen kiss, characters dying together and the freeze-frame ending.[29]

Gene Youngblood observes a similar connection between death and stunted motion, which he likens to strobe when reflecting upon the use of stop-motion in Ronald Nameth's short film *Exploding Plastic Inevitable*, which documented Andy Warhol's art and performance events of the same name. For Youngblood, "[w]atching the film is like dancing in a strobe room" as the freeze-frames "generate a sense of timelessness".[30] Referencing the photographic index of film, the static frame is literally the death of the image: we are instantly cut off from the illusion of cinematic life – the immediacy of motion – and the image suddenly is relegated to the motionless past, leaving in its place a pervading aura of melancholy.[31]

Youngblood suggests that the use of stillness hinders us from being swept up in the film's appearance of regular time. In particular, "the final shots of Gerard Malanga tossing his head in slow motion and freezing in several positions create a ghostlike atmosphere, a timeless and ethereal mood that lingers and haunts long after the images fade".[32] Unlike cinema's conventional movement that replicates regular time, stillness in film alerts us to how time has passed by breaking up movement to reveal the captured instant as halted and no longer animated, a slice of dead time rather than life resurrected.

120 BPM conforms to the narrative convention of returning to stasis as identified by Mulvey. During Sean's political funeral, strobe and its emphasis on stillness thematically join with the non-diegetic music's abrupt halt on the final cut to black. As Mulvey argues, "[t]he silence of 'The End' duplicates the silence of death itself but it also signifies total erasure, the nothing that lies beyond it".[33] In this gesture, *120 BPM*'s final moment manifests ACT UP's slogan SILENCE = DEATH by closing with a combined gesture of narrativised death and a pronounced muting of all sound, which does not resume even as the end credits roll. The silent, black screen encourages us to reflect on death in the context of HIV, including those deaths not portrayed in the film but whose vast numbers haunt the text. The extinguishing of the entirety of the representational plane that consolidates the film's depicted world enhances the poignancy of this final note. With singular and collective death situated in concert with the foreclosure of the filmic text, AIDS as an instance of historical trauma that cannot be contained by the specificity of the diegetic realm is evoked at the point that the field of signification reaches its limit.[34]

For Brinkema, darkness functions as an optical metaphor for mourning in the "long-standing Western philosophical and theological tradition of figuring suffering in relation to loss as a problematic of vision and visibility".[35] In the context of the AIDS epidemic, *120 BPM* suggests a corporeal precarity by introducing lighting schemas that emphasise optical opacity. As in *120 BPM*, artist Mat Collishaw offers up absence as a form of visual content to inventively examine how confusion at the borders of visibility suggests loss. Examination of Collishaw's installation *In Camera*, exhibited at the Library of Birmingham in 2015, sheds light on *120 BPM* by drawing attention to the photographic process which, as expressed by André Bazin, "embalms time" to present an aesthetic and temporal moment otherwise extinguished.[36]

Like *120 BPM*, *In Camera* utilises strobe to draw attention to the mechanism of photography on display and the representational substance of life and death that the content and context of the photographs negotiate.

Collishaw's installation consists of twelve photographic images featuring local crime scenes from the 1930s and 1940s. Having discovered the photographs in the Library of Birmingham's photography collections, Collishaw reprinted them in a phosphorescent ink that momentarily holds light before mounting them in Perspex boxes.[37] Freestanding lights intermittently turn on and off throughout the space, resurrecting the otherwise invisible images for a few seconds. The grain of the film's emulsion, similar to that of ashes, appears suspended in the cuboid structures. The illuminating bursts do not animate the photographs but exhibit otherwise forgotten scenes and remind viewers that the victims of whatever crimes the pictured environments are emptied of cannot return to either image or world. The photographic negative is reimagined in the negative space left behind after a burst of irregular brilliance allows for momentary glimpses of the pictures. As one navigates the erratic beams, the gallery is transformed into a shadowy maze that abruptly reveals ghostly images, inviting visitors to find contradictions and connections between the staging of light and the exposure of scenes emptied of life following some unseen crime whose remnants are captured 'in camera'. As with the strobing light in *120 BPM*, the site/sight of absence makes its mark in the spatial coordinates of the image to suggest death as an elimination of content, diminishing all trace of representation, including that of the body and the space it once inhabited.

If, according to Brinkema, "[t]he visual field, in mourning, is reduced entirely to its blind spot", then *120 BPM*'s strobing sequences can be interpreted as forging planes of uncertain opacity that set the stage for loss. It uses inconsistent lighting to introduce a gap in the field of vision, which lingers and repeats without obliterating the scene until the final cut.[38] As with Collishaw's erratic illumination of photographic scenes in *In Camera, 120 BPM*'s recurrent strobing and dust motif recode corporeal precarity by drawing attention to the cinematic apparatus, which is always in the process of resurrection. As Mulvey reminds us, the cinema "animates its still frames, so it brings back to life, in perfect fossil form, anyone it has ever recorded, from great star to fleeting extra".[39] *120 BPM* resurrects a time that resurrects a time; its historical past is retold in the moment of its making and then again in the time of its viewing.

The film's rendition of history maintains a pointed political evaluation of the time. Numerous scenes explicitly discuss how HIV spreads, including individual sexual practices and broader institutional regimes that neglect vulnerable populations. During their romantic relationship, Nathan and Sean disclose their different HIV statuses, are shown using protection during sex and engage in intimate conversations about how Sean contracted HIV and how Nathan managed to avoid it. Beyond engaging with personal narratives of transmission and living with the disease, the ACT UP group uses diverse tactics to inform people about the risk of infection. These include staging direct actions at pharmaceutical companies and schools, holding formal meetings and lobbying drug companies and governmental bodies.

At times, the deployment of different tactics creates tensions in the group, leading to scenes where members argue about the value of more or less 'diplomatic' modes of engagement. Viewers are offered an insight into the operations of various sectors, social pressures and politics at play in HIV infection and prevention. By presenting the disease through its associated activism, the film suggests that an individual's contraction is more complicated than personal responsibility. Instead, the systemic devaluing of lives – particularly those of gay men, sex workers, intravenous drug users and incarcerated people – produces circumstances that allow HIV to flourish, which the ACT UP members repeatedly draw attention to throughout the film. While offering a series of complex discussions concerning HIV, *120 BPM* is a localised and necessarily incomplete view of its historical period and resists locating a primary cause or solution to the public health crisis at its heart. In this sense, the strobing scenes offer a visual parlance of incompletion that is suggestive of the film more generally, as it does not purport to be a conclusive representation of its time and place. If stillness, silence and darkness are the absence of movement, sound and light and are used to infer varying registers of physical and symbolic death, strobe's volatility points to that which marks a stain on the surface of vision, that traumatic dimension of history that resists symbolisation and, here, finds its partial signifier in 'AIDS'.

Concluding with strobe lighting, *120 BPM* intensifies the stakes of absence in the cinematic plane of representation as we move closer towards the final sealing of the diegetic world previously constructed. Other films have also used strobe in their closing departure from their otherwise coherent aesthetic and narrative schemas to suggest how absence and presence hinge upon regimes of light and movement in the cinematic arts. For instance, the 'extreme cinema' film *Irréversible* is constructed in reverse chronological order, opening into the final scene of the fabula and closing with the earliest. Beginning with a gruesome fight involving a fire hydrant and a notoriously long mid-point graphic rape scene of one of the central characters, Alex (Monica Bellucci), the film ends with Alex reading in a park. The camera homes in on Alex as it travels through an open window in the previous scene, giving no immediate indication that we have retreated further back in time. With one of Noé's now-signature disorientating and remarkably long takes, the camera films Alex from above and upside down before rising upward and spinning as children play around a sprinkler below. As the camera's spinning increases, it tilts up to the sky until clouds bleach the screen and strobing fills it with increasing intensity. As with *120 BPM, Irréversible*'s use of strobe retreats from the realist address the film otherwise maintains. This effect is particularly striking during *Irréversible* as the hypnotic strobing takes over the frame. The result is similar to that generated by Tony Conrad's 1966 experimental film *The Flicker*, a thirty-minute piece comprised exclusively of black and white frames, which moves through rhythmic variations to create an intense strobing effect. In the case of all three of these film works, the screen is distilled to a pure surface that rejects the typical illusion of depth as it is patterned only with its most rudimentary element – light.

The Negative Present

To resituate *120 BPM*'s meditation on AIDS activism at the intersections of form and history, I turn now to Bersani's seminal essay "Is the Rectum a Grave?", which introduces the concept of enjoyment into the discussion of AIDS. The essay opens with a quote from Professor Opendra Narayan from the Johns Hopkins Medical School. Narayan claims that AIDS emerged as a consequence of gay men's capacity and excessive appetite for numerous sexual partners in a short space of time: "These people have sex twenty to thirty times a night. [...] When this is practised for a year [...] one can readily understand this massive epidemic that is currently upon us."[40] Bersani details the intersecting dynamics of race and sexuality in the social sphere of the then-contemporary United States before examining how enjoyment uniquely clings to homosexuality during this time. By concentrating on the discursive framing of homosexuals as killers, Bersani identifies media reports that present gay men as actively encouraging the spread of AIDS, despite this population being disproportionally affected.[41]

In locating the "fantasmatic logic" that reads homosexuals as homicidal, the essay highlights the "startling resemblance [...] to the representation of female prostitutes in the nineteenth century 'as contaminated vessels', conveyancing 'female' venereal diseases to 'innocent men'" and the "specific sexual heroics of their promiscuity".[42] Women and gay men are said to engage in sex that exceeds the limits of reproduction, distilled in "male fantasies about women's multiple orgasms" and anal sex's "potential for multiple orgasms having spread from the insertee to the insertor" as indicated by the essay's opening quote from Narayan.[43] AIDS and female sexuality become concentrated in a fantasy of promiscuity which, "far from merely increasing the risk of infection, is the sign of infection". Identifying a cultural connection between non-reproductive sex and death, Bersani cites the belief that "[w]omen and gay men spread their legs with an unquenchable appetite for destruction".[44] Acknowledging the sustained framing of homosexuality as moral deviance that Bersani establishes, *120 BPM*'s titular numerical value, '120', echoes the Marquis de Sade's 1785 erotic novel *120 Days of Sodom*.[45] While not a retelling of de Sade's book, the film establishes a numerical link to the biblical tale of Sodom and Gomorrah from the Book of Genesis, associated with the evangelical condemnation of homosexuality. The film's riffing off "120 Days of Sodom" is recontextualised by 'BPM/beats per minute', a dance music tempo that returns as a heartbeat leitmotif throughout the film.

Without endorsing the portrayal of gay men as killers or deserving of AIDS, Bersani investigates how enjoyment finds a subversive registration in the subculture of male homosexuality. Returning to Freud's "Three Essays on the Theory of Sexuality", first published in 1905, Bersani draws on the idea that "sexual pleasure occurs whenever a certain threshold of intensity is reached, when the organization of the self is momentarily disturbed by sensations or affective processes somehow 'beyond' those connected with psychic organization".[46] For Bersani, Freud's articulation of sexual pleasure "interrupts the more secure narrative outline of the history of desire" and

> return[s] to a line of speculation in which the opposition between pleasure and pain becomes irrelevant, in which the sexual emerges as the *jouissance* of exploded limits, as the ecstatic suffering into which the human organism momentarily plunges when it is 'pressed' beyond a certain threshold of endurance.[47]

This affective intensity, in which the self is 'shattered' and "the risk of the sexual itself [is] the risk of self-dismissal, of *losing sight* of the self", is read through the figure of the 'passive' male homosexual (who receives rather than penetrates during sex) and the woman.[48] Returning to the nightclub scenes of *120 BPM*, we encounter bodies that we *lose sight of* and who lose sight of one another under the pulsations of strobe. These sequences visualise Bersani's articulation of jouissance as that which exceeds the visible and situates enjoyment as an affect that writes the homosexual as a deviant figure.

The use of strobe produces a cinematic environment that brings enjoyment and subversion into the context of AIDS. A similar combination occurs in the opening scene of the vampire action film *Blade*, which follows the alluring Racquel (Traci Lords) as she leads an enthusiastic Dennis (Kenny Johnson) through an indoor meat market. Here, the naive and excitable Dennis glimpses suspiciously human-shaped carcasses hanging between the butchered animals, before a burly man opens a weighty door that leads into an underground nightclub. Inside, the room is full of dancing bodies. Time ripples in and out of slow motion as the DJ plays repetitive techno music. Strobe lighting hits the dancers from multiple angles, flickering across faces and carving silhouettes, distorting movement and time. The film cuts between medium shots of the crowd and close-ups from within it. Strobes form white highlights across an otherwise blue-washed room. Energetic bodies are pale as if cold to the touch, despite their tightly packed formations. Raquel's hair, Dennis's shirt and the opening credits at the edges of the screen are pops of red against the otherwise cool tones. By setting this opening scene in an underground club, the film introduces the crowd – soon revealed as vampires – as a subcultural community, with strobe visualising their nocturnal lifestyle that is awakened in darkness and put to sleep during daylight. Suggestive of cinema's ability to hesitate at the borders of stillness and movement, strobe reproduces figures as shifting between lively and inert, stilled before revving into animation once again. As in *120 BPM*, figures disappear and reappear under this dynamic lighting, thematising a liminal space between life and death that the characters negotiate in the narrative. While HIV is an explicit theme in *120 BPM, Blade* displaces the threat of infection on to the vampires who distil fears of contamination through the exchange of bodily fluids in the shadow of the AIDS crisis.

Neither alive nor dead, the vampires feed off human life to sustain their own. *Blade* stages a meeting of eroticism and horror as the opening scene sees Dennis's dancing become increasingly overconfident and out of place. His arms forge jerky lines among the ease of other dancers who bounce with the music's tempo and align with the dips in time. A woman, bleached out by her peroxide hair in two bouncing bunches, her shiny white jacket and skin that is almost blue, moves erratically. Unlike the homogeneous 'outside' perception in *120 BPM* that perceives all involved with ACT UP as HIV positive, Dennis's human (and, therefore, uninfected) blood is immediately detected by the vampiric crowd who peer at him with curiosity as drops of blood begin to land on his hands from above. As his glance moves upward, the arms of many dancers rise behind him before blood sprays from the overhead sprinkler system, raining down upon the room. At this moment, the building becomes an architectural body with blood running through its piped arteries before releasing to drench the crowd. The meeting of life and death that the nightclub proposes is not anxiety-producing for the club-goers but a deviant enjoyment expressed by their hedonistic appetites as they swarm to take a bite out of Dennis's flesh.

In concert with the self-reflexive qualities that strobe alludes to with its play of stasis of action, there is a vampiric quality sustained in the environment of the cinema itself as the viewing theatre omits natural daylight to better project its artificial light. The screen brings to life that which is otherwise inert and renders immortal the image of the filmed subject. As well as drawing attention to film's materiality, *Blade*'s use of strobe also suggests lighting's racialised history. As the flickering illumination accentuates the vampires' lightness of skin, the technical function of cinematic lighting becomes more noticeable. As Richard Dyer observes, Hollywood lighting techniques developed in part to give white skin a brighter appearance in pictures.[49] As film depends on light, and is indeed a medium *of* light, light and the racial category of whiteness inform one another in the early motion picture industry and its continued legacy. *Blade* alludes to the racializing effect of light by presenting the vampires' skin as illuminated by the quality of the artificial beams, in contrast to natural light, which would presumably dissolve this very organ and which the casting of black actor Wesley Snipes as the titular vampire-killing hero brings to the fore. The vampires appear drained of 'colour' and are juxtaposed with Blade, whom the film introduces as the opening blood frenzy reaches its crescendo.

As Dennis crawls along the floor in an attempt to escape the ravenous vampires in the nightclub, Blade's imposing frame blocks his path. The camera pans up to mimic Dennis's sightline, stopping short of the face; Blade is a pillar of black leather, black skin wrapping black skin. His body, reinforced by his armour-like attire, starkly contrasts with the patrons, whose blood-soaked appearance makes their insides and outsides indistinguishable. As such, strobe's flicker not only prefigures a vampiric embodiment but also gestures towards a concern with lightness and darkness that cuts across the film's representation of racialised difference.

In a later scene, haematologist Karen (N'Bushe Wright) examines a vampire's blood, producing a more obvious analogy between the figure of the vampire and AIDS. The screen fills with Karen's perspective through a microscope, demonstrating how the vampiric mutation occurs at a molecular level not otherwise apparent, much like the decreased white blood cell count that may indicate early HIV infection but that outside appearances may not show. Later in the film, Karen talks with Deacon Frost (Stephen Dorff), the leader of a vampire gang who refuses to assimilate into human society. During their conversation, Karen reinforces the vampire as a paranoid allegory for AIDS, stating that "vampires like you aren't a species, you're just infected, a virus, a sexually transmitted disease", a form of transmission established nowhere else in the film's narrative.

Blade and *120 BPM* are immediately distinct in their genres and framing of AIDS. Whereas *Blade* casts vampires as a metaphor for AIDS and the enjoyment associated with its transmission, *120 BPM* uses a realist address, centring ACT UP activists fighting against the systemic prejudices facing those who have AIDS and the marginalised populations at heightened risk of exposure. Despite such palpable differences, both films integrate scenes of enjoyment under the shadow of AIDS by employing strobe and flickering lighting. In *120 BPM*, the frame writes loss across bodies that teeter on physical precarity as they slip in and out of light's threshold. However, this inscription of loss extends to a broader negation of fixity in the visual field that implicates and exceeds the film's historical specificity and relates to the topology of the drive as developed in Lacanian scholarship.

Edelman offers the drive as a way to read queerness as the limit to, rather than an embodiment of, identity. In the opening chapter of *No Future*, "The Future Is Kid Stuff", Edelman sketches a paradigm of "reproductive futurism" that his formulation of queerness opposes. Here, the child stands for "the fantasmatic beneficiary of every political intervention" that attempts to foreclose the symbolic order's negative dimension.[50] The queer refuses this foreclosure by

> expos[ing] the obliquity of our relation to what we experience in and as social reality, alerting us to the fantasies structurally necessary [...] to sustain it and engaging those fantasies through the figural logics, the linguistic structures, that shape them.[51]

As outlined in the introduction of this chapter, the signifier installs a gap in meaning that functions as the support for desire and maintains lack as a structural and irrevocable dimension of the subject. Rather than seeking coherent identities through a disavowal of lack, Edelman – following Bersani – situates the queer as engaging in a jouissance registered in the failure of meaning inherent in symbolic organisation.[52] Edelman's understanding of queer echoes that structure of the Lacanian drive where the *objet a* is circulated but never attained, thus prying open lack rather than colluding in attempts to patch it over. The drive "marks the excess embedded within the Symbolic through the loss, the Real loss, that the advent of the signifier effects".[53] Within the tripartite Lacanian order of meaning (the real, the imaginary and the symbolic), Edelman emphasises the real when situating queerness. As the point of structural absence, the real implies a fragility in subjectivity that the fantasy of identity represses, and that commodities promising to help us realise 'our true selves' distil in the public arena.

Considering Bersani's and Edelman's interventions in queer theory, the formal coordinates of *120 BPM*'s numerous dance scenes can suggest a site of jouissance. In these sequences, viewers encounter absence as bodies drift through pockets of illumination that swirl across the surfaces of torsos and faces. Skin and fabrics bear light's brief impressions like screens, intercepting its travel to reveal glimmers of visual information. Figures are formally dissected and reduced to discrete, fleeting features. Light is cast in veins or specks in the nightclub, rendering the corporeal boundaries indistinguishable, reduced to the mass of shadow that dominates the frame, and causing bodies to disintegrate and partition – a shoulder, a chin, a face, a nose. Divided into pieces, they no longer appear whole. The erratic lighting makes the formal properties of movement indiscernible even as it remains comprehensible in the diegesis; as spectators, we can fill in the gaps of the image with the action we are not privy to visually. Nonetheless, strobe carves out spaces of relative darkness and creates temporal episodes that linger in obscured action and the repetitive beat of the soundtrack. Because of their formal distinction, these sequences are placed in relief from the rest of the film, even as they are integrated into its main body through editing. Rather than saddling action in narrative perpetuation, the two central nightclub scenes and the final strobe sequence become episodes of narrative decompression.

The film's diegetic concern with HIV situates bodies in pronounced proximity to death. At the same time, the mise-en-scène enacts Edelman's description of the queer's threat to the "hope [...] of filling the constitutive gap in the subject that the signifier necessarily installs" as distortive lighting renders bodies incoherent and fragmented.[54] Such framing problematises the imaginary wholeness of the figures by refusing to 'close the gap' in the image, creating a diagrammatic screen that uses the pictorial plane to describe the symbolic order's fundamental incompletion in the realm of representation. As with the topology of the Lacanian drive, the subject's perpetually 'missing piece' is not filled by the regime of the image but exemplified in the stark gap that is orbited and never resolved into visual clarity. The temporal illusion of strobing alludes to the construction of the cinematic image, allowing these scenes to traverse the impression of cohesion that the film format generally achieves. The distortive effect on movement and the perception of bodies in time come together in the diegetic depiction of enjoyment to coordinate an understanding of queerness as theorised by Edelman.

In conjunction with the sense of enjoyment that the nightclub scenes engender, *120 BPM*'s sexual encounters formally overlap with the strobe sequences. Nathan and Sean first have sex after dancing in the nightclub, and, when Nathan and Thibault have sex, it cuts through the film's closing stroboscopic scene. In both instances, strobe lighting admits a porous passage between distinct temporal and spatial planes. During the second nightclub scene, Nathan and Sean drop in and out of visibility as they move through textured pockets of coloured illumination on the dance floor. With cuts between medium close-ups of the two men, we detect the shrinking distance between them as their bodies bob and weave to the music, at times receding into black-on-black silhouettes. As they draw closer, the darkness of the nightclub and the editorial cutting become indistinguishable. Dancing becomes only a flurry of rustles in the dark as arms reach for one another: hands pull a shirt from a torso, the light from the nightclub faintly playing across a shoulder. Then, no dancing lights; a scramble out of clothes as bodies tumble across a barely perceptible bed, movement a glint in the faintest light on a white bed sheet, presumably seeping in from the dusky nighttime outside.

Preceding the later sex scene between Nathan and Thibault, the framing of the two men is reminiscent of a celluloid film strip. Sean has recently died, and, during the intimate wake at the apartment he and Nathan have recently moved into, Nathan asks Thibault to return later that evening. As they talk in the kitchen, a window separates them into neighbouring cells. The following shot repeats this formation as it coincides with Nathan's perspective of his fellow activists in one room and Sean's body in the next. The two spaces are separated by a wall partitioning the apartment, which stands as a dark mass that returns negative space to the frame and separates the living from the dead. The final scene depicting Sean's funeral is interspersed with shots of Nathan and Thibault's erotic encounter, initially filmed in a low light that contrasts with the well-lit hall where the group scatter Sean's ashes. By bridging these scenes, the film's editing closes the distance between distinct moments in time while retaining their formal heterogeneity that alternately privileges darkness and light to produce a formal precursor to the upcoming strobe which breaks from the diegetic realism as it floods both settings.

As well as constructing a mise-en-scène that suggests the cinematic format, *120 BPM*'s strobe scenes manifest Edelman's figure of the queer who stages a refusal of reproductive futurism, cast as the reigning metaphor for normativity. Before explicating this connection, foregrounded in Bersani, Edelman notes that the "conflation of homosexuality with [...] radical negativity" persists, despite widespread efforts to "normalize queer sexualities within a logic of meaning that finds realization only *in* and *as* the future".[55] The example of homosexual couples who enter structures of the nuclear family and child-rearing best exemplifies how 'queer sexualities' may engage with a process of normalisation that performs Edelman's schema of reproductive futurism.

In contrast to the proliferating of the family, Edelman returns to a view that positions homosexuals as "the gravediggers of society, those who care nothing [for] the future", as pronounced by François Abadie.[56] These are the homosexuals who bear "the lethal counterweight of narcissism, AIDS, and death, all of which spring from commitment to the meaningless eruptions of jouissance associated with the 'circuit parties' that gesture toward the circuit of the drive".[57] *120 BPM*'s characterisations recreate Edelman's queer as the film centres men with different HIV statuses having sex, edited in a visual continuum with dancing in the nightclub. In this move, *120 BPM* suggests an embodiment of homosexuality delinked from future 'progress' and relinked to AIDS and the parties Edelman names as registers of jouissance. Filmed with the prominent lighting design detailed, *120 BPM* inaugurates a sense of jouissance as bodies engaged in sex, dance and protest are simultaneously connected and distorted by the darkness that returns to stain the image.

(Turning One's) Back to the Future

In *Out of Time*, McGowan situates the "subject of the drive" as an ethical position that rethinks a relation between time and desire. The book analyses anachronic films such as *21 Grams* (2003), *The Butterfly Effect* (2004) and *The Constant Gardener* (2005) to establish a trend of non-linear narrative cinema that emerged in the 1990s and early 2000s, influenced by the increased ubiquity of the internet. For McGowan, cinematic atemporality departs from the logic of desire and instead performs the logic of the drive by elaborating narrative structures that repeat loss rather than depict satiation. For example, McGowan likens *The Constant Gardener*'s atemporal mode to the feminine position, embodied in the film by Tessa (Rachel Weisz), an activist investigating the corrupt British and American pharmaceutical industry operating in Africa.[58] Tessa's position is later taken up (in the film's fabula) by Justin (Ralph Fiennes), a British diplomat who develops a romantic relationship with Tessa and investigates the suspicious circumstances of her death. McGowan aligns the feminine with the drive, which he characterises as "one liv[ing] in a constant state of emergency in which no better future awaits and in which the necessity of the political act becomes exigent".[59] In this political drama, Tessa pursues that which can be effected in the 'here and now' rather than dismissing small changes as insignificant compared with an overall transformation of the broader socio-political system.

The drive formalises Tessa's characterisation that embraces partiality rather than totality in the social order, and the film's atemporal structure enacts this partiality by interrupting linearity and narrative completion. Justin's political transformation from the masculine to the feminine position, and from desire to drive, develops through his proximity to Tessa. As such, McGowan argues that *The Constant Gardener*'s anachronic structure "breaks from an everyday or ideological conception of time" that moves in a forward linear direction and communicates Justin's ethical reorientation.[60]

120 BPM does not fit into McGowan's category of atemporal film as its action occurs in chronological order, save for moments where characters recollect previous occurrences that the film relays. Neither does *120 BPM* reject the future per se as, it should be noted, ACT UP's strategy in the film includes alerting people to the risk of AIDS and its potential to cut their future short. Nonetheless, McGowan's thesis on atemporality develops a reading of cinema that introduces an important political slant to my interrogation of strobe lighting and its relation to loss and jouissance. For McGowan, atemporal films call attention to the gaps in narrative construction and curate a repetition of loss, interrupting capitalist fantasies of completion. By repositioning McGowan's analysis from syuzhet structure to mise-en-scène, strobe can indicate an ethical and political adjustment to absence and temporal distortion on screen.

In the introduction to *Out of Time*, McGowan succinctly compares drive and desire: Whereas "[d]esire represents a belief that a satisfying object exists and can be obtained [...] the drive locates enjoyment in the movement of return itself[,] the repetition of the loss, rather than in what might be recovered".[61] The shift from the logic of desire to drive suggests a reorientation to loss. Embracing lack, rather than seeking to remedy it, helps us to recognise that "[w]hat we have in common is what we don't have rather than anything we do".[62] In *120 BPM*'s nightclub scenes, strobe formally suggests McGowan's reading of absence as a social link as it transforms the image of the dancing crowd. In contrast with the scenes that centre the conversing, negotiating, planning and protesting around which the drama otherwise revolves, the nightclub maintains a visual commonality as figures merge in pockets of darkness.

McGowan's theorising of "[l]oss as our common constitutive event" designates drive as social, in contrast to Edelman, who establishes the drive as an *anti-social* modality.[63] While maintaining Edelman's thesis on queer as a relationship to the jouissance of the drive, McGowan's interpretation reframes *120 BPM*'s insistence on lack in the visual field as a social marker. Despite this seeming opposition between McGowan's and Edelman's interpretations of the drive, both read it as a radical departure from the paradigm of future satisfaction. McGowan articulates capitalism's reliance on the future as implicitly encouraging subjects to believe they "can see the realization of [...] desire":

> Though this future never comes – one obtains objects but never the object – and the subject's desire necessarily remains unrealized, the idea that desire might be realized has the effect of keeping desire alive, which is crucial to the functioning of capitalism as a socioeconomic system.[64]

Whereas Edelman associates the drive with a refusal of 'reproductive futurism', of which 'all politics' is on the side, McGowan interprets the drive as an ethical departure from the demands of capitalism. However, as outlined in this book's introduction, these theorists overlap as both propose the drive as a relationship to lack that refuses the promise of futurity.

McGowan considers how drive resonates with the cinematic apparatus in his chosen texts and studies the interdependence of syuzhet and fabula arrangements. Like Mulvey's analysis of the relationship between the drive, film endings and the mechanics of stasis and action, McGowan argues that cinematic editing can demonstrate "a gap in cinematic time in which an absence repeats itself", which "corresponds to the death drive".[65] As atemporal cinema uses editing to rearrange time in a pronounced way, the gap in chronology is emphasised in the films' constructions rather than hidden in continuity editing, designed to render seams between shots and scenes unnoticeable.

McGowan argues that conventional time in film corresponds to the logic of capitalism as both require investment in the illusion of linearity. As previously outlined, capitalism's appeal and success depend on a belief that acquiring commodities will be satisfying, even though this is an impossibility for the subject of language. Like capitalism's attempts to veil the insufficiency of the commodity, cinematic conventions rely on an inability to comprehend "the absence that constitutes the image".[66] Charting the development of motion pictures, Mary Ann Doane cites how the "deficiency of the human body" allows us to view photographic frames as in continuous movement rather than still images.[67] Similarly, McGowan maintains that "[s]uccessful film spectatorship relies on a certain failure of perception" that masks the stasis of the photographic index and editing's traversal of space and time.[68]

To synthesise a dual investigation into cinematic and capitalist time, McGowan reads the failure to perceive absence in the temporal and visual field as an optical and ideological blind spot. Not only are we unable to perceive how stasis underpins projected movement, but we also miss how the promise of satiation repeatedly staged by cinema's formal and social conventions veils our lack. McGowan summarises the relationship between cinematic and capitalist temporality by describing how the "traditional pleasure a film offers relies on a failure to recognize the illusory status of the promise of change" as it depicts subjects moving from dissatisfaction to satisfaction.[69] Across genres, it is overwhelmingly the formation of a monogamous heterosexual romantic couple that designates an end to the search for the object of desire, reinforcing how heteronormative relations serve to consolidate broader social relations in the capitalist arena. Capitalism's concealing of the impossibility of fulfilment echoes cinema's concealment of its discrete static frames and gaps in time. This comparison considers how the mechanics of the moving image coincide with the capitalist ideology that permeates the majority of conventional cinema.

In contrast with linearity, its psychic appeal and subsequent political orientation, *120 BPM*'s strobing mise-en-scène departs from the inscription of capitalist temporality by breaking up perceptible movement and creating a mimesis of static frames. During the nightclub scenes, lighting and music create an environment that maintains diegetic realism while introducing a distinguished soundscape and visual milieu. Dancing is not staged as an 'event' in the same manner as the protests are, with defined motives. Rather, the sequences become pressurised spaces of the 'now', released from the forward trajectory and anger that angle the protests as amplifications of the urgent need for change. Inside the nightclub, characters do not make demands. While one might assume that the club is a commercial space and, therefore, operates on a capitalist logic of exchange, the film's diegesis does not evidence this as we do not see characters pay a cover free to enter, nor are they drawn away from the dancefloor and towards the bar. Instead, they exist amid their dancing enjoyment, which turns away from the future – pessimistic or hopeful – that the depicted historical moment of the AIDS crisis otherwise inflects.

Preceding the first nightclub scene, the ACT UP participants pile into a metro carriage following their release from jail after protesting at the Melton Pharm offices, which are withholding "the toxicity results of its protease inhibitor".[70] Seen through the train's window, reflections of the moving cityscape pass over Sean's and Nathan's faces. Near the end of this scene, cross-cuts between the flickering Parisian city viewed from the train and the strobe light of the nightclub weave together, introducing the first nightclub scene as an extension of overt political action.

Other scholars have similarly read the nightclub in connection to the ACT UP demonstrations by examining this early transition from protest to dance. Alice Pember argues that the film's soundtrack brings heterogeneous spaces into contact as a "sound bridge connects the house track that the activists are shown dancing to in the club to the cityscape of Paris they pass through on the train".[71] This use of music "underscores the dancefloor's function as an extension of the Melton Pharm protest", developing "the connection between activism and clubbing".[72] Pember does not comment on the specific use of lighting as a self-reflexive cinematic motif. However, she describes how the film departs from linearity as its "sonic landscapes and phenomenological appeal of its dance scenes enmesh the viewer in an alternative temporality that approximates the disruptively queer club time experienced by its characters".[73] Pember specifies how the camera's mimesis of "the movement of a clubber on the floor" develops a distinct temporal schema as it "swirl[s] through the assembled bodies in a way that encourages the viewer to feel as if they are on the dancefloor themselves".[74] In this sense, the nightclub engenders an environment that formally departs from the film's more typical spatial and temporal coordinates while remaining tethered to the act of protest.

As discussed with reference to Mulvey, the film's flickering lighting distorts typical rhythms of sequential movement, emphasising cinematic time's illusory status. McGowan argues that atemporality in cinema can similarly bring the assembly of narrative film to the spectator's attention. In the film, *120 BPM*'s narratives of political resistance and the optical interruptions created by strobing operate in a similar mode to that which McGowan identifies in *The Constant Gardener*, whereby desire informs the film's arrangement of time and its narrative articulation of political and personal transformation. As strobe and editorial cutting combine to bring sites of protest and dance into a visual continuum, *120 BPM*'s narrative and aesthetic regimes coalesce to reframe political action and queer subjectivity on screen. In addition to amplifying a historical connection between activism and sexuality, the film suggests ways enjoyment redistributes political meaning, articulated by the distortion of strobe lighting.

Conclusion

On screen, strobe lighting introduces absence as a site of conceptual and visual importance that references cinema's mechanical development and history. By bringing together Mulvey's, Edelman's and McGowan's interpretations of drive, *120 BPM*'s incorporation of negative space is argued as manifesting a queer mise-en-scène that informs the film's portrayal of character, narrative and history. Combining the themes and aesthetic registers established throughout the film, *120 BPM* closes by employing strobe to stage an eruption that tears the diegetic 'reality'. During Sean's political funeral, which descends into a quasi-club scene cross-cut with Nathan and Thibault having sex, protest, death and sex coalesce under the formal insistence of strobe's negative space. The scene confronts viewers with a strobing that inexplicably fills the room, departing from the visual consistency that typically characterises the diegetic screen. As the stroboscopic image conflicts with the illusion of movement, it creates the meta-cinematic aesthetic of stasis to confront viewers with film's mechanical and narrative processes. Following Mulvey's analysis of the Freudian death drive and cinematic conventions, *120 BPM*'s closing sense of inertia cuts across narrative and mise-en-scène, as the funeral and the appearance of stunted motion both suggest a return to stillness. In this move, the film connects the poignant narrative of death with an allusion to cinema's history.

At the same time, the scene shares a formulation with Edelman's structural analysis of queer as that which is always outside meaning. By studying the partitioning of bodies that strobe creates during the film's nightclub scenes, the visual field undoes the image of corporeal consistency. In its place, *120 BPM*'s graphic shattering of dancing bodies figures the jouissance described by Bersani and the critical proximity to lack that Edelman suggests when evoking the figure of the queer. This framing is later pronounced in the final scene as the diegesis cannot integrate the absence elicited by strobe into its realist address. The pulsations of bright light and deep shadow rupture the bodies on screen and the broader textual system, causing a shattering of the cinematic body as characters plunge into the throes of grieving ecstasy.

Strobe's distortion also affects temporality on screen. Instead of consistent movement through time, action is broken and ruptured. Scenes in *120 BPM* featuring strobe become unrestrained by the linearity that indicates a continuation of time into the future. Regarding McGowan's analysis of atemporality in cinema, which argues that narratives that depart from linearity rethink desire, the strobe sequences and their proximity to scenes of protest suggest a political orientation that manifests in the film's aesthetic and temporal registers as well as the diegetic action.

The film confronts viewers with an absence that stretches across the film's thematic and narrative concerns without turning that absence into a metaphor for displaced content through the process of substitution. The strobing in the final scene rearticulates the space into one akin to a nightclub. As the protesters transform into a crowd of dancing bodies, strobe returns as a visual motif to disintegrate the borders of political action, spaces of enjoyment, the staging of death and the coherence of bodily agency. The film achieves this complex meditation by drawing attention to the system of representation and its limitations. Through absence being made a palpable feature of the screen, spectators are confronted with the failure of signification. The film conducts a sense of queerness as lack becomes a structural feature of the visual, temporal and conceptual field, one that cannot be filled but returns in stroboscopic form to repeat again and again.

Notes

1 'Revolution, n., Sense II.7.a', Oxford English Dictionary (Oxford: Oxford University Press, July 2023), https://doi.org/10.1093/OED/5824374224.
2 'Revolution, n., Sense I.1.a', Oxford English Dictionary (Oxford: Oxford University Press, July 2023), https://doi.org/10.1093/OED/1069339941; 'Revolution, n., Sense I.5.b', Oxford English Dictionary (Oxford: Oxford University Press, July 2023), https://doi.org/10.1093/OED/4824460772.
3 'Stroboscope, n., Etymology', Oxford English Dictionary (Oxford: Oxford University Press, July 2023), https://doi.org/10.1093/OED/1117527008; '-Scope, Comb. Form, Etymology', Oxford English Dictionary (Oxford: Oxford University Press, July 2023), https://doi.org/10.1093/OED/3121545158.
4 Eugenie Brinkema, *The Forms of the Affects* (Durham: Duke University Press, 2014), 216.
5 Sabina Spielrein, 'Die Destruktion Als Ursache Des Wedens [Destruction as a Cause of Coming into Being]', *Jahrbuch Fur Psychoanalytische Und Psychopathologische Forschungen* 4, no. 1 (1912): 465–503. See also Fátima Caropreso, 'The Death Instinct and the Mental Dimension beyond the Pleasure Principle in the Works of Spielrein and Freud', *International Journal of Psychoanalysis* 98, no. 6 (2017): 1741–1762, https://doi.org/10.1111/1745-8315.12630; Sigmund Freud, *Beyond the Pleasure Principle and Other Writings*, trans. John Reddick (London, New York: Penguin Books, 2003), 43–102. This chapter uses Jacques Lacan's designation of 'drive', except when referring to the explicitly Freudian understanding of 'death drive', which preceded Lacan's development.
6 Sigmund Freud, *Beyond the Pleasure Principle and Other Writings*, trans. John Reddick (London, New York: Penguin Books, 2003), 71.
7 Sigmund Freud, *Beyond the Pleasure Principle and Other Writings*, trans. John Reddick (London, New York: Penguin Books, 2003), 78, emphasis in original.

8   Laura Mulvey, *Death 24× a Second: Stillness and the Moving Image* (London: Reaktion Books, 2006).
9   Jacques Lacan, *The Four Fundamental Concepts of Psycho-Analysis*, ed. Jacques-Alain Miller, trans. Alan Sheridan (Harmondsworth: Penguin, 1979), 178.
10 Jacques Lacan, *Écrits: A Selection*, trans. Alan Sheridan (London: Routledge, 1989), 68.
11 Lee Edelman, *No Future: Queer Theory and the Death Drive* (Durham: Duke University Press, 2004), 8.
12 Lee Edelman, *No Future: Queer Theory and the Death Drive* (Durham: Duke University Press, 2004), 8, emphasis in original.
13 Lee Edelman, *No Future: Queer Theory and the Death Drive* (Durham: Duke University Press, 2004), 8, emphasis in original.
14 Jacques Lacan, *The Four Fundamental Concepts of Psycho-Analysis*, ed. Jacques-Alain Miller, trans. Alan Sheridan (Harmondsworth: Penguin, 1979), 167.
15 '"Man," Freud writes, first appeared on earth "as a feeble animal organism," and no matter how far the society into which he is born has succeeded in making this earth serviceable to him, "each individual of the species must once more make its entry ('oh, inch of nature!') as a helpless suckling."' Sigmund Freud, *The Standard Edition of the Complete Psychological Works of Sigmund Freud. Vol. 21 (1927–1931), The Future of an Illusion; Civilization and Its Discontents and Other Works* (London: Hogarth Press and The Institute of Psycho-Analysis, 1961), cited in Joan Copjec, *Read My Desire: Lacan against the Historicists* (Cambridge: MIT Press, 1994), 42.
16 Joan Copjec, *Read My Desire: Lacan against the Historicists* (Cambridge: MIT Press, 1994), 42.
17 Jacques Lacan, *The Four Fundamental Concepts of Psycho-Analysis*, ed. Jacques-Alain Miller, trans. Alan Sheridan (Harmondsworth: Penguin, 1979), 180.
18 Jacques Lacan, *The Four Fundamental Concepts of Psycho-Analysis*, ed. Jacques-Alain Miller, trans. Alan Sheridan (Harmondsworth: Penguin, 1979), 180.
19 Jacques Lacan, *The Four Fundamental Concepts of Psycho-Analysis*, ed. Jacques-Alain Miller, trans. Alan Sheridan (Harmondsworth: Penguin, 1979), 186.
20 Leo Bersani, 'Is the Rectum a Grave?', *October* 43 (1987): 197–222, https://doi.org/10.2307/3397574.
21 Lee Edelman, *No Future: Queer Theory and the Death Drive* (Durham: Duke University Press, 2004).
22 Todd McGowan, *Capitalism and Desire: The Psychic Cost of Free Markets* (New York: Columbia University Press, 2016), 21.
23 Todd McGowan, *Capitalism and Desire: The Psychic Cost of Free Markets* (New York: Columbia University Press, 2016), 22.
24 See Todd McGowan, *The End of Dissatisfaction?: Jacques Lacan and the Emerging Society of Enjoyment* (Albany: State University of New York Press, 2004); Todd McGowan, *Enjoying What We Don't Have: The Political Project of Psychoanalysis* (Lincoln: University of Nebraska Press, 2013); Todd McGowan, *Capitalism and Desire: The Psychic Cost of Free Markets* (New York: Columbia University Press, 2016); Todd McGowan, *Universality and Identity Politics* (New York: Columbia University Press, 2020).
25 Todd McGowan, *Out of Time: Desire in Atemporal Cinema* (Minneapolis: University of Minnesota Press, 2011).
26 Jonas Mekas, *Movie Journal: The Rise of the New American Cinema, 1959–1971* (New York: Macmillan, 1972), 253.
27 Laura Mulvey, *Death 24× a Second: Stillness and the Moving Image* (London: Reaktion Books, 2006), 67.
28 Laura Mulvey, *Death 24× a Second: Stillness and the Moving Image* (London: Reaktion Books, 2006), 67.

29 Laura Mulvey, *Death 24× a Second: Stillness and the Moving Image* (London: Reaktion Books, 2006), 71.
30 Gene Youngblood and R. Buckminster Fuller, *Expanded Cinema: Fiftieth Anniversary Edition* (New York: Fordham University Press, 2020), 105.
31 Gene Youngblood and R. Buckminster Fuller, *Expanded Cinema: Fiftieth Anniversary Edition* (New York: Fordham University Press, 2020), 105.
32 Gene Youngblood and R. Buckminster Fuller, *Expanded Cinema: Fiftieth Anniversary Edition* (New York: Fordham University Press, 2020), 105.
33 Laura Mulvey, *Death 24× a Second: Stillness and the Moving Image* (London: Reaktion Books, 2006), 79.
34 Kaja Silverman, 'Historical Trauma and Male Subjectivity', in *Male Subjectivity at the Margins* (New York: Routledge, 1992), 52–121. 'Historical trauma' is discussed in detail in Chapter Two of this thesis.
35 Eugenie Brinkema, *The Forms of the Affects* (Durham: Duke University Press, 2014), 54.
36 André Bazin, 'The Ontology of the Photographic Image', trans. Hugh Gray, *Film Quarterly* 13, no. 4 (1960): 8, https://doi.org/10.2307/1210183.
37 'In Camera · Mat Collishaw', *Mat Collishaw* (blog), accessed 19 June 2023, https://matcollishaw.com/exhibitions/library-of-birmingham/.
38 Eugenie Brinkema, *The Forms of the Affects* (Durham: Duke University Press, 2014), 54.
39 Laura Mulvey, *Death 24× a Second: Stillness and the Moving Image* (London: Reaktion Books, 2006), 18.
40 Opendra Narayan, cited in Leo Bersani, 'Is the Rectum a Grave?', *October* 43 (1987): 197.
41 Leo Bersani, 'Is the Rectum a Grave?', *October* 43 (1987): 211.
42 Charles Bernheimer, cited by Leo Bersani, 'Is the Rectum a Grave?', *October* 43 (1987): 210–11.
43 Leo Bersani, 'Is the Rectum a Grave?', *October* 43 (1987): 211.
44 Leo Bersani, 'Is the Rectum a Grave?', *October* 43 (1987): 211.
45 Sade, Marquis de, *The 120 Days of Sodom, or, The School of Libertinage*, trans. Will McMorran and Thomas Wynn (London: Penguin Books, 2016).
46 Leo Bersani, 'Is the Rectum a Grave?', *October* 43 (1987): 217. See also Sigmund Freud, *On Sexuality: Three Essays on the Theory of Sexuality, and Other Works*, ed. Angela Richards, trans. James Strachey (Harmondsworth: Penguin, 1977).
47 Leo Bersani, 'Is the Rectum a Grave?', *October* 43 (1987): 217.
48 Leo Bersani, 'Is the Rectum a Grave?', *October* 43 (1987): 222, emphasis in original.
49 See 'Light and the photographic media' and 'Lighting for whiteness' in Richard Dyer, 'The Matter of Whiteness', in *White: Essays on Race and Culture* (London: Routledge, 2013), 84–103.
50 Lee Edelman, *No Future: Queer Theory and the Death Drive* (Durham: Duke University Press, 2004), 3.
51 Lee Edelman, *No Future: Queer Theory and the Death Drive* (Durham: Duke University Press, 2004), 6–7.
52 Lee Edelman, *No Future: Queer Theory and the Death Drive* (Durham: Duke University Press, 2004), 7.
53 Lee Edelman, *No Future: Queer Theory and the Death Drive* (Durham: Duke University Press, 2004), 9.
54 Lee Edelman, *No Future: Queer Theory and the Death Drive* (Durham: Duke University Press, 2004), 9.
55 Lee Edelman, *No Future: Queer Theory and the Death Drive* (Durham: Duke University Press, 2004), 74–75, emphasis in original.

56 Cited in Lee Edelman, *No Future: Queer Theory and the Death Drive* (Durham: Duke University Press, 2004), 114.
57 Lee Edelman, *No Future: Queer Theory and the Death Drive* (Durham: Duke University Press, 2004), 75.
58 Todd McGowan, *Out of Time: Desire in Atemporal Cinema* (Minneapolis: University of Minnesota Press, 2011), 113.
59 Todd McGowan, *Out of Time: Desire in Atemporal Cinema* (Minneapolis: University of Minnesota Press, 2011), 119.
60 Todd McGowan, *Out of Time: Desire in Atemporal Cinema* (Minneapolis: University of Minnesota Press, 2011), 113.
61 Todd McGowan, *Out of Time: Desire in Atemporal Cinema* (Minneapolis: University of Minnesota Press, 2011), 11.
62 Todd McGowan, *Out of Time: Desire in Atemporal Cinema* (Minneapolis: University of Minnesota Press, 2011), 15.
63 Todd McGowan, *Out of Time: Desire in Atemporal Cinema* (Minneapolis: University of Minnesota Press, 2011), 15.
64 Todd McGowan, *Out of Time: Desire in Atemporal Cinema* (Minneapolis: University of Minnesota Press, 2011), 27.
65 Todd McGowan, *Out of Time: Desire in Atemporal Cinema* (Minneapolis: University of Minnesota Press, 2011), xi.
66 Todd McGowan, *Out of Time: Desire in Atemporal Cinema* (Minneapolis: University of Minnesota Press, 2011), 32.
67 Mary Ann Doane, *The Emergence of Cinematic Time: Modernity, Contingency, the Archive* (Cambridge: Harvard University Press, 2002), 72.
68 Mary Ann Doane, *The Emergence of Cinematic Time: Modernity, Contingency, the Archive* (Cambridge: Harvard University Press, 2002), 72; Todd McGowan, *Out of Time: Desire in Atemporal Cinema* (Minneapolis: University of Minnesota Press, 2011), 32.
69 Todd McGowan, *Out of Time: Desire in Atemporal Cinema* (Minneapolis: University of Minnesota Press, 2011), 32.
70 In the contemporary day of the film, protease inhibitors are still in development. This treatment later became effective in prolonging the life of people with HIV.
71 Alice Pember, 'This Party Is Political: The Moving Politics of the Queer Dancefloor in 120 BPM (2017)', *Modern & Contemporary France* 30, no. 2 (3 April 2022): 151, https://doi.org/10.1080/09639489.2021.2008337.
72 Alice Pember, 'This Party Is Political: The Moving Politics of the Queer Dancefloor in 120 BPM (2017)', *Modern & Contemporary France* 30, no. 2 (3 April 2022): 150–151.
73 Alice Pember, 'This Party Is Political: The Moving Politics of the Queer Dancefloor in 120 BPM (2017)', *Modern & Contemporary France* 30, no. 2 (3 April 2022): 152–53.
74 Alice Pember, 'This Party Is Political: The Moving Politics of the Queer Dancefloor in 120 BPM (2017)', *Modern & Contemporary France* 30, no. 2 (3 April 2022): 151.

References

Bazin, André. 'The Ontology of the Photographic Image.' Translated by Hugh Gray. *Film Quarterly* 13, no. 4 (1960): 4–9. doi:10.2307/1210183.
Bersani, Leo. 'Is the Rectum a Grave?', *October* 43 (1987): 197–222. doi:10.2307/3397574.
Bersani, Leo. *No Future: Queer Theory and the Death Drive.* Durham: Duke University Press, 2004.

Brinkema, Eugenie. *The Forms of the Affects*. Durham: Duke University Press, 2014.

Caropreso, Fátima. 'The Death Instinct and the Mental Dimension beyond the Pleasure Principle in the Works of Spielrein and Freud.' *International Journal of Psychoanalysis* 98, no. 6 (2017): 1741–1762. doi:10.1111/1745-8315.12630.

Copjec, Joan. *Read My Desire: Lacan against the Historicists*. Cambridge: MIT Press, 1994.

Doane, Mary Ann. *The Emergence of Cinematic Time: Modernity, Contingency, the Archive*. Cambridge: Harvard University Press, 2002.

Dyer, Richard. *White: Essays on Race and Culture*. London: Routledge, 2013.

Edelman, Lee. *No Future: Queer Theory and the Death Drive*. Durham: Duke University Press, 2004.

Freud, Sigmund. *Beyond the Pleasure Principle and Other Writings*. Translated by John Reddick. London and New York: Penguin Books, 2003.

Freud, Sigmund. *On Sexuality: Three Essays on the Theory of Sexuality, and Other Works*. edited by Angela Richards, translated by James Strachey. Harmondsworth: Penguin, 1977.

Freud, Sigmund. *The Standard Edition of the Complete Psychological Works of Sigmund Freud. Vol. 21 (1927–1931)*. London: Hogarth Press and The Institute of Psycho-Analysis, 1961.

Lacan, Jacques. *Écrits: A Selection*. Translated by Alan Sheridan. London: Routledge, 1989.

Lacan, Jacques. *The Four Fundamental Concepts of Psycho-Analysis*. Edited by Jacques-Alain Miller. Translated by Alan Sheridan. Harmondsworth: Penguin, 1979.

Mekas, Jonas. *Movie Journal: The Rise of the New American Cinema, 1959–1971*. New York: Macmillan, 1972.

McGowan, Todd. *Capitalism and Desire: The Psychic Cost of Free Markets*. New York: Columbia University Press, 2016.

McGowan, Todd. *Enjoying What We Don't Have: The Political Project of Psychoanalysis*. Lincoln: University of Nebraska Press, 2013.

McGowan, Todd. *Out of Time: Desire in Atemporal Cinema*. Minneapolis: University of Minnesota Press, 2011.

McGowan, Todd. *The End of Dissatisfaction?: Jacques Lacan and the Emerging Society of Enjoyment*. Albany: State University of New York Press, 2004.

McGowan, Todd. *Universality and Identity Politics*. New York: Columbia University Press, 2020.

Mulvey, Laura. *Death 24× a Second: Stillness and the Moving Image*. London: Reaktion Books, 2006.

Oxford English Dictionary. Oxford: Oxford University Press. Accessed July 2023.

Pember, Alice. 'This Party Is Political: The Moving Politics of the Queer Dancefloor in 120 BPM (2017).' *Modern & Contemporary France*, 30, no. 2 (3 April 2022): 149–163. doi:10.1080/09639489.2021.2008337.

Sade, Marquis de. *The 120 Days of Sodom, or, The School of Libertinage*. Translated by Will McMorran and Thomas Wynn. London: Penguin Books, 2016.

Silverman, Kaja. *Male Subjectivity at the Margins*. New York: Routledge, 1992.

Spielrein, Sabina. 'Die Destruktion Als Ursache Des Werdens [Destruction as a Cause of Coming into Being].' *Jahrbuch für Psychoanalytische und Psychopathologische Forschungen* 4 (1912): 465–503.

Youngblood, Gene, and R. Buckminster Fuller. *Expanded Cinema: Fiftieth Anniversary Edition*. New York: Fordham University Press, 2020.

Coda

Unfixed and Open-Ended

Throughout this book, I have sought to elaborate how queerness and neoliberalism structure desire in different ways by analysing contemporary moving image works that subvert generic, temporal and aesthetic conventions. When deciding what constitutes queer media, we are overwhelmingly met with films and television series containing clearly definable LGBT+ characters and social issues related to these positions. In recent years, strategies of LGBT+ visibility and narrativisation are increasingly met with slogans, such as 'love is love', and grouped within 'pride collections' that couple sexuality and gender categories with positive affective affirmations. In contrast, *Taking Back Desire* argues for the value of locating queerness at the point that formal subversions emerge on screen.

The assimilation of people structured as 'other' into mainstream productions proposes to encourage tolerance and acceptance. However, I contend that such gestures often uphold, rather than challenge, the power imbalance necessary for capitalism's continued functioning. As a political and rhetorical device, tolerance has its limitations. In discussing the production of race, Karen E. Fields and Barbara J. Fields argue that tolerance is "a political precept" with "unimpeachably anti-democratic credentials, dividing society into persons entitled to claim respect as a right and persons obliged to beg for tolerance as a favor. [...] Tolerance thus bases equal rights on benevolent patronization rather than democratic first principles".[1] As potentially well-intentioned but misguided political strategies, calls for tolerance and representation of LGBT+ identities continue to reify what are commonly called gender, sex and sexuality as inherent and immutable attributes, even if heterosexuality's claim to naturalism is to some extent undermined. While I sympathise with the urge to address representation, this approach has its limitations when taken as the essential component in assessing what constitutes 'queer' media. By supporting identity categories as reality, their fictitious and constructed status goes unchallenged. Similarly, this book reads neoliberalism not only in characterisations and settings but also in the temporal and aesthetic registers of the selected texts to further problematise the notion that on-screen representations function as the central vehicle for political content.

DOI: 10.4324/9781003527244-6

Neoliberalism is particularly adept at transforming that which appears outside the 'norm' into a consumer market and, thereby, imposes and defines its own norms. In this political and economic schema, we are all potential consumers if only we could find the right product to make us a better version of ourselves, a product that would help us express who we 'really are'. David Alderson responds to the incorporation and media sensationalism of sexuality by articulating how the "freedom we are said to enjoy" in contemporary Western capitalism "resides almost exclusively in freedom of choice in the marketplace":

> It is the freedom that turns 'object choice' into consumer choice and legitimates it as a lifestyle (and that includes the family lifestyle and the diversification of it under 'equal marriage'), but it is also the freedom governed by the compulsion of repressive incitement. It is the freedom that is bound ineluctably to exploitative production, the freedom that carries ecologically catastrophic implications in the abundance it is promised, and the freedom that transforms all value into the singular norm of exchange value.[2]

As Alderson describes, capitalism now presents a formation of market-based economic policies that continue traditions of exploitation (of labour, of the ecosystem and of planetary resources) combined with social relations that insist on individualism and yet reduce identifications to the role of the commodity, which must enter the circuits of value and exchange. Written in 2016, Alderson's critique specifically details how male homosexuality has been invited into the neoliberal schema, suggesting that "gay sexuality has become a – maybe even *the* – privileged sign of the diversified dominant".[3]

Part of the strategy of neoliberalism and its translation into media has been the co-option of structurally marginalised positions, including those who identify as 'queer', into narratives of capitalist success. At times, it has felt somewhat troubling to launch a critique at media that centre subjects whose stories have been historically undervalued and ignored, given that these instances hold importance for people. This (often deliberate) oversight in media is especially true for those who struggle to find on-screen examples of people who share similar identity markers as themselves in mainstream film or television. The significance of such gestures of representation, as I understand it, stems from an acknowledgement that, while lack is inherited by all speaking subjects as they are 'written' into the symbolic order, this does not negate the way social reality and political hegemony distribute resources and injury in discriminatory patterns. As Mari Ruti writes,

> [t]hough we are all traumatized by the signifiers of the Other's enigmatic desire, some of us are obviously much more traumatized than others, for signifiers do not function in a cultural vacuum, but rather communicate

and perpetuate deeply entrenched forms of socioeconomic, national, racial, ethnic, religious, sexual, and gendered power.[4]

Evidently, there remains a visual scarcity of subjects racialised, gendered and sexualised in particular ways in the media, and this, in turn, has created an emotional scarcity whereby shows such as *Pose*, that promise (and often deliver) the power of uplift, become precious sites of affective investment. In other words, I am not dismissing the resonance or importance of the work being done in such cases, even as I interrogate the methods that utilise the logic of identity and representation to harness neoliberal politics as a seductive and aspirational regime. As Lauren Berlant's work on "cruel optimism" attests, as well as much psychoanalytic literature, we often invest in structures that negatively impact us, and, indeed, my own desires for politics and desires for identity have often met in conflict.

Responding to this increasing co-option of queerness into the neoliberal framework that I have witnessed in the media, *Taking Back Desire* asks three main questions: How might queerness function to destabilise neoliberalism? How does this understanding of queerness manifest in moving image media? And why is Lacanian psychoanalysis so pertinent to this investigation? To answer these questions, each chapter turned to contemporary film, television or video art to analyse how the articulation of absence and uncertainty on screen can challenge the reproduction of neoliberal subjectivity. In this move, I return to a definition of 'queer' as that which resists identity, as argued in the work of Lee Edelman and other queer theorists associated with the 'negative' or 'anti-social' turn of this discipline.[5] However, *Taking Back Desire* extends this definition by re-signifying 'queer' as an *orientation to lack* that problematises the processes of neoliberal subjectification which have specifically attempted to embrace (and, therefore, distort) it. As a result, queer is claimed as a political modality that disrupts contemporary hegemonic arrangements of personhood, accumulation and sociality.

In other words, previous forms of capitalism have sought to exclude persons on the basis of gender, sexuality and race. Neoliberalism, however, has actively sought to include such persons, but only on the condition that they do not fundamentally challenge the operations of capitalism, which rest on the exploitation of labour and persons systemically drawn into this dynamic, who often embody race, class and gender in particular ways. While queerness-as-identity is embraced by neoliberalism, queerness as explored and defined throughout this book problematises this very process of inclusion. Thus, this book's object of critique and process of critique come into pronounced proximity as queer challenges the inclusion of queerness that neoliberalism attempts to establish.

The close textual analyses that form this project follow traditions of film and media scholarship and Lacanian psychoanalysis alongside queer theory to establish how desire plays a pivotal role in understanding subjectivity and social–political–economic life. This interdisciplinary approach investigates how desire manifests in visual representations and temporal structures on screen, including instances where these regimes become confusing and disorientating. Throughout, Lacanian psychoanalysis and queer theory inform one another as both position uncertainty and unknowability as central in their approach to subjectivity. Their insistence on the limits of knowledge and centrality of loss from within their disciplines contrasts with neoliberalism's promise that accumulating commodities, including the commodity of identity, can help subjects achieve coherence and completion.

There has also been an insistence on the future as a site of promise and potential fulfilment in the capitalist paradigm. Because of this, temporality has become a fulcrum for interpreting the politics of desire and subjectivity. Ergo, the moving image, as a visual medium with a durational structure, is uniquely situated to develop these discussions of how desire, identity and time come into alignment or disarray. Within this highly variable format, time, image and sound work to construct or deconstruct narratives and motifs. Central to *Taking Back Desire* is an understanding of how failure to secure meaning for the subject of language can come to problematise the neoliberal framing of personhood. With this in mind, my analysis often focuses on moments where signification falters or disrupts conventional modes of representation in ways that thereby queer them.

As the title of this book suggests, desire is crucial in the situating of queerness as a political mode, one which problematises the fantasy of fulfilment via the establishment of identity, accumulation and 'self-improvement'. The moving image comprises visual and temporal structures and features that typically combine in particular ways and translate into categories such as genre, theme and historical period, which refer to, reproduce and/or challenge the social worlds within which they are created. Though the moving image is transforming owing to social media, smartphone technologies and artificial intelligence, which are reducing the need for a large cast and crew to produce a piece, mainstream film and television still largely depend on industrialised processes and capitalist modes of production across their labour infrastructure. Despite this dependence on capitalist models, interpretation (and, in particular, psychoanalytic interpretation) brings out textual details that do not necessarily sustain the political and economic practices from which works emerge. If psychoanalysis strives to challenge and rethink the limits of knowledge, the moving image text can be a site for creative intervention that may challenge the enlistment of desire in support of capitalist relations. As the industrial scale of film and television production makes it an accessible and social format, reaching large audiences, such media often reflect and manifest the socio-political zeitgeist. As a result, the moving image – particularly film and television – is a privileged mode for considering the ways meaning is established and distributed in the contemporary world.

As the introduction to this book establishes, the work of Todd McGowan and Edelman emphasises the continued importance of Lacan when approaching subjectivity. By reading them together, their analyses are shown to be complementary and develop a queer challenge to neoliberalism. The combined interpretation of these scholars marks one of this book's main contributions to the intersecting fields of Lacanian psychoanalysis, queer theory and film and media studies as there has yet to be a substantial pairing of their texts. As a result, *Taking Back Desire* proposes that rejecting futurity positions queerness as a rupture to neoliberal regimes of subjectivity and investigates the ways this manifests on screen.

Central to my argument is that queerness denies the existence of a 'true self' that one could express and, thus, undermines the logic of identity to which neo-liberalism persistently appeals. This is not to say we can exist 'outside' of the political structures that shape our world: Queer is not a utopian gesture of rejection that leads to renewal. Instead, it is a window rather than a door; a plane through which to view the social world we encounter and are enmeshed within. However, it is not transparent to itself but, rather, draws attention to its own discursive strategies in attempts to resist redefining a position of mastery. In other words, the definition of queer developed and proposed throughout this book attends to the gaps in meaning, a scrutiny it is itself not immune to. It is, therefore, not the claim of this project to call for 'better' representations or expand the list of identities in service of recognition. In the end, I fall on the side of queerness as open, as a relation available to whoever, as it seeks to undo the strictures of identity rather than rename them. I want to challenge the notion of a subject determined by gendered, sexual and racialised positions, without dis-missing how important these ideas are in social reality, charged with the alter-nating weight of persecution and celebration.

Importantly, this understanding of queerness addresses a lack *we all experience* and is, therefore, not exclusionary. It is my own desire that we (in the broadest sense) approach lack in a way that seeks *not* to fill it with the trappings of consumer capitalism but rather to acknowledge, if not embrace, our very inability to garner closure. In this sense, I hold on to some optimism about queerness that manifests as a conviction that we have a right to chal-lenge capitalist hegemony, whether we either believe ourselves to be outcasts from it or benefit from it financially and/or socially. It is, in part, by rethink-ing or traversing a promise of fulfilment that this challenge partially takes place. The queer orientation to lack seeks to reach towards something expansive rather than particular and closed. As the world feels increasingly fractured and conflictual, I want to listen closely for the kernel of desire that embeds itself in every demand, in every statement and act. Queer offers but one way of negotiating the gap in meaning that we all are trying to fill in our different, inconsistent, failing ways.

Thus, it is desire, rather than identity, that must be 'taken back'. If desire is synonymous with lack, it is a relation to this unquenchable gap that needs to be pursued in ways that do not fall for the seductive qualities of neoliberalism. Despite now-conventional thinking that conflates our egoic 'personalities' with the truth of our subjectivity, identities are not internal to or inside us, even as they shape our communal and psychic lives. They are developed through symbolic and imaginary registers and, like language, are advanced in the external world to which we adapt. They often become deeply felt, as if they are the 'real' self. Yet categories of identity never properly 'fit'; we are never able to find the piece that would resolve our identity and make it self-evident to ourselves and others. In response, the preceding discussions of visual and scholarly works rethink such inscriptions to cast the subject as incoherent and unknowable rather than affirming them as positions of knowledge from which one can confidently speak. Importantly, the ideas and perspectives I have engaged with do not purport to speak from an immutable and consistent standpoint. Rather, the discrepancies in traditional forms of knowledge that have historically calcified around particular bodies establish queerness as a political mode of uncertainty and perpetual incompletion.

Notes

1 Barbara J. Fields and Karen E. Fields, *Racecraft: The Soul of Inequality in American Life* (London: Verso, 2012), 105.
2 David Alderson, *Sex, Needs and Queer Culture: From Liberation to the Postgay* (London: Zed Books, 2016), 291.
3 David Alderson, *Sex, Needs and Queer Culture: From Liberation to the Postgay* (London: Zed Books, 2016), 291, emphasis in original.
4 Mari Ruti, *The Singularity of Being: Lacan and the Immortal Within* (New York: Fordham University Press, 2012), 46.
5 Lee Edelman, *No Future: Queer Theory and the Death Drive* (Durham: Duke University Press, 2004).

References

Alderson, David. *Sex, Needs and Queer Culture: From Liberation to the Postgay.* London: Zed Books, 2016.
Edelman, Lee. *No Future: Queer Theory and the Death Drive.* Durham: Duke University Press, 2004.
Fields, Barbara J., and Karen E. Fields. *Racecraft: The Soul of Inequality in American Life.* London: Verso, 2012.
Ruti, Mari. *The Singularity of Being: Lacan and the Immortal Within.* New York: Fordham University Press, 2012.

Bibliography and Filmography

Bibliography

Åkervall, Lisa. 'Networked Selves: Ryan Trecartin and Lizzie Fitch's Postcinematic Aesthetics.' *Screen* 57, no. 1 (1 March 2016): 35–51. doi:10.1093/screen/hjw004.

Alderson, David. *Sex, Needs and Queer Culture: From Liberation to the Postgay.* London: Zed Books, 2016.

Andrejevic, Mark. *Reality TV: The Work of Being Watched.* Lanham: Rowman & Littlefield, 2004.

Andrews, Kehinde. *The New Age of Empire: How Racism and Colonialism Still Rule the World.* Dublin: Penguin Books, 2022.

Auerbach, Jonathan. *Dark Borders: Film Noir and American Citizenship.* Durham: Duke University Press, 2011.

Badr, Sarah. 'Re-Imagining Wellness in the Age of Neoliberalism.' *New Sociology: Journal of Critical Praxis* 3 (13 June2022). doi:10.25071/2563-3694.66.

Ballas, Anthony. 'Film Theory after Copjec.' *Canadian Review of American Studies* 51, no. 1 (2021): 63–81. doi:10.3138/cras-2019-010.

Banet-Weiser, Sarah. *Authentic TM: The Politics and Ambivalence in a Brand Culture.* New York: New York University Press, 2012.

Barnard, Suzanne. 'Introduction.' In *Reading Seminar XX: Lacan's Major Work on Love, Knowledge, and Feminine Sexuality.* Edited by Bruce Fink and Suzanne Barnard, 1–20. Albany: State University of New York Press, 2002.

Baudrillard, Jean. *Simulacra and Simulation.* Translated by Sheila Faria Glaser. Ann Arbor: University of Michigan Press, 1994.

Bazin, André. 'The Ontology of the Photographic Image.' Translated by Hugh Gray. *Film Quarterly* 13, no. 4 (1960): 4–9. doi:10.2307/1210183.

Bergstrom, Janet. *Endless Night: Cinema and Psychoanalysis, Parallel Histories.* Berkeley: University of California Press, 1999.

Berlant, Lauren. *Cruel Optimism.* Durham: Duke University Press, 2011.

Berlant, Lauren. *The Female Complaint: The Unfinished Business of Sentimentality in American Culture.* Durham: Duke University Press, 2008.

Bernstein, Jon. '"Nothing Like This Has Ever Happened": How TV Drama Pose Breaks New Ground.' *The Guardian,* 1 June 2018, online edition. Available at: https://www.theguardian.com/tv-and-radio/2018/jun/01/pose-ryan-murphy-transgender-actors-groundbreaking-new-show.

Bhattacharyya, Gargi. *Rethinking Racial Capitalism: Questions of Reproduction and Survival*. London: Rowman & Littlefield, 2018.

Borcherdt, Gesine. 'Ryan Trecartin.' *ArtReview*, 20 August 2014. Available at: www. https://artreview.com/summer-2014-feature-ryan-trecartin/.

Bordwell, David. *Narration in the Fiction Film*. London: Methuen, 1985.

Bordwell, David, and Noël Carroll. *Post-Theory: Reconstructing Film Studies*. Madison: University of Wisconsin Press, 1996.

Braunstein, Néstor A. 'Desire and Jouissance in the Teachings of Lacan.' In *The Cambridge Companion to Lacan*. Edited by Jean-Michel Rabaté, 102–115. Cambridge: Cambridge University Press, 2003.

Breckon, Anna. 'The Erotic Politics of Disgust: Pink Flamingos as Queer Political Cinema.' *Screen* 54, no. 4 (1 December 2013): 514–533. doi:10.1093/screen/hjt041.

Brennan, Niall. 'Contradictions between the Subversive and the Mainstream: Drag Cultures and RuPaul's Drag Race.' In *RuPaul's Drag Race and the Shifting Visibility of Drag Culture*. Edited by Niall Brennan and David Gudelunas, 29–43. Cham: Springer, 2017. doi:10.1007/978-3-319-50618-0_3.

Brinkema, Eugenie. *The Forms of the Affects*. Durham: Duke University Press, 2014.

Brown, Wendy. 'American Nightmare: Neoliberalism, Neoconservatism, and De-Democratization.' *Political Theory* 34, no. 6 (2006): 690–714. doi:10.1177/0090591706293016.

Buck-Morss, Susan. 'Hegel and Haiti.' *Critical Inquiry* 26, no. 4 (2000): 821–865.

Burch, Audra D.S. 'How a National Movement Topples Hundreds of Confederate Symbols.' *The New York Times* [online]. 28 February 2022. Available at: https://www.nytimes.com/interactive/2022/02/28/us/confederate-statue-removal.html [Accessed 10 October 2014].

Butler, Judith. *Bodies That Matter: On the Discursive Limits of 'Sex'*. Abingdon: Routledge, 2011.

Butler, Judith. *Gender Trouble: Feminism and the Subversion of Identity*. New York: Routledge, 2007.

Caropreso, Fátima. 'The Death Instinct and the Mental Dimension beyond the Pleasure Principle in the Works of Spielrein and Freud.' *International Journal of Psychoanalysis* 98, no. 6 (2017): 1741–1762. doi:10.1111/1745-8315.12630.

Carroll, Toby. 'Neoliberalism, Globalization, and Late Capitalism: Capital, Ideology, and Making the World Market.' In *The Oxford Handbook of Economic Imperialism*, edited by Zak Cope and Immanuel Ness, 135–152. Oxford University Press, 2022. doi:10.1093/oxfordhb/9780197527085.013.11.

Chandler, Raymond. *The Big Sleep and Other Novels*. London: Penguin Books, 2000.

Chandler, Raymond, and Etienne Chaumeton. *A Panorama of American Film Noir (1941–1953)*. San Francisco: City Lights, 2002.

Chetwynd, Phoebe. 'Postfeminist Hegemony in a Precarious World: Lessons in Neoliberal Survival from RuPaul's Drag Race.' *Journal of International Women's Studies* 21, no. 3 (2020): 22–35.

Chion, Michel. *Audio-Vision: Sound on Screen*. Translated by Claudia Gorbman. First edition. New York City: Columbia University Press, 1994.

Chion, Michel. *Audio-Vision: Sound on Screen*. Translated by Claudia Gorbman. Second edition. New York City: Columbia University Press, 2019. doi:10.7312/chio18588.

Chu, Andrea Long. *Females*. London: Verso, 2019.

Cooper, Melinda. *Family Values: Between Neoliberalism and the New Social Conservatism*. New York: Zone Books, 2017.

Cooper, Michael. 'Why Pose Is the Most Groundbreaking LGBTQ TV Show Ever.' *LA Weekly*, 19 July 2018.

Copjec, Joan. *Read My Desire: Lacan against the Historicists*. Cambridge: MIT Press, 1994.

Copjec, Joan. *Shades of Noir: A Reader*. London: Verso, 1993.

Copjec, Joan. 'The Orthopsychic Subject: Film Theory and the Reception of Lacan.' *October* 49 (1989): 53–71. doi:10.2307/778733.

Corner, John. 'Performing the Real: Documentary Diversions.' *Television & New Media* 3, no. 3 (2002): 255–269. doi:10.1177/152747640200300302.

Corner, John, and Sylvia Harvey. *Enterprise and Heritage: Crosscurrents of National Culture*. London: Routledge, 1991.

Crary, Jonathan. *24/7: Late Capitalism and the Ends of Sleep*. London: Verso, 2014.

Davis, Oliver, and Tim Dean. *Hatred of Sex*. Lincoln: University of Nebraska Press, 2022.

De Lauretis, Teresa. *Alice Doesn't: Feminism, Semiotics, Cinema*. London: Macmillan, 1984.

Derrida, Jacques. *Dissemination*. Edited by Barbara Johnson. Chicago: Chicago University Press, 1981.

Diawara, Manthia. 'Noir by Noirs: Towards a New Realism in Black Cinema.' *African American Review* 27, no. 4 (1993): 525–537. doi:10.2307/3041886.

Doane, Mary Ann. *Femmes Fatales*. London: Taylor & Francis, 1991.

Doane, Mary Ann. *The Emergence of Cinematic Time: Modernity, Contingency, the Archive*. Cambridge: Harvard University Press, 2002.

Durgnat, Raymond. 'Paint It Black: The Family Tree of the Film Noir.' In *Notions of Genre*, edited by Barry Keith Grant and Malisa Kurtz, 252–272. Austin: University of Texas Press, 2016. doi:10.7560/303757.

Dyer, Richard. *Only Entertainment*. New York: Routledge, 2002.

Dyer, Richard. *Pastiche*. London: Routledge, 2007.

Dyer, Richard. *The Culture of Queers*. London: Routledge, 2002.

Dyer, Richard. *White: Essays on Race and Culture*. London: Routledge, 2013.

Dyess, Cynthia, and Tim Dean. 'Gender: The Impossibility of Meaning.' *Psychoanalytic Dialogues* 10, no. 5 (15 September 2000): 735–756. doi:10.1080/10481881009348579.

Edelman, Lee. *Bad Education: Why Queer Theory Teaches Us Nothing*. Durham: Duke University Press, 2022.

Edelman, Lee. *No Future: Queer Theory and the Death Drive*. Durham: Duke University Press, 2004.

Ellis, Bret Easton. *American Psycho*. London: Picador, 1991.

Ferreday, Debra. 'From Dorian's Closet to Elektra's Trunk: Visibility, Trauma and Gender Euphoria in Pose.' *Queer Studies in Media & Popular Culture* 7, no. 1 (June 2022): 9–25. doi:10.1386/qsmpc_00065_1.

Fields, Barbara J. and Karen E. Fields. *Racecraft: The Soul of Inequality in American Life*. London: Verso, 2012.

Flynn, Gillian. *Sharp Objects*. London: Pheonix, 2007.

Fraser, Nancy. 'The End of Progressive Neoliberalism.' *Dissent Magazine*, 2 January 2017. Available at: https://www.dissentmagazine.org/online_articles/progressive-neoliberalism-reactionary-populism-nancy-fraser/.

Freeman, Elizabeth. *Time Binds: Queer Temporalities, Queer Histories.* Durham: Duke University Press, 2010.

Freud, Sigmund. *Beyond the Pleasure Principle and Other Writings.* Translated by John Reddick. New York: Penguin Books, 2003.

Freud, Sigmund. *On Sexuality: Three Essays on the Theory of Sexuality, and Other Works.* Edited by Angela Richards. Translated by James Strachey. Harmondsworth: Penguin, 1977.

Freud, Sigmund. *The Standard Edition of the Complete Psychological Works of Sigmund Freud. Vol. 2 (1893–1895), Studies on Hysteria by Joseph Breuer and Sigmund Freud.* Edited by Anna Freud. Translated by James Strachey. London: Hogarth Press and the Institute of Psycho-Analysis, 1955.

Freud, Sigmund. *The Standard Edition of the Complete Psychological Works of Sigmund Freud. Vol. 21 (1927–1931), The Future of an Illusion; Civilization and Its Discontents and Other Works.* Edited by Anna Freud. Translated by James Strachey. London: Hogarth Press and the Institute of Psycho-Analysis, 1961.

Freud, Sigmund. *Totem and Taboo: Resemblances between the Psychic Lives of Savages and Neurotics.* Harmondsworth: Penguin, 1938.

Gabbard, Krin, and Glen O. Gabbard. *Psychiatry and the Cinema.* Chicago: University of Chicago Press, 1987.

Galanas, Phillip. 'Ryan Murphy and Janet Mock on "Pose," Diversity and Netflix.' *The New York Times*, 23 May 2018, online edition. Available at: https://www.nytimes.com/2018/05/23/arts/television/pose-ryan-murphy-janet-mock.html.

Gawronski, Alexander. 'Art as Critique under Neoliberalism: Negativity Undoing Economic Naturalism.' *Arts* 10, no. 1 (2021). doi:10.3390/arts10010011.

George, Sheldon. *Race and Trauma: A Lacanian Study of African American Racial Identity.* Waco: Baylor University Press, 2016.

George, Sheldon, and Derek Hook. *Lacan and Race: Racism, Identity, and Psychoanalytic Theory.* London: Routledge, 2021.

Gherovici, Patricia. *Transgender Psychoanalysis: A Lacanian Perspective on Sexual Difference.* London: Routledge, 2017.

GLAAD. 'GLAAD Works with Hollywood to Shape Transgender Stories and Help Cast Trans Actors.' GLAAD.org, 12 May 2020. Available at: https://www.glaad.org/blog/glaad-works-hollywood-shape-transgender-stories-and-help-cast-trans-actors.

Gledhill, Christine, and Linda Williams. *Melodrama Unbound: Across History, Media, and National Cultures.* New York: Columbia University Press, 2018.

Goddard, Michael, and Christopher Hogg. 'Introduction: Trans TV Dossier, III: Trans TV Re-Evaluated, Part 2.' *Critical Studies in Television* 15, no. 3 (2020): 255–266. doi:10.1177/1749602020937566.

Goldberg, Leslie. 'Ryan Murphy Makes History with Largest Cast of Transgender Actors for FX's "Pose".' *The Hollywood Reporter*, 25 October 2017. Available at: https://www.hollywoodreporter.com/live-feed/ryan-murphy-makes-history-largest-cast-transgender-actors-fxs-pose-1051877.

Goldmark, Matthew. 'National Drag: The Language of Inclusion in RuPaul's Drag Race.' *GLQ* 21, no. 4 (2015): 501–520. doi:10.1215/10642684-3123665.

Gray, John. *Men Are from Mars, Women Are from Venus.* New York: HarperCollins, 1992.

Green, Treye. '"It Made My Walk a Little Taller": The Inspiring LBGTQ Legacy of Pose.' *The Guardian*, 8 July 2021, online edition. Available at: https://www.theguardian.com/tv-and-radio/2021/jun/08/pose-tv-show-fx-lgbtq-legacy.

Halberstam, Judith. 'The Anti-Social Turn in Queer Studies.' *Graduate Journal of Social Science* 5, no. 2 (1 January 2008): 140–156.

Halberstam, Jack. *The Queer Art of Failure.* Durham: Duke University Press, 2011. doi:10.1515/9780822394358.

Hammett, Dashiell. *The Maltese Falcon.* London: Orion, 2005.

Han, Byung-Chul. *Psychopolitics: Neoliberalism and New Technologies of Power.* Translated by Erik Butler. London: Verso, 2017.

Hartman, Saidiya. 'Venus in Two Acts.' *Small Axe: A Journal of Criticism* 12, no. 2 (2008): 1–14. doi:10.1215/-12-2-1.

Harvey, David. *A Brief History of Neoliberalism.* Oxford: Oxford University Press, 2005.

Harvey, David. *The Condition of Postmodernity: An Enquiry into the Origins of Cultural Change.* Cambridge: Basil Blackwell, 1990.

Heath, Stephen. 'Cinema and Psychoanalysis: Parallel Histories.' In *Endless Night: Cinema and Psychoanalysis, Parallel Histories*, edited by Janet Bergstrom, 25–56. Berkeley: University of California Press, 1999.

Heller, Meredith. 'RuPaul Realness: The Neoliberal Resignification of Ballroom Discourse.' *Social Semiotics* 30, no. 1 (1 January 2020): 133–147. doi:10.1080/10350330.2018.1547490.

Hill, Wes. 'The Automedial Zaniness of Ryan Trecartin.' *M/C Journal* 21, no. 2 (25 April 2018). doi:10.5204/mcj.1382.

Hook, Derek, and Stijn Vanheule. 'Revisiting the Master-Signifier, or, Mandela and Repression.' *Frontiers in Psychology* 6 (19 January 2016): 1–10. doi:10.3389/fpsyg.2015.02028.

hooks, bell. *Reel to Real: Race, Sex, and Class at the Movies.* London: Routledge, 1996.

Inwood, Joshua. 'White Supremacy, White Counter-Revolutionary Politics, and the Rise of Donald Trump.' *Environment and Planning C: Politics and Space* 37, no. 4 (June 2019): 579–596. doi:10.1177/2399654418789949.

James, Meredith. '"Nobody Wants to See That Fuckhead": Ball Culture and Donald Trump in FX's Pose.' In *Trump Fiction: Essays on Donald Trump in Literature, Film, and Television*, edited by Stephen Hock, 213–224. Lanham: Rowman & Littlefield, 2019.

Jameson, Fredric. *Postmodernism, or, The Cultural Logic of Late Capitalism.* London: Verso, 1991.

Joyrich, Lynne. 'Posing as Normal?' In *Ryan Murphy's Queer America*, edited by Brenda R. Weber and David Greven, 27–40. London: Routledge, 2022. doi:10.4324/9781003170358-3.

Jung, E. Alex. '"We Did Something Revolutionary": Janet Mock on the First Season of FX's Pose, Challenging Ryan Murphy, and the Politics of Desire.' *Vulture*, no date. Available at: https://www.vulture.com/2018/07/janet-mock-pose-season-one.html [Accessed 22 November 2022].

Kanter, Jake. 'Russell T Davies On How The Queer Casting Rule On HBO Max's "It's A Sin" Proved A Triumph.' *Deadline*, 2 March 2021.

Kaplan, E. Ann, ed. '"The Dark Continent of Film Noir": Race, Displacement and Metaphor in Tourneur's *Cat People* (1942) and Welles' *The Lady from Shanghai* (1948).' In *Women in Film Noir*, 183–201. London: Bloomsbury, 1978. doi:10.5040/9781838710163.

Kitamura, Katie. 'Ryan Trecartin: Any Ever.' *Art Monthly*, no. 349 (September 2011): 28–29.

Kornhaber, Spencer. 'Why Drag Is the Ultimate Retort to Trump.' *The Atlantic*, June 2017. https://www.theatlantic.com/magazine/archive/2017/06/rupaul-gets-political/524529/.

Kuhn, Annette. 'Women's Genres: Melodrama, Soap Opera, and Theory.' In *Feminist Television Criticism: A Reader*, edited by Charlotte Brunsdon, Julie D'Acci and Lynn Spigel, 145–154. Oxford: Clarendon, 1997.

Lacan, Jacques. *Anxiety: The Seminar of Jacques Lacan, Book X*. Translated by A.R. Price. Cambridge: Polity, 2014.

Lacan, Jacques. *Écrits: A Selection*. Translated by Alan Sheridan. London: Routledge, 1989.

Lacan, Jacques. *The Four Fundamental Concepts of Psycho-Analysis*. Edited by Jacques-Alain Miller. Translated by Alan Sheridan. Harmondsworth: Penguin, 1979.

Lacan, Jacques. *The Seminar of Jacques Lacan Book XVII: The Other Side of Psychoanalysis*. Translated by Russell Grigg. New York: Norton, 2007.

Lacan, Jacques. *The Seminar of Jacques Lacan/Book XX, On Feminine Sexuality: The Limits of Love and Knowledge: Encore 1972–1972*. Edited by Jacques-Alain Miller. Translated by Bruce Fink. New York: Norton, 1999.

Lacan, Jacques. *The Seminar of Jacques Lacan. Book 3, The Psychoses, 1955–1956*. Edited by Jacques-Alain Miller. Translated by Russell Grigg. London: Routledge, 1993.

Langley, Patrick. 'Ryan Trecartin: The Real Internet Is Inside You.' *The White Review*, April 2022. Available at: https://www.thewhitereview.org/feature/ryan-trecartin-the-real-internet-is-inside-you/.

Lawson, Richard. 'Stonewall Is Terribly Offensive, and Offensively Terrible.' *Vanity Fair*, 22 September 2015.

Lebeau, Vicky. *Psychoanalysis and Cinema: The Play of Shadows*. London: Wallflower, 2001.

Levine, Nick, and Russell T. Davies. 'It's A Sin Creator Russell T Davies: "Cast Gay as Gay".' *AnOther Magazine*, 20 January 2021.

Lewis, Justin. 'The Meaning of Real Life.' In *Reality TV: Remaking Television Culture*, edited by Susan Murray and Laurie Ouellette, 288–302. New York: New York University Press, 2004.

Lewis, Mary Grace. '23 Cisgender Actors Who Played Transgender in Movies.' *Advocate*, no date. Available at: https://www.advocate.com/arts-entertainment/2018/7/10/23-cisgender-actors-who-played-trangender-movies#media-gallery-media-1.

Lindop, Samantha. *Postfeminism and the Fatale Figure in Neo-Noir Cinema*. Basingstoke: Palgrave Macmillan, 2018.

Lippit, Akira Mizuta. *Atomic Light (Shadow Optics)*. Minneapolis: University of Minnesota, 2005.

Loren, Scott. 'Self-Fashioning, Freedom, and the Problem of His-Story: The Return of Noir.' *European Journal of American Studies* 3, no. 1 (21 January 2008): 1–18. doi:10.4000/ejas.1842.

Lott, Eric. 'The Whiteness of Film Noir.' *American Literary History* 9, no. 3 (1997): 542–566.

Lovelock, Michael. *Reality TV and Queer Identities: Sexuality, Authenticity, Celebrity*. Cham: Palgrave Macmillan/Springer, 2019.

MacCannell, Juliet Flower. *The Regime of the Brother: After the Patriarchy*. London: Routledge, 1991.

Manon, Hugh S. 'X-Ray Visions: Radiography, "Chiaroscuro", and the Fantasy of Unsuspicion in "Film Noir".' *Film Criticism* 32, no. 2 (2007): 2–27.

Martin, Alfred L. 'For Scholars … When Studying the Queer of Color Image Alone Isn't Enough.' *Communication and Critical/Cultural Studies* 17, no. 1 (2 January 2020): 69–74. doi:10.1080/14791420.2020.1723797.

Martin, Alfred L. 'Pose(r): Ryan Murphy, Trans and Queer of Color Labor, and the Politics of Representation.' *Los Angeles Review Books*, 2 August 2018.

Martin, Alfred L. 'The End of the "Best Actor" Discourse?' In *Ryan Murphy's Queer America*, edited by Brenda R. Weber and David Greven, 213–226. London: Routledge, 2022. doi:10.4324/9781003170358-18.

Marx, Karl. *Theories of Surplus Value*. New York: Prometheus Books, 2000.

Mat Collishaw. 'In Camera Mat Collishaw.' Available at: https://matcollishaw.com/exhibitions/library-of-birmingham/ [Accessed 19 June 2023].

McCarthy, Anna. '"Stanley Milgram, Allen Funt, and Me": Postwar Social Science and the "First Wave" of Reality TV.' In *Reality TV: Remaking Television Culture*, edited by Susan Murray and Laurie Ouellette, 19–39. New York: New York University Press, 2004.

McGowan, Todd. *Capitalism and Desire: The Psychic Cost of Free Markets*. New York: Columbia University Press, 2016.

McGowan, Todd. *Enjoying What We Don't Have: The Political Project of Psychoanalysis*. Lincoln: University of Nebraska Press, 2013.

McGowan, Todd. *Out of Time: Desire in Atemporal Cinema*. Minneapolis: University of Minnesota Press, 2011.

McGowan, Todd. *Psychoanalytic Film Theory and the Rules of the Game*. London: Bloomsbury, 2018.

McGowan, Todd. *The End of Dissatisfaction? Jacques Lacan and the Emerging Society of Enjoyment*. Albany: StateUniversity of New York Press, 2004.

McGowan, Todd. *The Racist Fantasy: Unconscious Roots of Hatred*. New York: Bloomsbury Academic, 2022.

McGowan, Todd. *The Real Gaze: Film Theory after Lacan*. Albany: State University of New York Press, 2007.

McGowan, Todd. *Universality and Identity Politics*. New York: Columbia University Press, 2020.

Mekas, Jonas. *Movie Journal: The Rise of the New American Cinema, 1959–1971*. New York: Macmillan, 1972.

Metz, Christian. *Psychoanalysis and Cinema: The Imaginary Signifier*. Translated by Celia Britton. London: Macmillan, 1982.

Metz, Nina. 'Why Trans Actors Should Be Cast in Trans Roles.' *Chicago Tribune*, 13 July 2018, online edition. Available at: https://www.chicagotribune.com/entertainment/movies/ct-mov-trans-actors-for-trans-roles-0713-story.html.

Michaeli, Inna. 'Self-Care: An Act of Political Warfare or a Neoliberal Trap?' *Development* 60, no. 1 (1 September. 2017): 50–56. doi:10.1057/s41301-017-0131-8.

Mirowski, Philip, and Dieter Plehwe. *The Road from Mont Pèlerin: The Making of the Neoliberal Thought Collective*. Cambridge: Harvard University Press, 2009.

Mulvey, Laura. 'A Phantasmagoria of the Female Body: The Work of Cindy Sherman.' *New Left Review* 188, no. 188 (1991): 136–150.

Mulvey, Laura. 'A Phantasmagoria of the Female Body: The Work of Cindy Sherman.' In *Death 24× a Second: Stillness and the Moving Image*. London: Reaktion Books, 2006.

Mulvey, Laura. 'Visual Pleasure and Narrative Cinema.' *Screen (London)* 16, no. 3 (1975): 6–18. doi:10.1093/screen/16.3.6.

Muñoz, José Esteban. *Cruising Utopia, 10th Anniversary Edition: The Then and There of Queer Futurity.* New York: New York University Press, 2019.

Murray, Susan, and Laurie Ouellette. *Reality TV: Remaking Television Culture.* New York: New York University Press, 2004.

Naremore, James. *More Than Night: Film Noir in Its Contexts.* Berkeley: University of California Press, 1998.

Neroni, Hilary. 'Confederate Signifiers in Vermont: Fetish Objects and Racist Enjoyment.' In *Lacan and Race: Racism, Identity, and Psychoanalytic Theory,* edited by Derek Hook and Sheldon George, 51–64. London: Routledge, 2021. doi:10.4324/9780429326790.

Nolan, Alan T. 'The Anatomy of the Myth.' In *The Myth of the Lost Cause and Civil War History,* edited by Alan T. Nolan and Gary W. Gallagher, 11–34. Bloomington: Indiana University Press, 2000.

Oh, David C. *Whitewashing the Movies: Asian Erasure and White Subjectivity in U.S. Film Culture.* New Brunswick: Rutgers University Press, 2021. doi:10.36019/9781978808669.

Orgad, Shani, and Rosalind Gill. *Confidence Culture.* Durham: Duke University Press, 2022.

Orwell, George. *Nineteen Eighty-Four.* London: Secker & Warburg, 1984.

Ouellette, Laurie, and James Hay. *Better Living through Reality TV: Television and Post-Welfare Citizenship.* Malden: Blackwell, 2008.

Oxford English Dictionary. Oxford: Oxford University Press, July 2023.

Pember, Alice. 'This Party Is Political: The Moving Politics of the Queer Dancefloor in 120 BPM (2017).' *Modern & Contemporary France* 30, no. 2 (3 April 2022): 145–160. doi:10.1080/09639489.2021.2008337.

Phelan, Peggy. *Unmarked: The Politics of Performance.* London: Routledge, 1993.

Piper, Helen. 'Understanding Reality Television: Reality TV – Audiences and Popular Factual Television – Reality TV – Realism and Revelation.' *Screen* 47, no. 1 (1 January 2006): 133–138. doi:10.1093/screen/hjl012.

Posner, Sarah, and David Neiwert. 'How Trump Took Hate Groups Mainstream.' *Mother Jones,* 14 October 2016. Available at: https://www.motherjones.com/politics/2016/10/donald-trump-hate-groups-neo-nazi-white-supremacist-racism/.

Puar, Jasbir K. *Terrorist Assemblages: Homonationalism in Queer Times.* Durham: Duke University Press, 2017.

Ragland-Sullivan, Ellie. *Essays on the Pleasures of Death: From Freud to Lacan.* New York: Routledge, 1995.

Rao, Rahul. *Out of Time: The Queer Politics of Postcoloniality.* Oxford: Oxford University Press, 2020.

Regnault, François. 'The Name-of-the-Father.' In *Reading Seminar XI: Lacan's Four Fundamental Concepts of Psychoanalysis.* New York: State University of New York Press, 1995.

Richard, David Evan. 'Episodes of Depression: Existential Feelings and Embodiment in SHARP OBJECTS.' *NECSUS European Journal of Media Studies* 8 (2019): 211–229. doi:10.25969/MEDIAREP/4174.

Rimke, Heidi. 'Self-Help, Therapeutic Industries, and Neoliberalism.' In *The Routledge International Handbook of Global Therapeutic Cultures,* edited by Daniel Nehring, 37–50. Abingdon: Routledge, 2020.

Robinson, Cedric J. *Black Marxism: The Making of the Black Radical Tradition*. Chapel Hill: University of North Carolina Press, 2020.

Ruti, Mari. *The Ethics of Opting Out: Queer Theory's Defiant Subjects*. New York: Columbia University Press, 2017.

Ruti, Mari. *The Singularity of Being: Lacan and the Immortal Within*. New York: Fordham University Press, 2012.

Sade. *The 120 Days of Sodom, or, The School of Libertinage*. Translated by Will McMorran and Thomas Wynn. London: Penguin Books, 2016.

Sadler, Landon. "'If You Can't Love Yourself, How in the Hell You Gonna Love Somebody Else?': Care and Neoliberalism on Queer Eye, RuPaul's Drag Race, and Pose.' *Journal of Popular Culture* 55, no. 4 (2022): 799–819. doi:10.1111/jpcu.13153.

Schjeldahl, Peter. 'Party On: Ryan Trecartin at P.S. 1.' *The New Yorker*, 20 June 2011. https://www.newyorker.com/magazine/2011/06/27/party-on-peter-schjeldahl.

Segal, Mark. 'I Was at the Stonewall Riots. The Movie "Stonewall" Gets Everything Wrong.' PBS News Hour, 23 September 2015. https://www.pbs.org/newshour/arts/stonewall-movie.

Sender, Katherine. *Business, Not Politics: The Making of the Gay Market*. New York: Columbia University Press, 2004. doi:10.7312/send12734.

Seshadri-Crooks, Kalpana. *Desiring Whiteness: A Lacanian Analysis of Race*. London: Routledge, 2000.

Shortland, Michael. 'Screen Memories: Towards a History of Psychiatry and Psychoanalysis in the Movies.' *The British Journal for the History of Science* 20, no. 4 (1987): 421–452. doi:10.1017/S0007087400024213.

Silver, Alain, and James Ursini. *Film Noir Reader*. 1. New York: Limelight, 1996.

Silverman, Kaja. *Male Subjectivity at the Margins*. New York: Routledge, 1992.

Sinwell, Sarah E.S. 'Showrunning Activism.' In *Ryan Murphy's Queer America*, edited by Brenda R. Weber and David Greven, 241–253. London: Routledge, 2022. doi:10.4324/9781003170358-20.

Slattery, James Lawrence. 'A Matter of Life and Death: Cinematic Necropolitics in "Arrival".' *Free Associations*, no. 79 (August 2020): 121–141.

Snorton, C. Riley. *Black on Both Sides: A Racial History of Trans Identity*. Minneapolis: University of Minnesota Press, 2017.

Spielrein, Sabina. 'Die Destruktion als Ursache des Werdens [Destruction as a Cause of Coming into Being].' *Jahrbuch für Psychoanalytische und Psychopathologische Forschungen* 4, no. 1 (1912): 465–503.

Spivak, Gayatri Chakravorty. *Can the Subaltern Speak? Reflections on the History of an Idea*. Edited by Rosalind C. Morris. New York: Columbia University Press, 2010.

Srnicek, Nick, and Alex Williams. *Inventing The Future: Postcapitalism and a World without Work*. London: Verso, 2016.

Stanton, Maya. "'Stonewall": EW Review.' *Entertainment Weekly*, 28 September 2015. https://ew.com/article/2015/09/28/stonewall-ew-review/.

Stavrakakis, Yannis. *The Lacanian Left: Psychoanalysis, Theory, Politics*. Albany: State University of New York Press, 2007.

Steyerl, Hito. 'In Defense of the Poor Image.' *E-Flux Journal*, no. 10 (November 2009): 1–9.

Stryker, Susan. *Transgender History: The Roots of Today's Revolution*. New York: Seal Press, 2017.

Styles, Rhyannon. 'Why, to a Transgender Woman, New TV Series Pose Seems so Incredible.' *Elle*, 7 March 2019. Available at: https://www.elle.com/uk/life-and-cul ture/elle-voices/a26745725/pose-tv-show-importance-transgender-community/.

Sykes, Pandora, and Sirin Kale. 'Unreal: A Critical History of Reality TV.' BBC, 7 May 2022. Available at: https://www.bbc.co.uk/programmes/p0c5w0zm.

Taylor, Jodie. 'Festivalizing Sexualities: Discourses of "Pride", Counter-Discourses of "Shame".' In *The Festivalization of Culture*, edited by Andy Bennett and Jodie Taylor, 27–48. London: Routledge, 2016. doi:10.4324/9781315558189.

Tinkcom, Matthew. *Queer Theory and Brokeback Mountain*. London: Bloomsbury, 2018.

Tokumitsu, Miya. 'Tell Me It's Going to Be OK.' *The Baffler*, no. 41 (2018): 6–11.

Tyrer, Ben. 'Film Noir as Point de Capiton: Double Indemnity, Structure and Tem-porality.' *Film-Philosophy* 17, no. 1 (December 2013): 96–114. doi:10.3366/film.2013.0006.

Tyrer, Ben. 'Film Noir as Point de Capiton: Double Indemnity, Structure and Tem-porality.' In *Out of the Past: Lacan and Film Noir*. Cham: Springer, 2016.

Wallace-Sanders, Kimberly. *Mammy: A Century of Race, Gender, and Southern Memory*. Ann Arbor: University of Michigan Press, 2008.

Ware, Vron. *Beyond the Pale: White Women, History*. London: Verso, 1992.

Waugh, Michael. '"My Laptop Is an Extension of My Memory and Self": Post-Internet Identity, Virtual Intimacy and Digital Queering in Online Popular Music.' *Popular Music* 36, no. 2 (2017): 233–251. doi:10.1017/S0261143017000083.

Weber, Brenda R., and David Greven. 'Introduction: Touching Queerness: Ryan Murphy's Queer America.' In *Ryan Murphy's Queer America*, edited by Brenda R. Weber and David Greven, 1–23. London: Routledge, 2022. doi:10.4324/9781003170358-1.

West, Cornel, and Sylvia Ann Hewitt. 'A Parent's Bill of Rights.' *Boston Globe*, 18 September 1998.

Wiegman, Robyn. *American Anatomies: Theorizing Race and Gender*. Durham: Duke University Press, 1995.

Wilson, Julie A. 'The Moods of Enterprise.' In *Neoliberalism*, 150–182. New York: Routledge, 2017. doi:10.4324/9781315623085.

Youngblood, Gene, and R. Buckminster Fuller. *Expanded Cinema: Fiftieth Anniver-sary Edition*. New York: Fordham University Press, 2020.

YouTube. 'Variety's Transgender in Hollywood Roundtable.' YouTube video, 7 August 2018. Available at: https://www.youtube.com/watch?v=6_oqeXz7vbc.

Žižek, Slavoj. *For They Know Not What They Do: Enjoyment as a Political Factor*. London: Verso, 2008.

Žižek, Slavoj. *The Metastases of Enjoyment: Six Essays on Women and Causality*. London: Verso, 2005.

Žižek, Slavoj. *The Sublime Object of Ideology*. London: Verso, 2008.

Zulueta, Ricardo E. *Queer Art Camp Superstar: Decoding the Cinematic Cyberworld of Ryan Trecartin*. New York: SUNY Press, 2018.

Zupančič, Alenka. *What Is Sex?* Cambridge: MIT Press, 2017.

Filmography

Abrahams, Jim, dir. *Big Business*. Los Angeles, CA: Buena Vista Pictures Distribution, 1988.

Aldrich, Robert, dir. *Kiss Me Deadly*. Los Angeles, CA: United Artists, 1955.

Atkins, Ed, artist. *Us Dead Talk Love*. 2012.

Bailey, Giselle, producer. *My House* [web-series]. New York City, NY: Vice TV, 2018.

Baker, Brent with Mark Busk-Cowley, Tom Gould and Joe Scarra, creators. *Love Island* [television series]. London: ITV2, 2015.

BBC. *What Not to Wear* [television series]. London: BBC, 2001–2007.

Brahm, John, dir. *Hangover Square*. Los Angeles, CA: 20th Century Fox, 1945.

Brooker, Charlie, creator. *Black Mirror* [television series]. London and San Francisco, CA: Channel 4, Netflix, 2011–2023.

Bunim, Mary-Ellis and Jonathan Murray, creators. *The Real World* [television series]. New York City, NY: MTV, 1992–2019.

Bunim, Mary-Ellis and Jonathan Murray, creators. *The Simple Life* [television series]. New York City, NY and Los Angeles, CA: Fox, E!, 2003–2007.

Cameron, James, dir. *Terminator 2: Judgement Day*. Los Angeles, CA: TriStar Pictures, 1991.

Campillo, Robin, dir. *120 BPM (Beats Per Minutes)*. France: Memento Films, 2017.

Capra, Frank, dir. *It's A Wonderful Life*. New York City, NY: RKO Pictures, 1946.

Chaiken, Ilene, Michele Abbot and Kathy Greenberg, creators. *The L Word* [television series]. New York City, NY: Showtime, 2004–2009.

Chaiken, Ilene, Michele Abbot and Kathy Greenberg, creators. *The L Word: Generation Q* [television series]. New York City, NY: Showtime, 2019–2022.

Chapman, Hannah Carroll, creator. *Heartbreak High* [television series]. Santa Clara, CA: Netflix, 2022-.

Collins, David, creator. *Queer Eye* [television series]. Santa Clara, CA: Netflix, 2018–.

Collins, David, creator. *Queer Eye for the Straight Guy* [television series]. New York City, NY: Bravo, 2003–2007.

Collins, David and Michael Williams, creators. *Queer Eye for the Straight Guy* [television series]. New York City, NY: Bravo, 2003–2007.

Conrad, Tony, dir. *The Flicker*. USA, 1966.

Cooper, Kate, artist. *RIGGED* [video art]. 2014.

Cowell, Simon, creator. *The X Factor* [television series]. London: ITV, 2010–2018.

Crichton, Michael, dir. *Westworld*. Los Angeles, CA: Metro-Goldwyn-Mayer, 1973.

Cronenberg, David, dir. *A History of Violence*. Los Angeles, CA: New Line Cinema, 2005.

Cronenberg, David, dir. *Maps to the Stars*. Canada: Entertainment One Films, 2014.

Davies, Russell T., creator. *Big Brother* [television series]. Netherlands: Veronica, Yorin, Talpa, 1999–2006.

Davies, Russell T., creator. *Big Brother* [television series]. New York City, NY: CBS, 2000–.

Davies, Russell T., creator. *Big Brother* [television series]. London: Channel 4, Channel 5, ITV2, 2000–.

Davies, Russell T., creator. *It's a Sin* [television series]. London: Channel 4, 2021.

Davies, Russell T., creator. *Queer as Folk* [television series]. Manchester, UK: Red Production Company, 1999–2000.

DiVillo, Adam, creator. *The Hills* [television series]. New York City, NY: MTV, 2006–2010.

Dunlop, Scott, creator. *The Real Housewives* [television series]. New York City, NY: Bravo Media, 2006–.

Dunn, Stephan, creator. *Queer as Folk* [television series]. London: All3Media, 2022.

Dusen, Chris Van, creator. *Bridgerton* [television series]. Santa Clara, CA: Netflix, 2020–.

Emmerich, Roland, dir. *Stonewall*. Los Angeles, CA: Roadside Attractions, 2015.

Feder, Sam, dir. *Disclosure*. Santa Clara, CA: Netflix, 2020.

Fiennes, Sophie, dir. *The Perverts Guide to Cinema*. London: ICA Projects, 2006.

Fleiss, Mike, creator. *The Bachelor* [television series]. Los Angeles, CA: ABC, 2002–.

Fleiss, Mike, creator. *The Bachelorette* [television series]. Los Angeles, CA: ABC, 2003–.

Fleming, Victor, dir. *Gone With the Wind*. New York City, NY: Loew's Inc, 1939.

Fuller, Simon, creator. *American Idol* [television series]. New York City, NY, and Los Angeles, CA: Fox, ABC, 2002–.

Funt, Allen, creator. *Candid Camera* [television series]. Los Angeles, CA, New York City, NY, West Palm Beach, FL: ABC, NBC, CBS, PAX TV, TV Land, 1948–2014.

Garnett, Tay, dir. *The Postman Always Rings Twice*. Los Angeles, CA: Metro-Goldwyn-Mayer, 1946.

Gateley, Liz, creator. *Laguna Beach* [television series]. New York City, NY: MTV, 2004–2006.

Gibson, Laura, and Charlie Bennett, creators. *Too Hot to Handle* [television series]. San Francisco, CA: Netflix, 2020–.

Gilbert, Craig, creator. *An American Family* [television series]. Arlington, VA: PBS, 1973.

Gilliam, Terry, dir. *Brazil*. Los Angeles, CA: Universal Pictures, 1985.

Godard, Jean Luc, dir. Histoire(s) du Cinema [film series]. Neuilly-sur-Seine, France: Gaumont, 1988–1998.

Godard, Jean Luc, dir. *La Chinoise*. France: Athos Film, 1967.

Godard, Jean Luc, dir. *Le Mépris*. Paris, France: Marceau-Cocinor, 1963.

Godard, Jean Luc, dir. *Tout Va Bien*. Neuilly-sur-Seine, France: Gaumont, 1972.

Graham, Will, and Abbi Jacobson, creators. *A League of Their Own* [television series]. Los Angeles, CA: Sony Pictures Television, 2022.

Groening, Matt, creator. *The Simpsons* [television series]. New York City, NY: Fox, 1989–.

Harding, C.B., dir. *The Osbournes* [television series]. New York City, NY: MTV, 2002–2005.

Harron, Mary, dir. *American Psycho*. Los Angeles, CA: Lionsgate Films, 2000.

Hawks, Howard, dir. *The Big Sleep*. Los Angeles, CA: Warner Bros., 1946.

Heckerling, Amy, dir. *Clueless*. Los Angeles, CA: Paramount Pictures, 1995.

Hitchcock, Alfred, dir. *North by Northwest*. Los Angeles, CA: Metro-Goldwyn-Mayer, 1959.

Hitchcock, Alfred, dir. *Spellbound*. Los Angeles, CA: United Artists, 1945.

Hooper, Tom, dir. *The Danish Girl*. Los Angeles, CA: Focus Features, Universal Pictures, 2015.

Huston, John, dir. *The Maltese Falcon*. Los Angeles, CA: Warner Bros., 1941.

Jarman, Derek, dir. *Blue*. New York City, NY: Zeitgeist Films, 1993.

Jenkins, Michael, and Ben Gannon, creators. *Heartbreak High* [television series]. Australia: Network 10, 1994–1999.

Jordenö, Sara, dir. *Kiki*. New York City, NY: IFC Films, 2016.

Kaplan, Jonathan, dir. *Bad Girls*. Los Angeles, CA: 20th Century Fox, 1994.

Kasdan, Lawrence, dir. *Body Heat*. Los Angeles, CA: Warner Bros., 1981.

Keighron-Foster, Dennis, and Amy Watson, dirs. *Deep in Vogue*. New York City, NY: FilmRise, 2019.

Kentis, Chris, dir. *Open Water*. Los Angeles, CA: Lionsgate Films, 2003.

Kertz, Rebecca, writer. *The Swan* [television series]. New York City, NY: Fox, 2004.

Kohan, Jenji, creator. *Orange is the New Black* [television series]. Santa Monica, CA: Lionsgate Television, 2013–2019.

Korine, Harmony, dir. *Spring Breakers.* New York City, NY: A24, 2012.

Landis, John, dir. *Trading Places.* Los Angeles, CA: Paramount Pictures, 1983.

Lang, Fritz, dir. *The Woman in the Window.* New York City, NY: RKO Pictures, 1944.

Lee, Ang, dir. *Brokeback Mountain.* Los Angeles, CA: Focus Features, 2005.

Lee, Spike, dir. *25th Hour.* Los Angeles, CA: Buena Vista Pictures Distribution, 2002.

Lee, Spike, dir. *Do The Right Thing.* Los Angeles, CA: Universal Pictures, 1989.

Lee, Spike, dir. *She's Gotta Have It.* London: Island Pictures, 1986.

Lehmann, Michael, dir. *Heathers.* Atlanta, GA: New World Pictures, 1988.

Levin, Henry, dir. *The Guilt of Janet Ames.* Los Angeles, CA: Columbia Pictures, 1947.

Livingston, Jennie, dir. *Paris is Burning.* USA: Off-White Production, Prestige Pictures, 1990.

Loach, Ken, dir. *I, Daniel Blake.* London: British Film Institute, 2016.

Luketic, Robert, dir. *Legally Blonde.* Los Angeles, CA: MGM Distribution Co., 2001.

Lye, Len, dir. *A Colour Box.* 1935.

Marker, Chris, dir. *Le Jetée.* France: Argos Films, 1962.

Marshall, George, dir. *The Blue Dahlia.* Los Angeles, CA: Paramount Pictures, 1946.

Marshall, Penny, dir. *A League of Their Own.* Los Angeles, CA: Columbia Pictures, 1992.

Marshall, Penny, dir. *Big.* Los Angeles, CA: 20th Century Fox, 1998.

Maté, Rudolph, dir. *D.O.A.* Los Angeles, CA: United Artists, 1950.

Mazon, Frankie, producer. *The Kardashians* [television series]. Los Angeles, CA: Hulu, 2022–.

Michaels, Lorne, dir. *Saturday Night Live* [television series]. New York City, NY: NBC, 1975–.

Mok, Ken, and Kenya Barris, creators. *America's Next Top Model* [television series]. Los Angeles, CA and New York City, NY: UPN, The CW, VH1, 2003–2018.

Morelli, Lauren, developer. *Tales of the City* [television series]. Santa Clara, CA: Netflix, 2019.

Murphy, Ryan, creator. *Glee* [television series]. Los Angeles, CA: 20th Century Television, 2009–2015.

Murphy, Ryan, creator. *Hollywood* [television series]. Santa Clara, CA: Netflix, 2020.

Murphy, Ryan, creator. *Nip/Tuck* [television series]. Los Angeles, CA: Warner Bros. Domestic Television, 2003–2010.

Murphy, Ryan, creator. *Pose* [television series]. Los Angeles, CA: 20th Century Television, 2018–2021.

Murray, Nick, creator. *RuPaul's Drag Race* [television series]. Los Angeles, CA, and New York City, NY: Logo TV, VH1, MTV: 2009–.

Myrick, Daniel, and Eduardo Sánchez, dirs. *The Blair Witch Project.* Los Angeles, CA: Artisan Entertainment, 1999.

Nameth, Ronald, dir. *Exploding Plastic Inevitable.* USA, 1967.

Nichols, Mike, dir. *Working Girl.* Los Angeles, CA: 20th Century Fox, 1988.

Noé, Gaspar, dir. *Irréversible.* France: Mars Distribution, 2002.

Nolan, Christopher, dir. *Memento.* Los Angeles, CA: Newmarket, 2000.

Norrington, Stephen, dir. *Blade.* Los Angeles, CA: New Line Cinema, 1998.

Parsons, Charlie, creator. *Survivor* [television series]. New York City, NY: CBS, 2000–.

Peck, Ron, dir. *Empire State*. UK: Miracle Films, 1987.

Pelecanos, George, and David Simon, creators. *The Deuce* [television series]. Los Angeles, CA: Warner Bros. Domestic Television, 2017–2019.

Reed, Peyton, dir. *Bring It On*. Los Angeles, CA: Universal Pictures, 2000.

Reeves, Matt, dir. *Cloverfield*. Los Angeles, CA: Paramount Pictures, 2008.

Reid, Alastair, dir. *Tales of the City*. London: Channel 4, 1993.

Reinholdtsen, Rik, dir. *Legendary* [television series]. New York City, NY: HBO Max, 2020–2022.

Rhimes, Shonda, creator. *Grey's Anatomy* [television series]. Los Angeles, CA: Buena Vista Television, 2005–.

Roeg, Nicolas, dir. *Bad Timing*. London: Rank Film Distributors, 1980.

Ross, Herbert, dir. *The Secret of My Success*. Los Angeles, CA: Universal Pictures, 1987.

Safran, Joshua, developer. *Gossip Girl* [television series]. Los Angeles, CA: Warner Bros. Domestic Television, 2021–2022.

Schultz, Howard, creator. *Extreme Makeover* [television series]. Los Angeles, CA: ABC, 2008–.

Schwartz, Josh, and Stephanie Savage, developers. *Gossip Girl* [television series]. Los Angeles, CA: Warner Bros. Domestic Television, 2007–2012.

Seacrest, Ryan, creator. *Keeping Up with the Kardashians* [television series]. Los Angeles, CA: E!, 2007–2021.

Sherman, George, dir. *The New Frontier*. Los Angeles, CA: Republic Pictures, 1939.

Shore, Jeffrey, producer. *The Anna Nicole Show* [television series]. New York City, NY: E!, 2002–2004.

Shyer, Charles, dir. *Baby Boom*. Los Angeles, CA: MGM/UA Communications Co, 1987.

Siodmak, Robert, dir. *The Killers*. Los Angeles, CA: Universal Pictures, 1946.

Soloway, Joey, creator. *Transparent* [television series]. Los Angeles, CA: Amazon Studios, 2014–2019.

Star, Darren, creator. *And Just Like That …* [television series]. New York City, NY: Warner Bros. Discovery Global Streaming & Interactive Entertainment, 2021–.

Star, Darren, creator. *Sex and the City* [television series]. New York City, NY: HBO Enterprises, 1998–2004.

Stone, Oliver, dir. *Wall Street*. Los Angeles, CA: 20th Century Fox, 1987.

Timoner, Ondi, dir. *We Live in Public*. Los Angeles, CA: Interloper Films, 2009.

Tourneur, Jacques, dir. *Out of the Past*. New York City, NY: RKO Pictures, 1947.

Trecartin, Ryan, artist. *Priority Innfield* [video art]. 2015.

Tucker, Duncan, dir. *Transamerica*. New York City, NY: The Weinstein Company, IFC Films, 2005.

Vallée, Jean-Marc, dir. *Dallas Buyers Club*. Los Angeles, CA: Focus Features, 2013.

Vallée, Jean-Marc, dir. *Sharp Objects* [television series]. Los Angeles, CA: Warner Bros. Television Distribution, 2018.

Vidor, Charles, dir. *Gilda*. Los Angeles, CA: Columbia Pictures, 1946.

Villeneuve, Denis, dir. *Arrival*. Los Angeles, CA: Paramount Pictures, 2016.

Wachowski, Lana, and Lilly Wachowski, dirs. *The Matrix*. Los Angeles, CA: Warner Bros., 1999.

Waters, John, dir. *Pink Flamingos*. Los Angeles, CA: New Line Cinema, 1972.

Waters, Mark, dir. *Mean Girls*. Los Angeles, CA: Paramount Pictures, 2004.

Welles, Orson, dir. *The Lady from Shanghai*. Los Angeles, CA: Columbia Pictures, 1948.

White, Sharr, creator. *Halston* [television series]. Santa Clara, CA: Netflix, 2021.

Wilder, Billy, dir. *Double Indemnity*. Los Angeles, CA: Paramount Pictures, 1944.

Wilder, Billy, dir. *Sunset Boulevard*. Los Angeles, CA: Paramount Pictures, 1950.

Wolf, Dick, creator. *Law & Order* [television series]. New York City, NY: NBC Universal Television Distribution, 1990–.

Wright, Craig, creator. *Dirty Sexy Money* [television series]. Los Angeles, CA: Buena Vista Home Entertainment, 2007–2009.

Wyler, William, dir. *The Best Years of Our Lives*. New York City, NY: RKO Pictures, 1946.

Zieff, Howard, dir. *Hearts of the West*. Los Angeles, CA: United Artists, 1975.

Zyl, Jenkin van, artist. *Looners* [video art]. 2019.

Index

120 Days of Sodom (novel) 153

For Product Safety Concerns and Information please contact our EU
representative GPSR@taylorandfrancis.com
Taylor & Francis Verlag GmbH, Kaufingerstraße 24, 80331 München, Germany